Just Looking, Thank You

Philip Marchand
Just Looking, Thank You

An Amused Observer's View of Canadian Lifestyles

Bruce R. Bartlett
Toronto / 12·6·81

Macmillan of Canada   Toronto

To my mother and father

© Philip Marchand

Canadian Cataloguing in Publication Data

Marchand, Philip, 1946-
  Just looking, thank you

ISBN 0-7705-1434-0

1. Canada—Social life and customs—1945-*
I. Title.

FC89.M37   971.06′44   C76-017153-X
F1021.M37

Printed in Canada for
The Macmillan Company of Canada Limited
70 Bond Street, Toronto M5B 1X3

ACKNOWLEDGEMENTS

Two editors made this book possible: Robert Fulford of *Saturday Night*, who first published my work in his magazine and has been a source of encouragement and support throughout my career, and Doug Gibson of Macmillan, who suggested the idea for this book a number of years ago and helped shape it through his canny and perceptive advice.

It would, of course, be impossible to mention all the people who were helpful when I was seeking information and enlightenment as a reporter, but I would like to mention those people in particular who showed great kindness and hospitality to me in the course of my travels, and made the writing of this book a much more pleasant task than it might otherwise have been: Donna Thorvaldson of Vancouver, Martine Becu and Seaton McLean of Ottawa, Helen Speight of Victoria, Dan and Germana Driscoll of Montreal, Pat and Len Sandrin of Calgary, Vic and Lori Davies of Winnipeg, and Catherine and Allen Shute of Edmonton.

I am also grateful to Robert Fulford for permission to reprint "Just a Little Love Between Two Swinging Singles", "Out of the Closet and Into the Gay Bar" (first published as "Send No Psychiatrists to Leo"), "Mating Dances Under the Basketball Hoop" ("Mating Dances of the 1970s Teenager"), "The Office Affair" ("The Love Life of the Alienated Office Worker"), and "That Old Family Feeling" ("The Trouble with Communes is They Don't Work") from *Saturday Night*; to Mildred Istona for permission to reprint "Snow White at the Glitter Palace" ("Glitter Palaces: The New Young Night Life"), and "You Lied to Us, Hugh Hefner" ("Can Men Take the Heat") from *Miss Chatelaine*; and to Don Obe for permission to reprint "Learning to Love the Big City" ("Swimming Upstream in the World") from *The Canadian*.

Thanks are also due to the Ontario Arts Council. Special thanks to Tom McNeil and Patricia Thorvaldson.

CONTENTS

INTRODUCTION

This book really began about five years ago when I was introduced to a group of ragged, young, true-believing Christians who were going under the name of "Jesus Freaks" and beginning to get a lot of attention in the media. The Jesus Freaks were interesting because many of them had been formerly deep into drugs — some peace and love, too, and revolution, but mainly drugs — and they had found themselves falling into voids no one had told them about or prepared them for, horrifying black holes of the psyche which led nowhere except to a nice clean room at the Addiction Research Foundation, if they were lucky. The Jesus-Freak form of Christianity was their last toe-hold on solid ground before they tumbled forever into that black hole. The fact that this movement was becoming so widespread among young people, particularly ex-hippies, was one more sign of the disintegration of the late sixties "youthquake" (as *Look* magazine termed it), the flower power revolution, and what Tom Wolfe called the "happiness explosion".

My encounter with the Jesus Freaks impressed on me two things. The first was the desperation with which people were trying to work up ready-made "lifestyles", credos, and brotherhoods, now that their society no longer offered them real communities, or work which could make them feel proud as men and women. The second was the amazing disparity, covered up by this desperate desire to *believe*, between what people said and what people actually felt. The Jesus Freaks acted out both of these depressing tendencies with a kind of dogged persistence. I would go and visit them in tattered houses, reminiscent of the homes of squatters, Okies, Alabama sharecroppers, and sit fidgeting politely, while around me people were bouncing off the walls and chewing the place mats on the kitchen table in fits of nervous agitation. Others, meanwhile, sat passive and as enervated as the stone Buddhas they had rejected in favour of Christ. Each person had his or her way of coping with the emotional chaos, the supercharged atmosphere in which they all lived and breathed. Of course, they were pretty well committed to feel love and joy, so it was hard for anybody to mention anything like "emotional chaos", or suggest that it wasn't so much fun to live with fellow Christians who would scold them like an angry headmistress for not doing the dishes, or bore them silly with long monologues about Moses and the Pentateuch.

The more I began to investigate lifestyles as a journalist, the more I found the pattern repeating itself, the perpetual gap — particularly in tightly knit or strongly ideological groups of people sharing the same idiosyncratic lifestyles—between what people *said* they were feeling and doing, and what they actually *were* feeling and doing. It was not a question of lying, of course. People were just unconsciously blotting out the most stark and overpowering facts of their existence, like one of those ancient southern ladies who keeps waiting for gentlemen callers to show up at her decaying mansion. Thus I would visit communes where young women would tell me how much more open they were becoming, how much their minds were being stretched, blown, and renovated from top to bottom, how gratefully they were learning a style of life which would some day prevail while the bourgeoisie crumbled all around them—at the same time as other young women, in the same commune, were walking around looking dazed and winded and bruised because some young man had gone temporarily berserk and tried to strangle them.

In one of the bedrooms of this particular commune, where

holes had been punched through doors in anger and frustration, two women were trying to read a message which had been scrawled on one of the walls, amongst various doodles, squiggles, and curlicues, by some long-forgotten soul who had once lived in the commune, some disturbed individual who had something to say, like a prisoner scratching a last testament on the stone walls of his dungeon. "Baby, you're frigid," one of the women said, deciphering the scrawl, and the other looked puzzled for a minute. "I always thought it said 'Baby, you're free.'"

"No, it says, 'Baby, you're frigid.'"

"Oh."

There it was, the writing on the wall! A clear statement, easy to read, easy to understand, although certainly not pleasant to think about. No wonder the poor woman who lived in the room had trouble with it, and confused the key word, the "free" which spelled out "frigid" when you looked closely at it. The incident was one of those moments, those little epiphanies, that provide the curious reporter with what Mary McCarthy calls the "natural symbolism of reality".

So the pattern kept repeating, as these groups came and went. But curiously the media in general — in Canada, at least — seemed to take a benign and credulous attitude towards each new emergent lifestyle, each new evangelical group to appear on the scene, from the Divine Light Mission to the Community Homophile Association of Toronto. The party line issued by these groups was faithfully repeated in newspaper feature stories, along with wide-eyed assurances from the reporter that the people in these groups were indeed breaking new ground, e.g., the people from the Divine Light Mission seemed to enjoy walking around totally blissed out, and gay men from CHAT seemed to be getting along nicely with their women co-workers in the organization, thus destroying the myth that homosexuality had anything to do with fear or hatred of the opposite sex, etc. Good news for Mr. and Mrs. Average Reader. Nice people out there doing their thing! Nobody, scanning the Family Section of the paper before going on to the Eaton's ads, could really be offended or jerked awake.

Of course, Canadian journalists were by now feeding off "lifestyles" like Israelites scrounging for manna in the Sinai Desert. As the seventies slouched on and it became more and more clear that there would be no revolutions, sexual, political, or otherwise — that the happiness explosion Wolfe predicted in the mid-sixties had not yet exploded north of the 49th parallel, and probably never would — no one in the media was really that keen on adding more gloom to the picture. After all, everybody has their expectations. People may lack real communities to live in, and they may lack satisfying, useful work, to be sure, but they will not stop demanding happiness! As Tom Jefferson said, it's an inalienable right. So the media encouraged these fledgeling groups, these liberated souls. Perhaps somebody, somewhere, had the key, after all.

So the reporters would come, interview, observe for an hour or two, and go back to write their pieces. The pieces were usually as innocent of irony as an interview with William Kashtan in the *Canadian Tribune*. They would often be couched in the form of . . . the liberated woman speaks! Saying something like, *Gosh, I don't need men, I'm happy modelling clay with my sisters in the Rosa Luxemburg Art Collective.* Or the swinging, high-rise bachelor speaks! *When I find a woman who gives me as much satisfaction as my Mercedes-Benz 450 SL, then maybe I'll keep one around as a long-term investment — till then, it's weekly trade-ins at the singles bar for this pussy cat.* Or the follower of gurus and swamis speaks! *Keep your eye on those transcendental bubbles, and be happy — it's as simple as that. Really! I mean it! Believe me! I've tried it and I know!*

All reported without irony, mind you. Reported as if there were, in fact, no substratum of desperation beneath the mobility and the freedom of choice and the whole array of lifestyles, and techniques for better living, and modes of consciousness-raising available to an urban, sophisticated, well-read, modern-day consumer. Reported as if people's official statements about what was going on with them were to be taken at face value. Reported as if the human capacity for self-deception was not almost limitless. There was certainly nothing wrong in a lot of the messages being laid on the public, from the gospel of St. John to the Vedic scriptures, but the people who embraced them too often seemed to disregard simple human realities, such as the fact that there are very few actual grown-ups walking around the streets these days, and a lot of bitter, disappointed children with chronological ages ranging from fifteen to ninety. And that even mature people find it exceedingly difficult to truly understand their own motives, much less follow through on their good intentions. And most journalists, as I say, seemed to disregard these facts as well, as if their editors had all had T.S. Eliot's dictum about mankind not being able to stand too much reality embroidered on samplers and hung above their typewriters.

Not that a reporter had to succumb to cynicism and pessimism. There were people out there who were managing to find unique and fascinating ways of carrying on the business of life, with stout hearts and a genuine zest for that difficult business. They ranged from Calgary oil and gas explorers who talked with southwestern American accents, to artists and musicians from the big city who were actually trying to make a go of living in the country, renovating old farmhouses, and so on. Of course, they worked like Trojans, but that was the price they paid for trying to turn fantasies — a rich motherlode of natural gas, say, or a home in the unpolluted hills — into reality. And as for the rest, those who were still caught up in some marvellous post-flower-power, post-youthquake fantasy and couldn't understand why things kept getting so *touchy* all the time — well, perhaps there were rich veins of comedy to be mined here, particularly in that yawning gap between party line and unruly fact — absurd and painfully funny contradictions, oddities, grotesqueries, pratfalls. The ancient and persisting human tendency towards self-deception certainly did not mean that henceforth every new social development had to be viewed as a tragedy. It did mean that new lifestyles and social creeds would probably turn out just as comic as the old ones.

Whether comic or tragic, the lifestyles and subcultures explored herein all seemed to me to be important, since they might well provide possible clues as to whatever larger twists and turns might be going on down there, under the mild, relatively composed, surface of Canadian society. Of course, if they were to provide such clues they would have to be approached carefully, entered into as fully as possible, looked at as intensely as the reporter's eye could stand. I wanted to see how far a reporter could go, really, in doing all these things. "Covering" a story until the shape and rhythms of the life within that story started to become clear, the patterns, the archetypal incidents— it was of course a very tricky thing to do, and I was constantly aware of the barriers, both inside myself and outside, that stood in the way of doing it right. Not least among them was my own diffidence in approaching people, particularly in situations where reporters were not necessarily welcome. I discovered, for example, that to introduce yourself as a reporter in a singles bar was one sure way to make yourself instantly unattractive. I remember two young and charming girls — they looked as if they could have posed as models, innocent but alluring, in a field of daisies for a shampoo ad — who minced no words in telling me to leave their table because I was interfering with their "hustling". One appreciates such frankness, in a way. You just have to wish them the best of luck, and leave. Generally, I found it inadvisable to come on as a reporter in situations where people felt even small amounts of guilt, conscious or unconscious, about what they were doing. In those situations, you have to talk to people as best you can, eavesdrop, mingle, strike up conversations in your capacity as a friendly stranger, and above all keep your eyes open.

The ideal for any reporter, of course, is to be perfectly straightforward about what he is doing, and yet blend into people's lives in such a way that they just come to see him as a sympathetic ear or even just as another person along for the ride. Basically, he wants to inform people that he is a reporter but not necessarily to keep reminding them of it. Of course, people never forget entirely that a reporter is a reporter. But at times their awareness of this fact recedes a bit, and at those times something more intimate, in a way, or just simply human, can often occur. It is not a question of people baring their souls, but of their allowing a reporter to be there in the middle of whatever small dramas they are playing out, to get as much first-hand exposure to what he is going to write about as possible.

For the most part, however, he has to rely on what people tell him about their dramas, and for that purpose it is essential to learn the skill of getting people to open up. Since attentive listeners are, in fact, rare in our society, a person—*any* person—who offers rapt attention to somebody talking starts off with a tremendous advantage right there. It's hardly an arcane skill. All it takes, really, is an enjoyment of an essentially childlike process of trying to construct a picture of what things look like or feel like from the casual, or not so casual, remarks people drop. If he gets really good at it, there is a possibility he can end up as the kind of reporter who meets one of Henry James's criteria for a good novelist—to be the kind of observer "on whom nothing is lost". That is something to aim for, anyway. In the meantime, the only thing he is sure of is that there is something going on here, more than meets the eye, and that he knows nothing about it, and that somewhere, there is somebody who does know and is willing to tell him about it.

If he can resist imposing his own preconceptions on the scene, checking madly during interviews to see if he has covered all the five W's, and asking questions that imply that he knows it all, anyway, chances are that he will succeed. Looking for people who *know*, who really do have something to say, is a search as interesting in its own way as digging up old Indian villages or hunting for wild asparagus, because when you find a person like that, the communication of information that can follow is pure pleasure for a reporter. It's like the reward for a dozen other interviews that have ended nowhere — the reward for the frustration of having to extract juiceless bits of information, like carious teeth, or discovering in the middle of an interview that the person being interviewed has nothing at all to say, has not got the tiniest degree of passion or insight or experience to communicate.

That, actually, is another lesson in life the reporter learns from his craft. There is a huge difference between people who respond to their experience, who seem to let their experience live inside them for a while, and people who either have no experience or allow it to drift through them like fog through a dense woodlot. The first kind of person really needs no encouragement from an interviewer because he is usually dying, anyway, to let somebody else know what he's seen or felt or experienced. The mere presence of an attentive listener is, again, the only necessary encouragement. I have felt this often enough in people to suspect that the communication of experience in itself is a human pleasure more essential to our lives than we usually recognize. People who have had no possible desire for, or hope of, publicity, have opened up and talked of their experience merely for the sake of this pleasure, to have their experience recapitulated, and so shared with and understood by someone else.

The second kind of person is pretty dreary, and there's no need to analyse his or her characteristics, except perhaps to say that you can get a good idea of what it's like to dwell in limbo, that region bordering on hell but not actually sulphurous, from trying to talk to them and get a feeling for a situation from them. Best admit defeat in such an interview and fill in the time with small talk — you can usually tell, after the first couple of questions, whether or not anything will be forthcoming. After all, you can't expect a person to tell you what a meal is like—if it's tasty or not, or what the precise nature of its taste sensations might be —if their meal consists of cold beans or stew devoured straight from the can.

To those people who did communicate their experience to

me, and feelings about that experience, I will always be grateful. I hope the book has not done an injustice to the full texture and feel of those experiences, and will stand as a faithful commentary on what is, essentially, everyday reality in their lives, and in the lives of thousands of people like them. That private reality — the reality of what goes on, not only in the heat of the singles bar, for example, but *after* people have left the singles bar and are driving home — was precious to me. It was my own fool's gold, worth every hour of its plodding pursuit.

P.M.
Toronto, June 1976

CIVIL SERVICE CITY

Ottawa! That's your real family town. Can there be a better place in the world for a man to settle down and provide for his wife and kids and hang his Eskimo print in the living room than this clean, wholesome, healthy, all-Canadian city? A city where you can skate to work on the Rideau Canal in the winter-time and bicycle to work on the bicycle paths in the summer-time. Where you can go cross-country skiing just across the river in the Gatineau Park, and make some piping hot cocoa afterwards in the huts along the trail they keep open until darkness falls, with plates and cups and hot water provided for you. Where you can rent a garden space in the Green Belt from the National Capital Commission and compare how your radishes and turnips are doing with your neighbour's. Where even the city library is equipped with Dor-o-matic Slide 'n Swing doors and a hanging sculpture made out of four hundred glass crystals. Ottawa, where the tulips grow in the spring. No comparison, say, to that other North American capital, Washington, D.C., where there are two black rapists for every white stenographer, and the cherry trees fade after a month or two.

Of course, as everyone knows, this is a company town, Civil Service City. This is not a town for swingers, hustlers, movers, studs, operators, hot dogs, chicken hawks, boardroom aces, and pin-striped carnivores. Which is not to say that such people do not live in Ottawa. They just don't leave their mark on it. They don't speed up the heartbeat of the city with their hyper-

1

metabolic juices, the way they do in Montreal, Toronto, Vancouver. The real Ottawa stud, the civil servant who is working on policy for federal-provincial relations in the Department of Finance, say, or keeping an eye on what kind of mileage the research boys are getting out of MAPIM (Macro-urban Program Impact Model) in Urban Affairs, blends into the cityscape in the same way as the retired staff sergeant who wears maroon pants with a white belt and white shoes to his office, the turkey with the pencil-thin moustache who keeps track of how many paper clips are being requisitioned by people in his division.

The deep drama of their lives goes unappreciated. People can plug into the fantasy of the Bay Street swinger who makes a killing in plutonium by day and picks up lonely receptionists at Malloney's by night — can savour the drama of this hot shot's liver being corroded by backed-up adrenalin and alcohol — but they are totally ignorant of the life-and-death struggles of the high-powered civil servant — the young man on the rise who is *not* into government so he can take half-hour coffee breaks in the morning and afternoon.

But how can outsiders be expected to understand these struggles, the intricate skill, for instance, with which a successful young civil servant will turn memo writing and committee discussions to his advantage. Committee meetings! Why has no one written a manual on the protocol and rules of the game for the ambitious civil servant sitting on a committee? Your average person on the outside would no doubt consider committee meetings rather stupefying, in the same way that a backgammon tournament will bore you silly inside five minutes if you don't know the rules. But if you *do* know the rules ... if you know, for instance, that a committee is not there to find a solution to a problem but to determine who is going to have *jurisdiction* over this problem ... if you know that a committee meeting is a chance to impress important people that your own boss would normally never let you get near to ... then meetings no longer become stupefying, but a true test of civil-service mettle, an occasion to display the lightning intellect as well as the armoured gluteal muscles.

To be successful in a committee meeting, of course, you have to speak. People who don't open their mouths are nothing. It is assumed that they have not opened their mouths because they can't do so without making fools of themselves. So you have to open your mouth, and usually it's best if you do it when the committee meeting is more than half over, and less than three-quarters over. That's important. The first half, you see, everyone is feeling each other out. The last quarter everyone is starting to think where they're going to go for lunch. So that time slot is critical, and you have to be on your toes to make full use of it because you've usually got a lot of competition from other speakers.

Michael Pitfield is a master of timing in this respect. Michael Pitfield is Clerk of the Privy Council and Secretary to the Cabinet, which makes him Trudeau's number-one civil-service honcho, and the biggest ace in the whole government service. In important committee meetings, Michael Pitfield usually doesn't say much, except for the odd perfunctory question during the first three-quarters of the meeting. Because of this silence a certain amount of expectation — even suspense — builds up around him. He is the number-one honcho, after all. He *has* to say something. So two-thirds of the way through he makes his move. He will say something like, "I take it, then, the consensus that has been building up here is that we should . . . " and proceed from there to sum up what everyone has been saying, only twisting it slightly in whatever direction he wants the committee to go. It is a very subtle, tricky art. The twist, the slant, is there, all right, but he has to do it in such a way that nobody can pinpoint exactly where he has started to bend things — everybody will have to say, yes, by geez, those *were* the main points, and they'll all be so busy trying to think just what he left out or just how he paraphrased what they said that suddenly he's got them supporting something they were pretty well dead-set against when the meeting began.

Of course, not all ambitious civil servants can hope to rival Pitfield in this art while their careers are yet young. If they can just make some key Director, or Chief, or Co-ordinator, or

Adviser, notice them at a meeting, for the while they will consider it time well spent. Or they will devote their energies to that other great object of committee meetings, getting a piece of the action for their particular department or division. Getting a piece of the action: one must understand here the underlying teleology of the civil service. The whole civil service, of course, is there with the one settled purpose of solving problems for the taxpayer. Problems are continually arising. Frequently they arise in areas where there is no exact precedent to determine which government department should handle them. Therefore inter-departmental meetings are held to consider these problems, to draft "terms of reference" for them, and, in effect, to decide who is going to get their hands on them. A department with a new problem to solve is a happy department—there are possibilities in it for increased budget, increased staff, increased responsibility, and prestige for the department officials.

The ambitious civil servant who sees a problem coming around the bend knows that it is time to start writing memos. A problem — let us be fanciful here — like enforcing the twelve-mile limit off Canada's shores. A problem, obviously, that the Defence Department alone, or External Affairs alone, could not tackle. An inter-departmental task force, drawn from members of both departments, therefore becomes necessary. But let us assume that a quick thinker in the Department of Communications gets word of the impending task force and realizes that this imminent yawning conundrum of enforcing the twelve-mile limit cannot begin to be resolved — *begin* to be resolved — without experts on communications there to provide input on the inevitable problems that will arise in this area. I mean, what happens once our men in uniform are out there on the high seas and they're looking down on a Russian trawler big enough to house half the population of Leningrad that is backing into Canso Bay? We have here nothing less than the *communications dimension*. So this bright, alert, young civil servant starts working on the memo ... *strongly recommend, in these preliminary meetings, that a representative from our department be on hand to provide input and help clarify any questions relating to the communications dimension. . . .*

Who can object? Who can fight the Communications Dimension? You can never nail *that* door shut—or shut it tight enough that at least one Department of Communications man can't slip by it, right into the vortex of pipe smoke and knit eyebrows which is your task force. Once he's sitting there, this man will show no mercy. "Well now," he will say at some convenient gap in the conversation, "this point reminds me here that one vital problem will be the problem of communications between our naval and air forces offshore and our people back at the base. Now, we've done some preliminary work on this in our department, and we'd be glad to provide some of the information we've been able to come up with . . ." and the rest of the committee members are thinking, *Sure you have. There's no way you've done some preliminary work on this, because there's no way you could have found out about this task force until the last minute, which is the way we planned it—Jesus!—in hopes that keeners like you wouldn't find your way onto it.*

But of course no one calls the bluff. Perhaps the DOC man has even done some softening up of the terrain beforehand—talking to a few of the committee members over the old office electric kettle, and saying how, if there was anything he could do for them, in the way of representing their viewpoint in the future, why don't hesitate—I mean, it's all communications, when you get right down to it — and he'd sure appreciate their showing a positive response, you know, not breaking his balls when he opens his mouth in this forthcoming meeting. . . .

Perhaps in the meeting he volunteers to take the minutes. This chore, this joe-job — he'd be glad to take it off somebody else's hands. Only, being a skilled communications expert, he knows how to do this joe-job right—taking the minutes down in such a way that nobody is misquoted, nothing is blatantly distorted, but that the right parts are given their — well, their proper perspective. What he says, for instance, is quite unmistakeably clear and well-expressed in these minutes. And any implied opposition to it is somewhat . . . muted. These minutes, the draft minutes, are then circulated to all the parties involved, the Deputy Ministers, etc., of the Departments represented at the meeting. If they want to head off this Trojan from the DOC, or if they just start having second thoughts — *what the hell do we want Communications in this for, anyway?* — now is the time they must act.

Unfortunately, Deputy Ministers are extremely busy. Draft minutes are extremely boring to read. Chances are good they will be approved, almost automatically, by all concerned, and so will become "official" minutes. And once he's there in the official minutes — or once he's there in the "terms of reference" — you can't pry him out of this with chisels, crowbars, or claw hammers. Nobody's going to act after it's all down there on paper — having something down on paper is like the First Principle of Actuality in the metaphysics of the civil service. If you complain after you see it down in the official minutes you look like a sorehead — as well as (aha!) making it obvious that you didn't really read the draft minutes.

It's all part of getting your way without resorting to gauche and self-defeating measures like telling them they can't do this to you, you'll have your Deputy Minister write to *their* Deputy Minister, etc. You can get away with being obvious and gauche in some areas of life, but you can't get away with it in the upper echelons of the civil service. These upper echelons train you in an exquisite sensitivity towards nuance—particularly nuance pertaining to status. In committee meetings, for example, you can often watch the subtle comedy called who-will-take-off-their-jacket-first. If someone takes off his jacket and then everyone else gradually takes off his, that first person obviously has scored a point. He has proved himself a leader. But if a person takes off his jacket first, and it is clear that he does not have sufficient cachet to assume this role, the rest will probably bloody well keep their jackets on. The poor fool who took off his jacket first will then have to suffer through the rest of the meeting in his shirt sleeves. He might as well be sitting there in his all-action sport shorts. Even if he's only the *second* one to take off his jacket, the person who *should* have been second to take it off, according to status rank, may decide to keep his on, and a silent message will go through the room: nobody else take your jacket off. Let Junior here start to sweat, as he sees it's just him and the Boss, and he looks like the sycophant he is.

Status sensitivity. The court mandarins of the Ch'ing Dynasty, after whom our own lords of the bureaucracy have been named, made it into an art as stylized and elegant as the stage movements in a Japanese Noh play. If you saw one of these mandarins walking around the Forbidden Palace wearing a red coral button on his official cap, an embroidered golden pheasant on the breast of his official robes, and a gold clasp set in rubies at the back of those robes, then you knew you were dealing with an official of the second rank ... definitely an ace, a High Potentate, the equivalent of an SX (senior executive) in the Ottawa bureaucracy, or even an ADM (Assistant Deputy Minister). If, however, he was wearing a sapphire button, an embroidered peacock on his breast, and a clasp of worked gold on his back, then he was just an official of the third rank, the equivalent, in Ottawa, of someone next in line for an SX—perhaps—a mere FI8 or FI7, say, if he worked in the Treasury Board. This went all the way down to officials of the lowest rank, the ninth rank, who went around wearing a silver button on their cap, an embroidered long-tail jay on the breast of their robes, and a clasp of buffalo horn at the back — the equivalent, say, of a graduate of Carleton University Journalism School just hired as a copy-editor by Information Canada.

Nobody was embarrassed about status in those days. Nobody felt there was anything wrong in making sure everybody was visibly in his place. Nowadays, of course, people are. Blatant status trappings are not encouraged. Ottawa mandarins, therefore, have to content themselves with merely their ratings—the initials SX or ADM—and a few visible symbols of high position. A real office in La Place Bell, for example, instead of a seven-foot-square plot of pea-green Tecton carpet marked off by buff-coloured dividers, in the middle of an "open landscape" floor plan . . . a schefflera growing in the corner of the office, instead of a philodendron . . . a few trappings, as I say, nothing fancy. But they would probably have felt at home in the Forbidden Palace just the same, since elegant and stylized arts of putting people in their place are not unknown at La Place Bell, or Tunney's Pasture. Indeed, they are practised daily, and refined with true mandarin subtlety, and you can take the true measure of a high civil servant by how well he can cut off your balls and grind them into his Tecton carpet for plant food without your even realizing it. Again, the gauche, the obvious move here is not only politically inexpedient (nobody wants to make enemies if they can help it) but bad form, like smoking a cigarette at a funeral.

So one must look for the small signs. When you go in to see a mandarin, does he just sit behind his desk and wave you to a chair? Or does he get up and go over to a couple of armchairs in the corner, where you both sit down and have an intimate, tête-à-tête conversation? If he is busy when you call, does he come out to the door personally and tell you he'll be a few minutes, or does he tell his secretary to tell you? Of course, if he tells his secretary to tell you, that probably means you'll get the wave-from-behind-the-desk treatment when you do go in. But not necessarily. You might go in, and he'll be behind his desk and he'll jump up vigorously like some high-coronary-risk executive and leave his desk and sit down with you on the corner sofa, and you know you've been set up for the I-would-have-shown-you-in-personally-you're-such-an-important-individual-to-me-but-as-you-can-see-I-am-fantastically-almost-inhumanly-busy scenario. And then, of course, when it comes time to leave, you also have to watch the signs: does he see you to the door of his office? (Not too bad —he could have just shaken hands with you and pointed his pipe stem to the door.) Does he see you to the door of his outer office/reception area? (Pretty good.) Does he walk you to the elevator? (Terrific— you're up there with the best of them.)

And there are pitfalls—my goodness, there are pitfalls! Worse pitfalls than failing to get on an ad hoc committee, or being waved out of an office by a superior instead of being shown to the door. You can be programmed out of the information stream, for example. In Ottawa, if you are a civil servant with any ambition and you find yourself being programmed out of the information stream, you might as well decide to shave your head and devote yourself to chanting hymns to Krishna on the corner of Bank and Laurier with the rest of the losers and drop-outs. Being programmed out of the information stream is like being gently prodded out of a top spot in the herd by the number-one buffalo.

What happens when you are being programmed out of the information stream is that basically you never get sent copies of the really good memos circulating around the office. I don't mean the bullshit memos, like "Please co-operate with our cleaning staff and make this a more pleasant work environment by not dumping your cigarette ashes in the potted plants". I mean the really *good* memos, the ones that tell you between the lines, like a notice in *Pravda*, what is really happening, who is getting the money ("utilization of priorities in resource alloca-tions"), who is supporting the guys who are getting the money, etc. Memos that outline strategy and provide ammunition for our Stakhanovite members of ad hoc committees.

What happens sometimes is that two or three like-minded civil servants will get together and come to an . . . *understand-ing* . . . nothing too brutal like a paper with a list of names and a little round black ball after certain ones, but a kind of informal consensus . . . old Bill over there isn't too clued-in, is he? Not that you can blame him, the poor bugger — he thinks "synec-tics" is something you do with the word order in a sentence . . . and pretty soon, when the question of putting Bill's name after the "cc" in a key memo comes up, one of these two or three civil servants will clear his throat and say, well, do you think Bill is really in a position to provide input here? . . . and pretty soon after that the question of putting Bill's name after the "cc" does not come up at all. One says to one's secretary, uh, we won't be sending a copy of this memo to Bill, and one hopes she will get the picture without the instruction having to be repeated too many times . . . *this guy is not on our mailing list.*

It's a question of power, when you get right down to it, though nobody ever gets explicit about it. *Let's pull a squeeze play on Bill, why don't we* . . . no, no civil servant would use such language, any more than a swinger at a soirée would say, boy, am I dying to get laid tonight. Too crude, too embarrassing. Too reminiscent of funky whiffs from our ancestral simian home-land — the whole atmosphere of Ottawa is permanently deodorized to prevent such whiffs from troubling the human sensorium. And usually it's the old guard who gets sacrificed in such power plays, programmed out of it by trendy young McLuhanites and Organizational Development freaks, young men in corduroy suits who want to restructure the whole de-partmental matrix to provide for a number of meaningful work alternatives not present already in the big ball of wax. . . .

Although it must be said, too, that the civil servants who are into this, and into rising up through the ranks to reach, some glorious day, the PCO, or the PMO, or the level of DM, are probably only about five per cent of your government work force in Ottawa. The other ninety-five per cent are your civil servants who have decided all they want to do is to settle into the Ottawa life, with all its soothing and life-enhancing bonuses. The Ottawa life! All one has to do, it seems, is sign on with the government, hang that Eskimo print in the living room, and then claim your ticket . . . a lifetime prize offered nowhere else in Canada. Security for you and your family. All the healthy outdoor facilities, every season of the year, one half-hour drive away. The R.A. Centre on rainy days, where civil servants and their families can get involved in activities ranging from broomball and curling to philately and health and charm courses. The R.A. Centre — now that's worth a word or two. Open to all members of the Ottawa Civil Service Recreational Association, it's a two-storey brick building surrounded by football fields, baseball diamonds, and a few stray bleachers, while the building itself has that certain atmosphere that causes the visitor walking along the linoleum corridors to feel that he should be checking into the principal's office. Very, shall we say, *organized.* Civil servants who are really into the R.A. Centre have usually taken a long look at what's ahead of them in their lives as civil servants, they've seen that they will never be a Michael Pitfield, or a DM, or an ADM, or even an SX, they'll always be what they are now, intelligent, moderately conscientious, moderately skilled office functionaries, and they'll probably stay in Ottawa for the rest of their days — or at least until those Public Service Superannuation cheques start rolling in.

There's no doubt about the seductiveness of this organized life. A civil servant is usually well paid for his work. He is probably better paid than he could hope to be in private industry, though this is a proposition resentfully disputed by many in the civil service and subject to no real proof, since jobs in the civil service have an exotic life of their own, with their own exotic skills, and you can't compare them with anything on the outside. The pension, though, is certainly better than you'd get in private industry. So, as the years go by, the civil servant feels less and less able to pull up stakes and move on to something different. His family likes it in Ottawa. He has settled into a work routine which is comfortable, free of any possibility that the boss will call him into his office one day and tell him that they're restructuring his department, and his own position is outside the new management flow, and he'll have to leave in two weeks—free of all this, and every year he stays, his munificent superannuation credit builds up, and perhaps he and his wife decide, what the hell, we'll move out into the country and buy some old farmhouse full of character, near Jockvale or Twin Elm or Johnston Corners, and spend the next few years renovating it, so that Bill and Sue living in their condominium in

Mississauga will eat their hearts out when they come and visit. The countryside around Ottawa, which for years had been Jukes Family territory as far as the Ottawa civil service was concerned, inhabited by people who ate in kitchens with the local auto-repair-shop calendar hanging on the wall and flies buzzing around the butter dish, has now been invaded by trendy young civil-service couples who drive in to Ottawa for work, and for the latest cultural offering at the National Arts Centre, and who are also trying to live out a separate existence as combination country squire and back-to-the-earth-honest-black-soil cucumber-growers.

As for their workaday civil-service existence—no one can say it is not without its modest pleasures. The high drama of the ambitious, power-driven civil servant is lacking, of course, but there are the broader, more human dramas of life in the middle echelons. In this respect, the open-landscape office-plan, with moveable area dividers instead of walls, has been a great boon. In an open-landscape office you can hear *everything*. The girl who's having a fight with her lover over the telephone. The guy who has long, fruity conversations with *his* lovers and friends over the telephone —*I tell you, Max, he was positively insatiable. I don't know how I dragged myself out of bed this morning.* The neurotic, anxiety-ridden husband who calls home to his wife every twenty minutes.

He's one in particular who can drive his office neighbours crazy — his "Hi Suzy" over the telephone hits half a dozen people around him at once, and they all start thinking, okay, *now* what's the problem with the Bert-and-Suzy household. It all penetrates the brain pan, and you have to be very careful to remember what you've heard officially, and what you've heard unofficially, wafting over the area dividers. If you confuse the two, if you ask Bert during coffee break, for example, how his wife is getting over her hysterectomy operation, and you suddenly remember—*uh oh, that was something I heard over the open office airwaves and wasn't really supposed to listen to —* well, you can see how it all adds a certain piquancy to the work routine.

Dramas of status-life also lack the critical urgency one finds in the corridors of power, but they're still played, however faint-heartedly, back in the corridors of routine and just getting by till pension time. Often they take place at parties where strangers get together and try to feel one another out. In other cities this universal process lacks the peculiar focus and excitement it has in Ottawa. In Ottawa you know it's much easier to get a fix on that stranger at the party because you can safely assume he's working for the same employer you are, and you can narrow down the prestige of his occupation immediately to the categories of *department* (the Finance Department is definitely sexy; with something like Supply and Services, on the other hand, you might as well wear maroon pants to work), and rating within that department. The problem, of course, is that you can ask what department he works for, but you can't come right out and ask what his rating is — that's the equivalent of asking him what his salary is, in precise figures. Therefore you start off by asking what department he's in, and then what division, and then — *ah yes, the personnel services division* — one raises the pensive eyebrow a notch or two, like it's all coming back to you now — *who did you work for there? George S——, eh? Well, isn't that something. George and I used to play squash together at lunchtime a few years ago. Terrific guy.* The message, of course, is: you used to be buddies with his boss, that's how far ahead of him you've climbed in the jungle-gym of this bureaucracy. You have got this fellow pegged precisely, you know where he stands in relation to you, and you can continue your pleasant conversation with him on that basis.

It's a world where all the boundaries are laid out for you like that. Bureaucracies, of course, are famous for the regard in which they hold artificial boundaries, clearly defined rules of the game, and so on, and in Ottawa, this traditional bureaucratic respect is intensified because of the fact there is no other game in town. It's a company town. The bureaucracy is *it*. The Perfect Memo Spirit emanates from the warm-air duct in every office building in town. You just can't resist, defy, or blaspheme against it.

A new employee comes into her division, settles into her work area, and spies a nice oak-veneer credenza left by a departing employee. Just standing there in a deserted corner of the office. Now this little piece of furniture, thinks the new employee, is exactly perfect for storing her reference materials, dictionaries, phone books, all the clutter and paraphernalia of her job that won't fit into her tiny desk, and so she asks a fellow employee to help her lug the credenza over to her work area. He looks at her as if she is suggesting they go shoplifting on their lunch-hour together.

"Oh, uh, this credenza belonged to Mr.——."

"But he's gone, isn't he?"

"Yes, I know, but I don't think it's supposed to leave his work area."

"Why not? I mean, he left, didn't he?"

"Yes, he has, but . . . but he wasn't even in your *division*!" Finally he promises to help her move it after five o'clock when everybody else in the office is gone. It's as if he's afraid Somebody Important is going to mark it down in the little book of employee infractions and misdemeanours, the two of them doing this thing in broad daylight. She tells him to forget it, and asks one of the Fine's Florist men spraying the office philodendrons to help her with it.

A frustrating experience, but you can't expect free-wheeling spirits in a ballpark designed for anal compulsives—in a "work environment" geared for men and women who never handed in book reports with messy ink splotches or words crossed out when they were sitting behind a desk in the seventh grade, and later grew up to be civil servants. In a way, the city they inhabit is also such a ballpark, one Canadian town that will never jump at you, or set you up for a painful disillusionment, like a pimp who vanishes after he takes your money. It is tidy, well-ordered, and delivers nothing more or less than it promises, like any good bureaucrat. It drives artists, gypsies, and high-living folk in general quite insane. Few good restaurants (perhaps two or three)—only a plague of steak houses throughout the city. No jazz clubs open until three, or coffee houses, or small, folding-chair theatres doing raunchy experiments with a black-box stage—only the Arts Centre putting on plays by George Bernard Shaw, or someone equally unknown and untried.

The kids practically desert Ottawa after six p.m. for Hull, which is positively funky compared to our nation's capital. The Sparks St. Mall, which at noon is full of strollers and browsers and oglers and layabouts and office workers on their lunch-hour — as full of life as the waterfront of any Mediterranean city — looks as empty as a defunct railroad terminal by night. High-school students, young workmen, secretaries, eighteen-year-olds on welfare, are all off doing the disco scene across the river, or exploring other delights of Hull — some of the kids who are into weightlifting at John A. Macdonald C.I. like especially to go over and beat up the waiters at La Chaudière.

Whatever your pleasure, you're more likely to find it in Hull than back home in Ottawa. The only competition, in fact, for the patronage of anyone under twenty-five in Ottawa is something like the Carleton University Pub. It's an incredible place, actually, full of students in a sort of mass coma, students anaesthetized daily by the Dead Orgone Energy floating around the campus's underground concrete tunnels who then come in at night to finish off the job and push their expiring brain cells over the edge by drinking eight or nine quarts of beer. An incredible place — and one understands why anything, even a tacky Hull discotheque where they've bribed the fire marshal to let them stay open, is preferable to it as a night spot.

Well, that's all right. As I say, Ottawa's not for teenagers or young swingers anyway, or for Bohemians and artists who can bloody well stop their crabbing and move to Montreal or Toronto. Of course, it's easy to see why these people are not into the Ottawa life, why they don't have, say, a cottage on Lac Plombagine where they can unwind on weekends and invite their neighbour, who's in the Planning, Research and Evaluation division of their department, over for a beer and the two of them can indulge in the pure undiluted pleasure of shop talk —

the sweet arcana of bureaucracies — about task forces, policy reports, inter-departmental liaisons, planning programs, the very words themselves proof that these two shop-talkers are grown-up, important people, and not children playing games after all. Such intimate pieces of information they share—only a very limited and select species of human will ever begin to understand. And that, actually, is the Ottawa life right there, or one part of its tangless essence.

A great place to live, this city, but you wouldn't want to visit there. After working late in the office the servant of the taxpayer with the cottage on Lac Plombagine strolls past Parliament Hill and the eternal flame—indisputably majestic against the fading light of the early evening, Canadian Gothic at its best — and he takes a long look at the Château Laurier and the Arts Centre and Confederation Square, where the warriors surge through the stone arch dragging an 18-pounder behind them, and he thinks — yes, I'm on top of this town. I'm on top of it in a way I could never be on top of Montreal or Toronto or Vancouver, and who cares if there are only two or three good restaurants in the whole damned city. He passes a Chevrolet pick-up truck stopped by an RCMP officer, driven by an old bucheron wearing a ski parka smeared with motor oil and shouting gibberish French at the cop who is trying to see if there's an open bottle of liquor in the front seat somewhere in the middle of a pile of empty Kentucky Fried Chicken boxes, and he gives the cop a look as he passes by that seems to say — yes, officer, perform your duties! Don't be buffaloed by one of these wetbacks from Hull. Let him be grateful that he's in a city where you won't drag him off to the police station and break his knuckles with his own jack handle. Let him know that he's in *my* city, my kind of town, Ottawa! Where we will be as gentle and kind as we can be ... and clean ... and orderly ... and organized ... as long as that Ottawa life is ours for the living.

OUT OF THE CLOSET
AND INTO THE GAY BAR

That's right, Bill, you conceited male chauvinist boor, brag about it. The rest of us guys sitting around the office coffee percolator are all ears. We are simply amazed, let me tell you, that the girl you went out with last night, the one we all thought was the shyest little creature imaginable, came right out and asked you if you wanted to ball when you took her home. Simply amazing!

Bill, sexual conquistador without peer in the ranks of lower management, is around thirty and still has a few post-acne scars. He is not terrifically handsome, in other words, but he does all right because he is definitely charming with women. He is charming with them despite the fact that he despises them, as he will tell you anytime. "I've never met one who was really intelligent," he will say. "Even the ones with college degrees are dumb, once you get to know them."

This is still a bit of a puzzle to Leo, how someone can despise women like that and still turn on the old charm when he wants to. But then, Leo, one of Bill's co-workers, has not had a great deal of experience with women. He has not gone on a date with a girl since high school, in fact. Leo's sex life has consisted of masturbation fantasies, and these have not centred on women. Not exactly. Leo is rather the type of person who can get sentimental over Johnny Weismuller in the old Tarzan flicks. (No intellectual, that Johnny, but there's something sympathetic in his face, after all, an unmistakable trace of a subdued sorrow, a

17

touch of niceness, even as he prepares for a dive into the crocodile-infested waters.) Actually, Leo happens to be almost as much a source of fascination to Bill as Bill is to Leo. Bill frankly used to wonder if Leo was a queer, but he decided that, for all practical purposes, he wasn't. This was partly on the principle that a man is innocent until proven guilty. True, Leo never went out with girls and still lived in somewhat cozy fashion with his parents, at age twenty-four, and that was certainly, in Bill's book, pretty damaging evidence. But he could also pronounce the letter "s" without difficulty, and his wrists were fairly firm, and so, what the hell, he could pass. Bill watched him for a while to see if he were laying a friendly hand on guys' shoulders a little too often (since the other infallible sign of homosexuals, according to Bill, was the fact they were "always touching each other"). When he was satisfied Leo wasn't, he allowed himself to be a little chummy, even, with Leo.

Once, on a weekend afternoon, they got together for a drink. A terribly depressing Saturday afternoon it was, and they both got stinking drunk. Towards the end, Bill, riding some stray current in the channels of his brain, devious and remarkable channels, suggested that they drop in at the St. Charles, favourite Yonge Street haunt of Toronto's gay male population, for a look at the queers. Just for a giggle, you understand. And Leo, who up to this moment had never really known that gay bars existed in Toronto, who had never really encountered a genuine, flesh-and-blood, self-admitted homosexual, agreed.

Strange and wonderful world of gay love at the St. Charles! Most of the guys there looked—exactly—no different from the customers sitting around the Men's Beverage Room of some hotel in outer Scarborough. Of course, there were a few boys there whose blond Malibu sun 'n surf style locks were a little too exquisite, and whose faces looked like they would collapse pretty soon from the strain of giving long and meaningful looks in the direction of every mirror in sight. Basically, however, the only difference between this beverage room and any other was the almost unnatural quiet. It was quiet because the men there (those who were not sitting by themselves) were huddled in groups of two, three — at most, four — and they were not discussing their supervisors at work, their hockey favourites, or their girlfriends in loud, public voices, but were into little intense conversations. And this quiet began to affect Bill and Leo. Two men who ordinarily enjoyed talking very much, they became very silent, they were lost in thought. Leo, quite simply, was thinking that there were several men there he would like to go to bed with.

Listen, what does Leo know about sleeping with men? When he was thirteen or fourteen, his father, a man in a condition of permanent terror before all the mysterious processes of life, all the subterranean movements of feeling and desire, told him simply "If you masturbate too much, you'll become a homosexual." Well, Leo masturbates a great deal, and always has, in fact: is this why, when he does masturbate, it is with no vision of a woman in bed there beside him, no ripe girl with wanton eyes and billowing tresses? But of course excess of masturbation does not a homosexual make because there was never a moment in Leo's whole masturbatory career when the fantasy partner was a woman. No. If all his fantasies were turned to reality, he would be one damned busy homosexual.

The reality of his life is that he lives in a house with his mother and father who are very concerned for him, and he never stays out much later than closing time at the local pub and he has never actually touched a man with intent to make love with him. But this little trip to the St. Charles, this lark with the number-one office hetero, is just possibly a turning point in his life, he thinks; yes, what else can it be—and he sees before him the Rubicon of his sexual life, the whole territory laid out in front of him of pick-ups, and affairs, casual liaisons, and prolonged relationships between men, and all he has to do is work up the courage to cross into that territory, that tantalizing world right in front of his eyes.

Leo, you don't know it yet, but if you actually cross that

Rubicon you won't just be having your first homosexual experience, you'll be casting a vote for the legions of the Polymorphous Perverse, yes indeed, you'll be right in there with the shock battalions of the sexual revolution (whether you like it or not). Poor anonymous white-collar closet case! It's been your great fortune or misfortune (and what great sexual prophet has yet appeared to decide which it will be?) to have been born in late-twentieth-century North America, where one's innermost anxiety, the most private anguish or joy of the psyche, now becomes dramatic public evidence for use by the partisans of sexual politics. That, however, will all come later. In the meantime very personal, very secret, resolutions are being drafted in Leo's head.

The next weekend he is back on Yonge St. catching an afternoon movie by himself, and when he steps out he heads for a dirty book store, and buys a magazine — Johnny Weismuller without his loin cloth, at last — filled with photographs of spoiled and furious young men posing by waterfalls like debauchees from a Charles Atlas orgy. Leo is psyching himself up for his second visit to the St. Charles, this one for real. Three times he has to pass in front of the door before he feels ready for it. He has the mistaken notion, actually, that just walking into a gay bar wanting to go to bed with someone means that you'll be grabbed on the spot, probably by some fat queer wearing a see-through shirt and a dynel wig.

No, it's not like that, Leo. You just walk in through the door and sit at the bar and order a beer and if somebody happens to give you the eye you don't even have to look back at him, you can spend your whole evening watching the overhead colour TV (Tony Randall of "The Odd Couple" doing his borderline queer routine for Middle America, perhaps), if you want to.

So Leo does sit down and sets a speed record downing two bottles of beer, and notices that he hasn't even moved far enough into the bar to get beyond the vision of passersby walking by the glass doors of the St. Charles, so that the whole world, actually, could walk by at this moment, maybe Bill and his friends coming back from an evening of admiring the topless go-go girls at the Zanzibar Tavern, and see that he is, in fact, a queer, Leo who never goes out with girls, a homosexual drinking beer at the St. Charles.

At this point Leo must admit to himself that things are getting ridiculous. If he wants to meet somebody he is going to have to make himself available. So he goes to the beverage room and sits at a table in a row of tables which customers have to walk by to get to the main part of the room. He sits there for a few hours, sinking further into a depression every time a man who looks halfway attractive walks by and ignores him, and every time he has to ignore someone else making friendly faces at him whom he is frankly not ready to climb into the sheets with. Good God! There are representatives here from the lower depths after all, hustlers looking like they've come fresh from a twenty-four-hour engagement at the men's room of the Bloor-Yonge subway, tough guys with real grease in their hair, desperate middle-aged men with no hair at all and a slight cringe in the shoulders—yes, if one wanted to, one could get into a hell of a depression.

Meeting a suitable partner at a gay bar is, in a way, more problematic than trying to hustle a chick at the Straight Arrow Discotheque ever was, since one is both, so to speak, hunter and quarry. And yet Leo is not totally out of luck this evening, not even after four hours of sitting by himself. This moment, after all, represents the turning of a large wheel in the mechanism of whatever fate rules his life, he is thinking — it *has* to. The build-up of such excitement, such sheer stimulation, as he has been feeling tonight cannot conclude with nothing. There is no way it is not going to happen.

So shortly before closing time Leo makes the second great decision of this evening. He goes up to another table where another young man is sitting, a pleasant-faced young man wearing eyeglasses and an outfit—corduroy sports jacket included—that would pass inspection before the personnel department of the tightest-arsed corporation imaginable, and asks him simply "Can I join you?" When he says yes, Leo sits down and the rest is easy.

They leave the St. Charles and go for a coffee somewhere, and have a nice chat, the details of which Leo will never remember, but he is surprised it is so comparatively effortless. The other man is almost the same age as Leo, bland in his conversation without being a bore, quite friendly, helpful, willing to please—they might be tourists from the same locality who have met by chance in some exotic foreign country, thrilling in its hint of unknown perils, except the one has been around for a while while the other is still totally amazed that he is there in the first place. Amazed, and grateful now that he has found someone he can hold on to. Finally the other man suggests, with a minimum of strain in the voice, that they might go to bed, and Leo says yes, it's time.

"Uh, I'm living in an apartment with my sister. Do you think we could go to your place?" To ... Leo's place. Leo cannot believe it. He has seized the time, followed the bidding of his fate, his true fate, and yet ... as usual, that unknowable, unchallengeable fate is fucking him over for his trouble. No place to hop into the sack! After all this! Leo living with his mom and dad, who even now are beginning to expect the cheering sound of his footsteps coming in the front door, his lover living with his sister. Too much.

They are too far into this thing, however, to give up easily. As it happens they drive out of the city a bit in Leo's car, ending up in as reasonably secluded a suburban lane as one could hope for. It is, by any measure, a wondrous moment, the payoff of a lifetime when countless fantasies are to be redeemed—yes, any time now — by a few minutes of reality, and Leo hasn't a clue what to do. Not a clue. The unhappy truth of the matter is that he has never quite been able to imagine in any explicit terms what homosexuals actually *do* with each other when they make love. He has, of course, heard a few of the terms with which one man will implicate another in homosexuality, a few standard insults of the working class, but the reality of fellatio, for instance, is as foreign to him as the trickier breathing exercises in Pranayama Yoga.

There has to be an analogy here with the situation where the callow youth is taken to bed by the wise, true-hearted whore, the woman who can soothe the fears of a boy and lead him gently through the portals of the Sacred Mystery. Leo could sure use something like that, he is absolutely petrified. Fortunately his friend, while perhaps not entirely wise and true-hearted, is at least somewhat sensitive to Leo's fearfulness, and is generous enough to take the initiative and not expect Leo to do all that much in return. No, all Leo has to do is settle back and be brought to sexual climax by this man doing what he, Leo, has always had to do by himself. In truth, Leo does not feel all that radically different experiencing this as he had felt experiencing nothing but the fantasy with the orgasm — no new heaven, no new earth—but this has got to be real, after all, this has got to be profoundly significant. It means he has become one of *them*, he has taken out full membership in the guild of practising queers. . . .

So for the next few days he is practically a nervous wreck. At home he can't eat, all he can think of is the night he got off in his own car with this stranger touching him. At work he can't concentrate, he is positive Bill is giving him hostile glances, is avoiding him, talking to the other guys in the office about him, how he, Bill, has seen the word "homosexual" written in lurid magenta letters over Leo's guilty visage. And he is also thinking of the weekend ahead — each weekend has suddenly become unreal, now, a rendezvous with his destiny—he knows he will be back at a bar, or perhaps a club which plays records and has fish nets hanging from the ceiling and go-go boys with hairless chests for decor.

Leo is not completely aware of it but he is in the process of what is called in gay liberation circles "coming out". It will take a few weeks yet, but before long he will be in the life, and everyone will know it. (Well, almost everyone. Perhaps Bill will never find out, because Leo will leave his job soon, not out of fear of what the other guys will think, exactly, but because the job was a drag and he has plenty of unemployment insurance coming to him, anyway.) Leo's next partner will be another conservatively dressed gentleman, of sensational good looks, who will, in truth, know how to soothe his fears and lead him gently through the portals of the Sacred Mystery; their first night together he will merely cuddle him in his arms. They will have an affair lasting one month, until this gentleman gets a little weary of Leo looking as if the sky is going to fall on top of him any minute, every time they are out together in broad daylight. And Leo will still have problems to face, worries about how attractive he is, how able and willing to satisfy other men ... hangups not altogether different than those of heterosexuals trying to proceed from fantasies of masterful sex with the grateful girl of wanton eyes and billowing tresses to real encounters with real women.

But if you ask him now he will assure you that he is indeed happy in his new-found identity, his new lifestyle. One day he hopes to get involved in a truly smashing love affair, of course ... already he knows the pangs of unrequited love, the sweet despair of longing for that unattainable young man. One day, though, he'll find his true love. In the meantime, send no psychiatrists to Leo, recent recruit to the growing ranks of Gay Liberationists, unashamed practitioner of the love which, aeons ago, dared not speak its name—relaxed beer drinker, finally, at the dear old St. Charles.

SUNSET STRIP

Marigolds, roses, tulips, hydrangea, daffodils, chrysanthemums — all those flowers fit for the Queen Mum. They can be found, every one of them, growing in Victoria's Beacon Hill Park. Begonias and pansies and sweet alyssum flourish in the heart of the city, Victoria, B.C. You can't keep spades and trowels away from good British stock. Fifty years ago, after all, this was Tea and Crumpet City. An outpost of the empire, more English than England, etc. As English as George here, walking through Beacon Hill Park assisted by his ashplant cane, smiling at all the polychrome plants around him. "This is the part of the park the old ladies love," he says. Bless their marigold and hydrangea hearts! George himself is not into that *Better Homes and Gardens* scene. But he is English nonetheless, and will remember until his dying days—not such a distant prospect, now, actually—his childhood spent among the fields of Lincolnshire, where every scrap of land was cultivated, every blade of grass tended (except where the hedgerows grew, with the oak, and the ash, and the beech trees). Now *there* was a race of cultivators, those turn-of-the-century Lincolnshire farmers. Everything "kept up", every farm husbanded as if it were a woman who must not lose her shape even though she gives birth every year. A bit different, say, from farms in eastern Canada today where they tear down a little more of their barn each year so they can sell barnboard to some guy who's driven up in his station wagon from Poughkeepsie, N.Y.

Anyway, George is one authentic English-born resident of this city which still clings to whatever images of Englishness it can salvage from its past. Its trees and gardens in the middle of the city are a genuine legacy of that English past. Of course, they've overdone this, too. In the course of anglicizing the terrain, they imported some Commonwealth flora and fauna, Australian laurel, broom from the Scottish highlands, English starlings. The broom has spread all over Beacon Hill, unkillable, ugly as bristle on a pig, though it is said defensively that the bushes do hold the soil together. The English starlings have spread, too. Mean and predatory, they have practically driven away the native population of sparrows and thrushes, and now they, too, are as indestructible as cockroaches. And the Australian laurel! Green, glossy laurel — it grows like the broom. A little more handsome, and serviceable as a hedge in front of your house, but after a while you have to keep hacking away at it or else it will take over your lawn, the sidewalk, and half the street. Victoria is full of these Australian laurel hedges, sheltering Tudor-style stucco houses from the noise of the traffic.

That's another British import that has proved unkillable, as a matter of fact — Tudor-style houses. They have not, like the starlings, driven away the competition — you can see lots of Georgian-style houses, split-level ranch houses, houses done in New England Colonial, Bauhaus Modern, Bel Air Spanish, at least one in Moorish Delight, with seraglio arches and medieval tessellae gracing its façade. But Tudor is dominant. Even one-bedroom bungalows have three or four stripes painted on the stucco to suggest a little of that Tudor half-timber work. You don't really need gables, wooden shingles, oak doors with iron hinges, elaborate brick chimney stacks, oriel windows, and all the rest of the design features built in to the more true-to-life replicas. Three or four narrow stripes painted on the stucco and you have your instant Tudor dwelling.

So George fits in, a Lincoln man, from the land where Captain John Smith grew up among houses with real gables and oriel windows and Tudor-style half-timber. Victoria is a city, like

Williamsburg, Virginia (fruit of that captain's labour), dedicated to preserving memories, and George has more or less the appropriate ones — Lincolnshire farms, Lincolnshire horses, a Lincolnshire choir school where you could get that old-time classical education, with no frills like a laboratory, gymnasium, industrial shop, or home ec. class for the girls. A Lincolnshire Anglican church, where the choirmaster got into trouble by trying to do a Christmas carol with the phrase "Christus natus hodie" in it — too many echoes of popery for the Lincolnshire *petite bourgeoisie*. He fits in this city, where widows face the end of their days watering their African violets and occasionally dusting off the shelves where the porcelain nymphs and the old choir-school textbooks are kept. Dr. Goldsmith's *History of England* , for example, *With Questions for Examination at the End of Each Chapter* — sixty years ago they were knitting their brows over tough ones like, "What race of people infested our dominions in the East Indies?"

Yes, there are still memories of England and the empire, but they are fading by the minute. Victoria tourist literature likes to conjure up pictures of elderly English couples walking their bulldogs through the streets of the city, and British army colonels retired from India sipping tea in the Bengal Room of the Empress Hotel. When the last retired colonel died, they should have set his mummified remains in a glass case in the Bengal Room, like they did to Jeremy Bentham, who has been sitting up behind glass in University College, London, for these past hundred and forty years. As it is, the colonels are long gone, and have really left few traces behind them. As in Williamsburg, the historical resonances, the collective memories of the past, have lost any actual hold on the living, except when they've been lacquered and touched-up as museum artifacts. No one takes tea at the Empress Hotel any more except people from Spokane.

And George, when you get right down to it, despite his Lincolnshire roots, has small use for Tudor half-timber work and oriel windows, or tweeds and bulldogs, or the British raj, or even marigolds, hydrangea, and daffodils. He left Lincolnshire, after all, when he was nearing twenty, when the soldiers were being demobbed after the First World War, and there was no work for a fresh young choir-school graduate — left Lincolnshire to spend most of the rest of his life working in a bank in the Maritimes. If he, like the thousands of other retired people living here, clings to memories, as Saul Bellow says, to keep the wolf of insignificance from the door, these memories are more concerned with those forty-odd years of slugging away at the Royal Bank. Forty years of doing everything from cleaning the rust out of the sidearms they used to protect the tellers, to attending endless, stupefying meetings of the local Rotary Club. He had to do the Rotary Club, you see, to keep his managers from breathing down his neck about "being active in the community". Forty years of that boring, mechanical fox trot called "being active in the community" . . . no wonder George can't be bothered, today, to get involved in The Silver Threads or the New Horizons or any of these other programs which are designed to inspire older people to keep on living.

Forty years! One can easily understand why the Little-England, tweed-and-bulldog, colonial motif has little to do with anything in George's past, or his present. In a curious way, George has more in common with the hordes of wandering flower children who pass through Victoria every summer on their way to some organic vegetable commune halfway up the island. George, after all, is a fan of Thoreau's and knows something about the simple life, and the unfettered spirit, and the kind of human existence philosophers have always thought to be desirable. No one has to remind him that when he was doing things like sketching Walden Pond (he can draw like an angel, by the way) he was more alive than when he was sitting in on the Rotary Club luncheon. If only he had grown up in an era when doing your own thing was gospel — instead of growing up in an era when doing your duty, and paying your grocery bills on time, and avoiding the poor house at all costs, was gospel.

There is definitely some philosophical bond between George, the retired Royal Bank employee, and these flower children, although George, who grew up in an era when it was also considered a grace to be articulate, could doubtless explain that philosophy more intelligently and coherently than most of these kids. But there is an even more striking and visceral bond between them, which is hard to explain, exactly. It has to do, in a way, with this one-act play George was in about forty years ago, a play by Lady Augusta Gregory called *The Travelling Man*. George played the title role when they put it on at the Dominion Drama Festival in Ottawa in 1935. The play is one of these literary portraits of the simple, humble faith of the Irish peasantry around the days of the Celtic twilight. An Irish lass, cast out from her home, is saved one rainy, stormy night by Christ appearing before her eyes. He sends her to this peasant cottage where she finds herself a husband, and He promises that one night He will return. Well, of course, when He does return He comes back not in His magnificent Christ-like robes, or with His aura glowing, or anything, but as a barefoot, mud-spattered wretch, the "travelling man". Of course, the woman kicks this bum out of the cottage without a second thought. George, in an old white flannel shirt ripped to shreds for the occasion, and a pair of old gabardine trousers spattered with huge glops of sienna paint to suggest the mud, got to cry out heartfelt lines like, "I will go. I will go back to the high road that is walked by the bare feet of the poor, by the innocent bare feet of children. I will go back to the rocks and the wind, to the cries of the trees in the storm!"

Strong stuff for a lifer in the Royal Bank of Canada. More, I'm sure, than his employers bargained for, when they urged him to get involved in the community. I mean, Christ-like figures were *not* wanted behind their wickets. No, sir. You just keep your waistcoat buttoned and your tie on straight, George. . . . It must have been an effort for him, really, to keep that old travelling-man spirit, that banked down passion for freedom and simplicity, in check. These days the spirit, after those forty years of servitude, still adds a faint luster to George, the luster of a candle flame seen through one of those ancient, fragile windows made out of sheets of horn. You get the feeling that if you touch the window with the least bit of roughness it will crumble into powder, and the candle flame will be blown out instantly. But in the meantime, of course, the flame is still in there, shedding its bit of light.

Basically, the visceral bond between George and these kids is the fact that, like the travelling man, they are really not much in demand in this city. Not really. It doesn't matter what they might have to offer in the way of spiritual refreshment for the solid citizenry, the contented peasants in their Tudor cottages. The kids, for example, walk around in knapsacks, living off a jar of peanut butter and a loaf of stale bread for a month, and whenever they walk into a store the manager keeps stealing glances at the anti-shoplifting mirror. The cheerful smiles of waitresses turn hard and sullen when they walk into the lunch counter. There are still many people who are disgusted merely by the sight of their long hair and beards and Army and Navy wardrobes.

With many old people, it's not much different. You can trust them not to steal anything, of course, but you can also trust them not to be big spenders. And, like the ragged children, they are not usually the kind of people you'd want to stick in a Pepsi-Cola commercial on TV, the ones that show people bouncing around having a good time. I mean, they are generally not an advertising agency's idea of what constitutes an attractive person. George, for example, despite the luster of his travelling-man spirit, is at the stage where his mortality as a human being is becoming more and more obvious. He is at that stage of masculine physical decline where the sternum seems to buckle inwards and the belly stands out as a nice, rounded ball of cracked vinyl stretched over the abdominal viscera. When he takes off his glasses, the red marks on the bridge of his nose look like erosions in granite. And when he walks along the street, in his old man's uniform of charcoal grey suit-jacket, and polo shirt buttoned up to the top button, and standard old-man straw hat with tiny brim — no one has to guess where this travelling man is going. When he walks into one of those restaurants that have red glowing candles on the table for lighting—George with his eyes slowly succumbing to glaucoma, eyes that can no longer adjust to the gloom of intimate restaurants—it is like walking into that everlasting night promised us all. He can't see a bloody thing. Of course, the waitresses are not as rude as the Irish peasant woman. They whip past him on all sides as he stumbles and gropes through the black nothingness, but they don't kick him out. They just ignore him, usually. You can talk about your rocks and wind and cries of the trees in the storm, but a restaurant in the busy hour is murder. Sooner or later, he'll fall over an empty table, or something, and sit down.

In Victoria there are thousands of men like him, walking around wearing suit-jackets in shades like midnight green or pigeon-wing grey . . . the sun can be sizzling overhead, but these jackets don't come off. Travelling men, all of them. Any day one expects them to be gone, removed from the scene. Of course, George is different from most of them, because he doesn't really have much worry about money. Some of these fellows live in 7' x 5' rooms with a hot plate and a few cans of Campbell's Cream of Tomato soup. And maybe a bathroom at the end of the hall which they share with five or six other people. For contact with the outside world they visit places like the Senior Citizens Activity Centre, formerly known as "The Silver Threads", where they can do everything from crewel embroidery to lapidary work to making little Canada-goose mobiles out of balsa wood . . . or they drop in at the New Horizons place, where they can play whist, sing hymns, go on picnics to James Bay. Since this is Victoria, dedicated to fading memories, they can do all these things under the benign gaze of Queen Elizabeth and Prince Philip, or—at the New Horizons—under the sterner gaze of Winston Churchill. At the New Horizons there is, besides the Churchill portrait, a portrait of Vimy Ridge, with its barren earth and sky painted in a dark, death-like blue tint. At the crest of the ridge there is a marble or granite monument, bathed in an unearthly cream light. Death was never so solemn, so poignant, so lovely. Solemn, poignant, lovely Death! This is something anybody can appreciate, here in the heart of anglophilia . . . this collective memory of Death, from out of the English past.

As I say, however, such awe-inspiring nostalgia really doesn't have that great a hold on the living here. Victoria is still part of late-twentieth-century North America, however much many of these people might sincerely regret that fact. And that means a day-to-day concern, like rising prices, now takes up more of their attention than this kind of memory possibly can. If money is the blood of the poor, as Leon Bloy said, it is corpuscles and hemoglobin to these old people, as well. And inflation means that they bleed more frequently every day—they who can least of all afford the loss of rich, red blood. Of course, the government understands. The government helps provide them with activity centres. It also likes to keep them on their toes, employing students during the summer to interview old people and "assist" them in re-applying for their Mincome grants (minimum income)—in the process, of course, making sure that they aren't pulling a fast one on the government. No telling what these old girls might have stashed away under the floorboards. So university students who otherwise would have been forced to spend their summers smoking hash in grubby communes or fomenting revolution now go around in the summer months knocking on the doors of old people's apartments and going through these interviews on behalf of the B.C. provincial government.

Needless to say, the old people are terrified of this intrusion in their lives. Few people who are not old realize the extent to which many old people, particularly those who are poor, live in fear almost every day of their lives. Thank God they are not yet fearful of muggers, like they are in St. Petersburg, Florida, and other retirement havens in the United States. But they are afraid of things like the traffic, afraid of landlords raising their rent or selling their houses to some guy building young-executive condominiums, afraid of waking up in the middle of the night and hearing their hearts beat a strange new tattoo, afraid of any breakdown in their TV sets because prices are so high for repairs now that if their sets start acting up they may as well say goodbye to them, goodbye to their faithful companions, more tireless and soothing than any spouse, friend, or nursemaid — afraid, most of all, that the government which helps support them will cut off the blood supply, will stop sending cheques through the mail — because of computer error, or some obscure bureaucratic regulation, or because someone, somewhere, has become displeased with them.

They are truly fearful, and also — perhaps for that reason — the most scrupulously honest of any class of citizens. They will agonize for hours trying to pin down the exact date of a change in residence that occurred fifteen years ago because that is what the application form demands. And so there is the young man in their doorway, smiling intently, and being as polite as a mortician, and it doesn't matter if he explains to them a million times in his kindest, nicest, most patient and polite voice, "The purpose of this interview is, uh, just to make sure you understand clearly what constitutes a source of income. I'm not here, you know, to check up on you, or anything," in their minds he could just as well be grabbing them by their cut-glass chokers, brandishing a rubber hose in the other hand, and shouting, "Okay, lady, where are the dividends from AT&T! Where's your husband's insurance policy! Where's your Christian Science annuity! We're the government and we want to know!"

Ah yes, the helplessness of inflation cutting your veins open, one by one. Couples who slaved for years, did without vacations, without second cars, without dinner at the local French restaurant because they figured that the long winter of retirement was close by and they might as well prepare for it so they could be warm and cozy like the industrious ants, and not freezing and destitute like the foolish grasshoppers who went off to the Côte d'Azur every summer, now find they're freezing and destitute *anyway*. A nest egg of one hundred thousand dollars, which fifteen years ago seemed like a guarantee of comfortable middle-class life for the rest of one's natural life (post retirement), now means a comfortable middle-class existence for maybe six or seven years. All over Victoria people examine their bank accounts and their budgets and think — please don't let me live to be eighty. Please, God, don't let me live to eighty-five. Please, oh please, whatever You do, don't let me live to be ninety! They're in the situation of the old fisherman in the Santa Cruz Islands who realizes that he is getting to be more and more of a burden to his family, and decides to head out to sea in his worn out old Te Puke canoe, never to be seen again ... only, of course, this is British Columbia and such things are not really seriously considered as options.

There aren't that many other options, however, for our travelling men. That's the long and short of it. Old age cuts off the number of your choices. Even a second legal marriage, say, for two old people who want to live as cheaply as one — two old people who like each other and think it might be nice to move in, and cut their rent in half—is a doubtful option. "Living together", for a generation brought up to regard common-law marriage as the first wave of social anarchy, is now seen as preferable to going through a wedding ceremony. It's just wisest not to disturb the Mincome computers by having the data on your card changed, however slightly. Of course, for old men one of the few remaining solaces of their last years may be the fact that they've never had such a wide field to play. Men die younger than women, and Victoria is actually more a city of widows than of "senior citizens". At The Silver Threads and the New Horizons the ratio runs about four-to-one in favour of women. So if a man lives past seventy and is single his chances of finding a mate are good, providing he really wants one and suffers from no obvious defects, like acromegaly or dementia praecox.

George has a lady friend, strictly platonic of course, who likes to twit him on this subject. George lives in an apartment building where there are a lot of unattached women of his age, and his friend, over dinner at a restaurant one night, starts going on about this potential menace to George's health and security. "I worry about you, George, you know," she says, "with all those good-looking women. There's a woman in my golf club, as a matter of fact, who lives right on your floor. But I'm not telling her about you." George looks at her like somebody being tickled once or twice between the ribs. She has put on this determined expression, like the chairman of the Metropolitan United Church Entertainment Committee vetoing a proposal for some girl to jump out of a cake and kiss George, happy birthday. "I know, Edith," he says, "but you see . . . none of them can *cook!* " And he starts laughing hard, which comes out like a high-pitched, excited moan.

But what's a joke to one man is deadly serious to another. Alliances do occur late in life, and they are not infrequent here in Victoria. Some women are convinced, in fact, that a man who is over sixty-five and single has "something wrong with him". Of course, they will also remark to each other over tea and Arrowroot biscuits, sitting by the African violets, that a woman, unless she is desperate to share the rent with someone, might do better than have a man under foot in her apartment once again. One does not want to be trapped into becoming an unpaid nursemaid and housekeeper for some old fellow rapidly slipping into invalidism — particularly if one has already been through that scene. And some of these widows know intimately what it is like to care for someone who is in a wheel chair or bed-ridden. Being alone is not the most crushing fate that can befall you.

One lady recalls waiting in the lobby of a hotel for the limousine to take her to the airport, and there's this old guy slumped in the leatherette sofa giving her the eye. Not some old bum, you understand—he has a dark blue, three-piece suit that looks like it's recently come back from the cleaners, and a good Irish blackthorn cane. Anyway, all of a sudden he starts addressing her, in these shouts. He's nearly deaf, of course, and he just wants to hear a little bit of what he's saying. So he shouts out to her in the middle of the lobby, "Hi! Have you been to Alaska?" Now she has to make one of these split-second decisions as to whether she's going to ignore him or not, and she decides—well, she doesn't really decide, it's just sort of a conditioned reflex on her part, based on an instantaneous, unreasoned hope that if she replies in a calm, adult voice, he will see that he doesn't need to shout, and, of course, the guy is deaf, there's no way he's going to stop shouting — but she replies, anyway, "No," and the guy shouts back, "I've been there twice! Been to Mexico?"

By now it's hopeless. She replies, "Uh, yes," and he shouts, "Yeah, I've been there too. . . . Been to Spain?"

"No."

She starts to open her purse and rummage through it, as if there is something in it she just has to find, and also to look anxiously at the door of the lobby — the damned bus is two minutes late — and here she is, stuck with this guy talking nonsense to her because the blood vessels feeding his brain have obviously become clogged beyond repair . . . and he shouts again triumphantly, "I've been there! My niece is there now. I lent her forty thousand dollars—for income tax purposes, you know." A smile of idiot cunning spreads over his face. And then he looks up at her, as if remembering now the purpose for which this conversation was initially commenced. "Say," he asks, "would you like to marry me? I've got lots of money." Mortification! But the worst is yet to come. "The thing is, all the women want to marry someone who can —— them. But I'm eighty-five. Can't cut the mustard any more."

So all this is shouted out in the middle of the lobby, and she can't stand it any more, the bellboys are smirking, the little children are staring, other elderly couples are looking at her as if she were some retired streetwalker who deliberately got this poor senile old gentleman aroused, and she grabs her two suitcases and walks out to the sidewalk to wait for the limousine. Reflecting later, she supposes he might actually have been in the market for a wife. More precisely, for that unsalaried, lifetime nursemaid. Well, there's no way any of these ladies, as I say, will be trapped into *that* once again — it could be the Aga Khan proposing, but if he needs somebody to spoon-feed him his tapioca pudding every day, forget it. But in his peculiar way, this loony gentleman did put his finger on one aspect of post-retirement marriage that has nothing to do with sharing rent, or pooling income, or the question of money at all. The loony gentleman who could no longer meet the sexual demands of some passionate seventy-year-old bride probably understood the situation very well, and the fairly major problem rising out of it.

If older people are being deprived of financial nutrients, they are also not exactly encouraged to get their share of the action in our on-going society-wide sexual free-for-all. A curious phenomenon. Everybody, from the thirteen-year-old girl desperately washing her face four times a day with Phisohex to clear away tiny zits, to the middle-aged businessman waiting at the airport, is reading *Playboy, Penthouse, Viva,* etc., and grasping the subtle message that if they are not enjoying thirty orgasms a night they are definitely Missing Out. Even newspaper readers now receive humourless advice from psychologists and clergymen to the effect that "sexual fulfilment is a profound need in human beings". No excuse for frigidity these days, ma'am! But somehow it all stops short of one class of humanity, the folks over sixty, all those women, say, who were a little too vigorous for the gentleman in the lobby. Somehow the readers of *Playboy, Penthouse,* and *Viva* don't like to think of the old wrecks snorting and wheezing in passion, or making the earth shake once a week. It's hard to put one's finger on it. I mean, just because their wrinkled torsos don't have the glossy look of *Playboy/Viva* models is no reason to exclude them from the fun … but still the squeamishness is there.

And more than squeamishness. When two old people come together in a common-law relationship they don't usually get any hassles from their friends, the people who grew up with them in the days of the stifling, pre-Hefner morality we all despise so much. But watch out for the kids, their own enlightened offspring. One woman in Victoria who moved in with a man who is now divorced, wife back home in Nova Scotia, answers the phone with a cheerful hello, and hears this "Oh" on the other line from Sudbury or Penticton or wherever her lover's children are now residing—an "Oh" as in "Oh—it's *you*." Then there is this slight pause, and a voice that could chill your whipped egg whites all the way from Sudbury, Ontario, asking, "Is, uh ... Mr. *Macpherson* there?"

Such hostility! Needless to say, the kids are not anxious to drop in on the old man in Victoria these days—even less anxious than they might be, say, to drop in on their college-age son shacking up with a girl off-campus. With the son you never know—his girl might turn out to be "nice", after all, and they'll get married and have kids, and it's best not to alienate permanently a potential source of grandchildren, a potential family to drop in on *them*, come holidays and family reunions. But Dad is another matter. These allowances do not apply to him. Perhaps there is even a touch of Hamlet's petulant outburst to his mother — "at your age/The heyday in the blood is tame, it's humble,/And waits upon the judgement". Come off it Hamlet, you hopeless neurotic. That's not the *real* reason you're angry with your mother for sleeping with Claudius. ... Anyway, for whatever reason, this common-law relationship means that Dad might as well forget about visits from relations for a while. He is not about to kick his woman out for a week or so, make her stay at the Y while his kids are in town.

A not unusual situation here in Victoria ... this city which no longer belongs (if it ever did) to English couples walking their bulldogs, or retired colonels writing furious letters to the London *Times* or *Daily Telegraph* every time Willie Hamilton attacks the monarchy. It's just a city of old people, period. They count their dimes and they look for love. It's very simple really. They just have more trouble, sometimes, getting a hold of those dimes, and finding that love. And they are more conscious than most of the fact they are travelling men and women, and that they live in an impermanent world.

That's okay. That's not the tragedy. If there is a tragedy in their lives it is probably that too many people are like that obtuse peasant lass who wants the travelling man out of her kitchen, who won't *look* at them long enough to notice the light — subdued and faint, but still flickering there—within people like George, who have never given up on life. Never given up despite the many temptations to do so, over the long and painful years. And because people like George have not given up they are not yet completely powerless; they have, in fact, something to give, if people would only go out of their way to receive it. A subtle and understated message to the effect that we weren't all born yesterday, kids. Some of us older people have travelled along much the same road you're taking. Some of us have been travelling for a long, long time. Don't forget us. Don't forget to learn from us that no destination, certainly not this beautiful city here on Vancouver Island, is more important than all that hard and ceaseless travelling you're doing.

SNOW WHITE AT THE GLITTER PALACE

Rock'n'roll performers always lead the way. David Bowie, with the sour look of a child who would dearly love to throw a colossal temper tantrum, became the very model of the new teen-age decadence, the new satin set, in the same way Elvis Presley, in his "Jailhouse Rock" days, became the model for the fifties greaser, and the Beatles, in their "Sergeant Pepper" and "Yellow Submarine" days, became prophetic lights for the sixties flower children. David Bowie is indeed perfect for this role. Better than Alice Cooper or the New York Dolls or Elton John with his round rainbow glasses, better than any of them, because he is so . . . because, oh David, it is so obvious you don't *care*! Even sex means nothing to you. A pretty young man here, a bored-looking girl with green lipstick there, animals, inanimate objects — does one really have to get specific about what sort of love objects will do? Of course not! Only one thing really matters to David. That is the attention of his audience — not necessarily rapt admiration, you understand, but simple attention. You can all continue with your outrageous sex lives, bisexual, pansexual, omnisexual, whatever label you wish to hang on it, but whatever you do, don't take your eyes off the main show.

Bisexual chic. In a way, it doesn't have a great deal to do with sex. It's more that desire for being seen, for attention, for the looks you get when you walk into the room with your dynamite rhinestones and furs, say, and your friends give them a cool, almost professional appraisal — *Honey, that dress would look tacky on anyone else but you.* Right! That's good. Do it up one night like Marlene Dietrich at *The Blue Angel*, the next night like Sidney Greenstreet at *The Blue Parrot* — for you, this is chic, and only incidentally may one call it "bisexual".

In Canada, we are undoubtedly behind in all this. To be more precise, a city like Toronto is four years behind New York City. At least, that's what Murray tells me, sitting in his apartment cluttered with various art objects, like the framed relievo sculpture of a female torso done in what looks like white Bakelite. Murray, who reads the French, Italian, and British editions of *Vogue*, and therefore has some notion of what goes down in the world of chic, assures me, in fact, that the situation in Toronto is "pretty grim". Those are his very words. Murray makes his living right now, or part of his living, doing things like curling and setting wigs, choosing wardrobes, and helping make basic life decisions for some wealthy women in the city, but he is more famous for being a kind of entrepreneur in the field of Toronto nightlife. One of the clubs he ran, *Mama Cooper's*, was the first "homosexual-heterosexual environment" in the city, meaning a club which was basically derived from your standard gay discotheque with its late hours, absence of liquor, and non-stop music and dancing, but a club where straight couples were welcome, for the first time, to share in the fun. "Homosexual-heterosexual environments" are very big now, but when Murray says the situation is grim, he means there are few, if any, clubs that attract the really classy bisexuals who have the money and the taste to actually *look* like a sultry blonde from the silent-screen era, or a dashing young man from the thirties with the Prince of Wales look, or whoever else they happen to feel like on any given night.

That leaves the field pretty much to the less than classy admirers of David Bowie and the clubs they frequent like *Mrs. Night's* in Toronto. There the height of chic consists of clothes sold in stores along Yonge Street. The interiors of these stores seem like booths slapped together with two-by-fours and

Masonite, run by patent-medicine salesmen who keep them open until the local rubes get suspicious and then leave town. Anyway, they sell things like satin blazers in gleaming-metal raspberry tints, or emerald green with gold brown-cinnamon lapels; and flash items like slinky, black-satin torchsinger gowns complete with accessories such as a white fur boa and matching India-ink jacket with accentuated Rosalind Russell shoulders. Terrific stuff. I'm not even mentioning the glitter boots with the eight-inch heels that, along with ubiquitous satin, are the very trademark of the satin set, the David Bowie rhinestone fiends — those boots that give the gentlemen who wear them their characteristic look of slumping cervical vertebrae.

Thursday, Friday, Saturday, and Sunday nights, they're all there at *Mrs. Night's*, dancing to the music. It's bisexual chic, all right. Although most of the couples on the floor are male-female, there are the occasional two girls doing the undulating hip and groin thing with each other, a torrid version of the Bump where you nudge your hip not only against your partner's hip, but her thighs, knees, lower abdomen, and *mons veneris* —all to the rhythm of the music, of course, if you really get into it—and there are plenty of girls here who do. Then, about two in the morning, shock troops of gay fun-seekers often bounce in, blowing little plastic whistles and tearing up the dance floor. The "heterosexual-homosexual" environment starts to heat up. One fellow walks in with shades, a beach hat, cut-offs, and a sweat shirt, as if he'd just come in from sunning himself on the beach at Fire Island, and starts walking down the line of men lounging against the wall on one side, giving each one a hot, burning, how-long-ya-gonna-be-in-town-sailor? full-length stare. This is not considered cool. Heavy cruising in a "heterosexual-homosexual environment" can annoy a lot of people, for different reasons. Raymond over there, a portly, middle-aged black man wearing Kresge's slacks and the top half of a jogging suit, is trying to hustle this young guy, only he has obviously picked the wrong person here. He looks at Raymond with the horror of a tourist bumping into a street beggar, of the sort who tries to arouse sympathy by displaying his syphilitic sores. Only Raymond, for some reason, doesn't seem sensitive to this and keeps moving in, and finally, the young man tells him to —— off. Raymond is hurt and outraged. He finds it hard to believe such uptightness can exist in this world. "I was only trying to be friendly. You don't have to be an asshole about it."

This is not typical, however. Most of the customers respect the subtle boundaries of the place. It's just too bad Raymond picked out some kid who probably heard about *Mrs. Night's* from his buddies on the afternoon shift at the warehouse, and had a vague notion that *Mrs. Night's* was a good place to pick up girls. In reality, *Mrs. Night's* is probably one of the worst places in the city to try to pick up girls, if you have never really gotten heavily into the satin set. I mean, you take a girl like Snow White, sitting at a table at *Mrs. Night's* smoking Matinées with two of her girlfriends and making those little dip-and-roll shoulder movements to the beat of "Rock the Boat". A slender, young East Indian, wearing a white stretch-weave shirt unbuttoned to the umbilical region, approaches her and asks her to dance. Snow White thinks about it for a second. Usually, she automatically rejects such requests from obvious ethnic types. Not that she has anything against ethnic types. It's just that they usually seem to have this not-so-subtle notion derived from ancient, steamy Mediterranean or Asiatic wisdom, that women, *bwana*, are either good girls, meaning virgins, wives, or widows, or else — here one starts to roll the eyeballs and inhale the faint scent of musk in the evening air — abandoned women, concubines, dispensers of forbidden delight. A girl who goes to *Mrs. Night's* obviously falls into the latter category. *Quelle drag!* Nothing could be further from the ultra-advanced ethos and outlook of the satin set.

However, Snow White decides to dance with him anyway. Sure enough, after the dance, he trails Snow White back to her table. He sits there with his hands on his knees, watching her out of the corner of his eye, fidgeting with a cigarette, trying to think of something to say. Snow White is no help. The music is no help. Its pounding, relentless volume seems positively designed to discourage conversation, so that you can only communicate if you are already into the whole dip-and-roll, moving-to-the-beat thing where words are completely unnecessary because we all know each other already and nobody's too impressed, right, so why say anything? Finally, he asks her if she'd like something to drink, a coffee or soft drink perhaps, and she shakes her head, not even looking at him. He goes to get a coffee for himself, and when he comes back, she gets up and dances with this other couple she knows, the three of them forming a little space of their own, a radioactive zone for people like this character with the virile unbuttoned chest who has actually put his coffee down and is now hovering about, looking at them fearfully across the radioactive line like some child who has just been excluded from the marbles play-offs at recess. Three minutes later, he is walking out the door with the two guys he came in with.

This is the whole point, though! The swinging single thing where the old aggressive male comes on and tries to hustle the girl is completely dead at *Mrs. Night's* and other "heterosexual-homosexual environments". It's as if feminist dreams have triumphed, at this establishment anyway, and the woman is as dominant as one could wish. The washrooms are labelled "Ladies" and "Boys", and there, in a way, you have it exactly. Men can jolly well go in their own corner and play by themselves if they don't like it. Hustling is done-with. The traditional man-woman couple, where the man is supposed to be protective and a bit possessive with his woman, is done-with. Snow White, dancing with a male friend, has often had another male friend—Jamie over there, for instance, with his beautiful, pouty Mick Jagger lips, and cheeks as soft and pure as the baby's on the Ivory Snow box—stop her and hold her by the waist and kiss her full on the mouth, *Snow, you bitch, where were you last Friday? I never forgive friends who don't show up at my parties, honey pie*, and her first partner just keeps dancing away by himself, as if Snow White has just been temporarily made invisible by an ultra-stroboscopic light from the *Mrs. Night's* ceiling or whatever, and will reappear any moment. Nothing unusual, as I say.

It's more than the simple presence of homosexuals and heterosexuals on the same dance floor that has this corrosive effect on traditional sexual relationships between men and women. After all, the "bisexual" atmosphere, or whatever, of a place like *Mrs. Night's* is, when you come right down to it, almost completely derivative of the old-style, homosexual, gay-disco atmosphere. Gay discos, as far as anyone knows, were the first to emphasize this continuous loud playing of music, each rhythm'n' blues record blending into the next seamlessly, Barry White fading into Love Unlimited, Love Unlimited swinging right into Gladys Knight and the Pips, so that you don't have to shift gears between records, much less stand around with your hands in your pockets for a few seconds of silence, wondering whether the next number will be a fast free-style, or a slow one, necessitating putting your arms around your partner. Such emphasis makes the actual dancing more important, and social interaction, including things like conversation, much less important. (It almost wipes out of existence, of course, such antique considerations as the "approach" or the "line" one takes in hustling somebody — indeed, as I have been trying to point out, it almost wipes out the art of hustling itself.)

At *Mrs. Night's*, bizarre and extravagant forms of dancing flourish in this atmosphere. There is the mechanical style, in which dancers twitch and jerk across the floor like those wooden figurines rotated every hour on German clocks. There is the virtuoso style, in which dancers give themselves over to athletic feats, like bending backward from the knees and pushing the palms of their hands up and down at the ceiling, or doing wild free-form kicks and gyrations with the foot.

These various styles, of course, hardly require any partner, and therefore carry further a tendency which has been noticeable since the days of the Twist. Indeed, it is not unusual to see someone dancing alone at these places. It is, again, part of the whole package — the feeling of dancing in the darkness, with perhaps the strobe lights going, and a wall of bouncy, hard-driving soul music surrounding and practically vacuum-sealing your field of consciousness. You can switch partners in the middle of the number, or simply switch off the partner; it doesn't matter, he doesn't matter, you just have to keep *moving*. And if you rarely even look at your partner, you can still be assured of seeing yourself — "homosexual-heterosexual environments" are big on mirrors for the walls, where you can find yourself from time to time, take a breather and inspect the costume you've assembled for the night. Snow White, for instance, glimpses herself just as she turns around to face the mirrored wall, in her walnut corduroy knickers and beige cashmere pullover, as tight as tight can be, and the cream-coloured scarf with tasselled ends hanging loose—well, she's not bad, especially with that cigarette held at a slight angle from her arching fingertips, glowing there in the darkness. She could even see that Jamie's boyfriend Gino was looking over her ensemble earlier in the evening, Gino the male model whose sartorial judgment is worth more than five dozen—*five dozen!* an infinity at least! — of admiring glances from stretch-woven shirts unbuttoned to the navel. And of course, Sara Lee, her girlfriend — in a marvellous hat with elegant swooping brim, such as might have been worn by a stenographer trying to come up with something to match the Bauhaus chic of her office in the Chrysler Building thirty-five years ago, and a second-hand blouse with cameo brooch, and floor-length skirt—Sara Lee had looked at her out of her moist, wounded eyes—she had admired Snow White too. Knowing that was enough to make Snow White feel secure for a whole evening.

Bisexual chic? You would only tire Snow White by talking to her in terms of that, or "homosexuality", "heterosexuality", any kind of sexuality. Snow White doesn't really *know*, for example, if she is really geared up for a life of making it with men, or if she might basically prefer, when all is said and done, to stick to friends like Sara Lee, or dear Jamie, or Maxine, a statuesque blonde who has a habit of putting a friendly arm around Snow White's shoulder and then, suddenly, like Victor Mature grabbing diaphanous old Gina Lollabrigida in a late Cecil B. de Mille epic, whirling her into her arms and planting a scorching kiss. Not that Snow White has yet experienced what one might certify as an official lesbian coming out—but still, let us examine the men Snow White has been most deeply involved with to date, including the most hated individual in her whole universe, her father.

Her father. A charming man who has worked at a variety of jobs in his lifetime, but whose mental-energy currents seem to have gotten wired into all the wrong circuits — like heavy daydreaming and fantasy, for instance. Snow White tells me once they're driving along and a police car passes by, a yellow Toronto cruiser with *To Serve and Protect* written on the side, and Snow White's father snorts, *"To Serve and Protect*—what a bunch of malarkey that is."* Snow White asks him what he has against the police, and he just says, "If it hadn't been for them, I'd be rich now." Now it is impossible for Snow White to figure out this remark. Her father sometimes brings home spare parts for his car that he's filched from inventory at work, but so far as she knows, he has never had any big money-making schemes that the police have interfered with. A potential big-time bookmaker or numbers runner he's not. So what is this weird fantasy about the police standing between him and great wealth?

That is not what truly bugs Snow White about her father though. What truly used to bug her were the not-infrequent occasions when Dad came home with a twelve-pack for an evening of what he would call "some well-earned ree-laxa-tion", and sooner or later, if Snow White were home, he would walk into her room, sit down beside her, hold her by the wrist with a wet, beery grin on his face and tell her that she should trust him more, she should open up to him—he knew all about boys, for instance. There's only one thing they want, he would say, as if this bit of immemorial schoolgirl wisdom was actually news to Snow White. And there he would sit, going on like this, with poor Snow White catching a whiff of the suds whenever he exhaled a breath — no wonder she still can't stand the taste or smell of beer.

Anyway, Snow White wasted no time, from fourteen on, getting out of the house and taking up with those evil-minded boys her father seemed so knowledgeable about. If he could only have seen some of the goings-on! She and a boyfriend would be waiting for a subway on a Saturday night, and he would be leaning against the tile wall while she clutched his waist and kept bouncing up against his chest, the two of them exchanging passionate kisses while the subway hordes walked around them. Such looks they would get! She was not being what you'd call promiscuous, but she did manage to collect a few of those boyfriends on her way to *Mrs. Night's*. Teen-age subway loiterers, with their faces half-covered by clumps and wiry knots of hair, and a few tiny inflamed spots on the corners of their mouths, and a look of feeble resentment in their eyes, like six-year-olds wondering how they're going to get back at their mothers for yelling at them. She remembers Bernie, in particular, who couldn't sit on a subway seat without doing a bongo drum routine on the space between his knees — dear old Bernie! At least, he had a little bit of energy. Ten or twelve years ago, he would have been a certified greaser, walking around in a T-shirt, jeans, and hair with the telltale sheen, but now people take one look at him and his flowing locks and the leather thong tied around his forehead, and they mentally classify him as a "hippie". Actually, Bernie has as much to do with your classic Haight-Ashbury hippie as Fulton J. Sheen has to do with Daniel Berrigan. In his heart and soul, Bernie is a genuine greaser — not, I might add, the romanticized greaser of *American Graffiti* or "Happy Days" . Real greasers were not the kind of posturing fools portrayed in these and other specimens of fifties nostalgia. Real greasers nobody could possibly get nostalgic about, not in a hundred years. One might describe them as being basically sullen, nasty, incapable of realizing anything productive or lasting in their aimless lives, and genuinely threatening because they would actually maim or mutilate if it came right down to it. Now Bernie would not maim or mutilate anyone, but you take the rest of that description, and it would fit him pretty well. Dear old Bernie, who soon developed a real talent, a knack almost, for making Snow White feel, in the company of his buddies, like somebody's Mongoloid brother who tags along with the rest of the gang because he has no place else to go. Bernie, who seemed even more prone than Snow White's father to making odd, unconnected little statements out-of-the-blue, so that one really wondered just what thoughts were whipping across the lunar landscape of his unapproachable mind, precisely what fantasies were germinating behind those pale eyes of his, staring right through Snow White and beyond, into the distant nothingness. Once, he astonished Snow White by informing her that, given a chance, he'd really like to become a cop — it was almost his ambition, one might say. He with his dope-smoking and long hair. That just about killed Snow White. She thought, well, he should get together with my father, and they can have it out, my father the cop-hater, and my boyfriend the potential crime-stopper.

But of course, all these boyfriends now belong to Snow White's distant past, about a year and a half ago. Snow White's last serious boyfriend was Dave, a young man in his late twenties who seemed several lifetimes more mature than Bernie and that crew. He introduced Snow White to the delights of cocaine for one thing. Dave and Snow White would be sitting at the counter at Dirty Louie's, a famous all-night grill in Toronto, not far from *Mrs. Night's* as a matter of fact, and a couple of the old, teen subway-loitering crowd would wander in, looking bored and resentful as usual, and Snow White would burst into this outlandish, this . . . *hearty* laughter — *Well, sit yourself down, boys! Long time no see* — and her two larger-than-life eyeballs would be just sparking, *fizzing* with vivacity and goodwill. Her old friends couldn't believe it. The blood was spurting through her veins like water from a squirt gun, from the cocaine and all, and they had no idea.

Well, that whole thing didn't last long. One night, Dave and Snow White were sitting at a restaurant when some girls walked in, one of Dave's old girlfriends among them, and Dave got up and picked a fight with her. Snow White can't remember what it was about, but Dave started shouting at her, and he reached over at one point and took a swing at her. He wouldn't even stop when the night manager came over and muttered helpfully, in a heavy Budapest accent, "You fight with girlfriend outside, please." It was quite a scene there for a while, the girl shrieking and Dave grinding his teeth and the night manager playing the befuddled straight man. When they walked home, Dave was limp as a tea towel, and couldn't do or say anything except flop on the chesterfield and mumble soft and tender curse words to himself until he fell asleep. That was the point at which Snow White decided it was time for this particular number to wind up.

Yes, and now with the music thumping away at the weary tympanum in Snow White's ear — *Love, sweet love is the aaaanswer*—Snow White looks at Jamie dancing with Sara Lee, and she thinks, Jamie is *nice*. He will never beat anybody up, and he doesn't have those weird fantastic ideas about what he's going to do with his life. He knows what he likes—which is not girls, okay—but what's so bad about spending one's life looking through antique shops for some prize porcelain cabinet plates and living with a beautiful Narcissus of a male model? Jamie can keep you entertained for hours with his conversation, and go into these routines where he's treating you like some fantastic, spoiled little debutante, glamorous to the end like Bette Davis in *Dark Victory*. There's always the fine edge of mockery to it, of course, but it sure beats being treated like a greaser's old lady.

That is why Snow White is not exactly sure she's cut out for this life of heterosexual relationships. Maybe now and again, but when the most agreeable men she knows are out-and-out homosexuals like Jamie, what can she say? The other alternative, of course, is her friends like Maxine. And Sara Lee. Sara

Lee, of course, is not her real name, any more than Snow White is Snow White's real name. Snow White was christened Beverley, and Sara Lee was something like Lou Ann, but disregard that. They took their names about a year ago as a sort of farewell gesture to their past lives, which they'd as soon forget about completely, thank you. The name change was also a kind of passport into the world of what we have been calling, for lack of a better term, "bisexual chic". New names, new identities. Jamie and the boys call her "Snow White" with a wonderful kind of sardonic fag lilt, as in "Oh stop it, Snow White, pul-*lease*," and Snow White thinks that is, well, good.

Anyway, Snow White and Sara Lee at one point discussed becoming lovers, but one can hardly be dead serious about these things. Now they just giggle and tease each other about it. They don't really *want* to get into bed with each other, but they have this understanding which occasionally flashes between them, with a certain look and half smile in the darkness of *Mrs. Night's*, saying something like, well, boys, we're keeping our options open. Actually, one does look at boys with a certain fresh perspective in the light of such an understanding. Dear creatures, one wishes to inform them, you are not all that necessary in this world of ours. Do keep that in mind, will you? Do realize that we are not utterly, heart-and-soul, emotionally, spiritually, and physically dependent on you. For emotional support, I have my friend Sara Lee here, the two of us walking hand in hand to the Ladies' Room, and as for basic bedrock sex, well, we do know that it's not always as terrific as it's supposed to be, don't we?

And Snow White has her dancing and her clothes, which keep her amused for the duration, and help to confirm her new identity. Snow White. "Snow" is an agreeable allusion to the champagne of the drug world, as they say — her favourite illicit substance, cocaine. "Snow White", of course, is an ironic reference to all that is pure and maidenly and innocent and antithetical to the ethos of the disco. People who dwell in this ethos appreciate cutting little ironic references like that.

Snow White also cherishes another, rather private, connotation of her name. She likes to think of herself as a white princess forever out of bounds to any of the black guys hanging around *Mrs. Night's*. She means it. She doesn't broadcast this fact, but she really doesn't like those black guys. Like, she knows they're a big part of the scene here, and she knows they carry off the flash-and-trash style of dressing a lot better than the white boys, and they can dance a lot better, too, because they're closer to the jungle, right? But those guys — especially the mean dudes with the pimp outfits — have a few nasty habits, like beating up their women. They look like real tigers, you know, tough gangsters, but in reality they are strictly pussycats when it comes to other men. It's just with women that they get tough. And they never, *ever* spend money on a woman. Hell, they expect *you* to spend money on *them*. Snow White won't touch any of those guys, even though they also come up to her like Super Fine and You number *one*, baby, and all that shit.

But that's just part of the game, anyway. Don't tell Snow White this is not some far-out game she is playing. Where else is anybody heading these days? The counter culture is dead, stone dead, interred with the corpses of Jimi Hendrix and Janis Joplin. The old suburban split-level and blacktop-driveway, middle-class dream is still alive, but it's just lurching along, waiting for someone or something to put it out of its misery. That leaves the cultural void most of the rest of us are lost in and little febrile lifestyles going under the label of the new decadence or the new bisexual chic, and epitomized by people like David Bowie and Lou Reed. These lifestyles, which are a complete reaction against the sixties, against the sixties idealism, the cosmic consciousness, the back-to-earth naturalness ideology, the sixties girl with her long straight hair, her denim skirt, and face without a trace of lipstick or makeup. A reaction against the sixties notion that sex might be salvation for us all, after all, the route to the free and natural way of living, and marigolds in the springtime and sharing and gentleness and concern for one another. No, we can all forget about that now. That is definitely not what's happening. So don't tell Snow White that the music and dancing won't last and the mirrors won't always be up there. Don't tell her that dress-up night will be over eventually, and we'll all be having to peer into the light of day where our costumes look hopelessly tacky. Don't tell her that, unless you can offer her something different, prove to her that something else is shaping up out of this great, shapeless, menacing decade.

YOU LIED TO US, HUGH HEFNER

Who is this writer, George Gilder, anyway, with his "naked nomads", and his talk about the sorry lot of our North American single males? Listen to a sample of the man: "So, violence and crime join with 'madness', mild neurosis, depression, addiction, venereal disease, chronic disability, psychiatric treatment, loneliness, insomnia, institutionalization, poverty, 'discrimination', unemployment, and nightmares" — Gilder is in high gear now, ticking off these choice afflictions like a Bolshevik doing a survey course on the capitalist economy — "*as part of the specialized culture of the single man in America.*" Can one believe it? Gilder, in his book *Naked Nomads: Unmarried Men in America*, seems to be saying that these dreaded maladies of the twentieth century — depression, insomnia, etc. — are just waiting to embrace the man who stays single after his twenty-fifth birthday. Each year of bachelorhood after twenty-five and the odds against you get better and better . . . no amount of swinging or grooving or moving or making it can chase away that bad bachelorhood karma. Depression, insomnia, and so forth, are just about the least of it too. "The climax of this grim story," Gilder continues, "is death. It is not surprising that the single-male mortality rate also is the highest of all."

Yes, it's the ballad of the sad singles bar once again. Gilder has statistics, too. Most of your criminals and vicious psychopaths are single men and most of the men in mental hospitals and unemployment lineups are single too, and all in all, one can say that the singles lifestyle as portrayed and advocated in *Playboy* and *Penthouse* is definitely not quite the routine for most men who are unwilling or unable to marry.... Still, let's not get carried away. Gilder is basically constructing an argument here for marriage as the great maturity-builder for men, the instrument that turns them from callow predatory wanderers to settled, productive, faithful, and loving mates, and a lot of single men, while not into the *Playboy/Penthouse* fantasy either, are not about to swallow *that* number. My friend Wyatt — a single man of about twenty-five, in fact — gives me a disgusted look when I mention Gilder's theories. "Yeah, of course, it's great for a man to be married," he says. "A wife to take care of all your needs, you know, like ironing your boxer shorts every night. Come off it. The guy's obviously a right-winger. I mean, with all that stuff about men being hairy-chested killer apes and saying that unless we settle down and marry a good woman and all that shit, we're gonna become antisocial — I mean, no woman's gonna believe *that* nowadays."

Well, Wyatt should know. The woman he lived with gave him a few lessons in just what the modern liberated woman of today is going to believe. She is one of those girls who, instead of a purse, carries a shapeless khaki handbag that looks like it's made out of the same material as the covering on your army-surplus canteen. When she isn't wearing jeans, she's wearing a floor-length denim skirt and maybe an Oxford-blue shirt tied in a knot around her navel — the kind of shirt that has a few white splotches here and there from the time she wore it doing the kitchen walls in semigloss. Denise. Six months before she and Wyatt split, before any such thought ever occurred to either one of them, one night when they were sitting in the living room of their flat, sprawled out on the corduroy-covered floor cushions, reading or something, she told Wyatt she was going to "take up a little more psychological room around here." That was her way of expressing what she had learned from poring through half a dozen feminist anthologies.

The way she said it, of course, she had to be joking. That's what Wyatt assumed. *Taking up more psychological room.* Sure thing. We're all crazy here, what with the summer heat and our cramped living quarters in the middle of one of those lively Toronto "ethnic" streets — houses painted acid green, hemoglobin red, orange sherbet, lime, houses with porches where the patriarch sits, stubble on his face, wearing a strap-style undershirt and a grey felt hat with a narrow brim like the kind old men wear to the race tracks, giving you the stare cultivated by centuries of hairy, bigoted, muscular, salt-of-the-earth, male-supremacist peasants—*look at that kid. He lets his girl walk in public with her* mammellas *bouncing around*—and meanwhile his wife is sitting by him, round and sturdy as a soccer ball, in a dress with geraniums printed on it, holding on to a squirming six-year-old boy and — Wyatt has the highest regard for New Canadians, really, but in some of these neighbourhoods it seems like they have a dozen vocal children per family, and if you like good old Anglo-Saxon tranquillity, it just gets to be too much, and . . . how was Wyatt to know that Denise really meant it, and it wasn't just their hot, muggy flat with the shrieks and the yelling coming through the Gyproc walls every night.

Shortly after that, they're having dinner at a draught-beer-and-Wiener-schnitzel restaurant, where some kind of happy, Tyrolean-mountaineer polka music is issuing from a record player behind the meat-slicer, and the waitresses are wearing peasant blouses with short skirts, and when they have to pay the bill, Denise insists on giving the waitress her portion of the tab instead of slipping it under the table to Wyatt. The waitress cannot understand this. "You should let the man pay," she says reproachfully to Denise, and Denise can't think of a thing to say back to her; she just shakes her head and grins a little nervously. The waitress is standing over them with that fixed jaw cultivated by centuries of women wearing babushkas and carrying sacks of turnips over their shoulders, who see wars come and go, famine, social upheaval, bloody revolution, and they know that a lady allows the gentleman to pay, unless he's a rapist or something. Wyatt himself stares at his butter patty. He is sure the waitress is thinking, *what kind of a man lets his girl be so pushy and aggressive in public?* He is also afraid Denise is going to take the incident out on him by not talking to him for the rest of the evening, or bringing up a touchy subject, like who's going to wash the kitchen floor and clean the oven this time around.

Wyatt, at any rate, is in no space to appreciate Gilder's arguments on behalf of traditional monogamous marriage and against the liberated, fancy-free, singles life. That would be to see himself as an even bigger fool than he has already admitted he is. That would mean the sequence of events leading up to the breakup of his relationship with Denise would appear not only painful but downright unnatural. They broke up because Denise turned on to this guy, and started sleeping with him. Or more precisely, they broke up because Denise insisted on being honest about the whole thing. Wyatt, of course, became quite upset when she told him. He knew the guy, a wiry, cerebral-looking young man who played acoustic guitar in a group doing the *cappuccino*-hard-cider-and-cinnamon-stick circuit, around various folk clubs in southern Ontario. The sneaky son of a bitch, with his cerebral wire-rim glasses and folksy cracker-barrel moustache.

Wyatt and Denise had a scene in a restaurant, with Wyatt biting his fist and refusing to look at Denise, and Denise trying to soothe him—*I'm sorry, Wyatt. . . . I never wanted to hurt you, I never did . . . but* — but this is the age of women's liberation, kiddo, and exclusive relationships are *out*. Denise can't help it if Wyatt reacts badly. She is sorry about it, of course. If only he could see she doesn't love him any less, she's just turned on to this guy; it's only temporary, a brief funky diversion, nothing serious. The funny thing is, that night, they go home and make love and they both feel so . . . *into it*. It's the most feelingful love they have made in months, absolutely first-rate.

Yes, but next morning, of course, Wyatt keeps running the whole situation through his mind. Denise and this guy—unbelievable. In the next few weeks, he spends a few tormented nights lying in bed while Denise is out somewhere, and he doesn't know whether she's going to come home or stay the night with her friend. It's tough on the nervous system all right, lying there in the darkness of their bedroom with his heart pounding and his ears as fine-tuned as a bat's, waiting for Denise. Wyatt hears a noise on the street outside their house, and the blood starts spurting and pushing against the walls of his two beating ventricles—*oh footsteps, stop walking as you pass our door, stop there and be Denise putting her key in the lock, Denise coming home.*

The nights that she doesn't come home, Wyatt resolves, in the morning, to make a big show of not responding to her when she does return. Usually, he carries this out, and Denise notices, and she thinks, well, what the hell — it's his problem.

This goes on for a few weeks until one weekend Denise's friend actually drops by to pick Denise up for a night out. Well, Wyatt is there and he's damned if he's going to hide in the bedroom while this fellow's talking with Denise. So, the two of them actually sit down face-to-face, and wouldn't you know it. Denise's lover is friendly and sincere and upfront. No word is spoken about the weirdness of the situation; there is just some friendly, sincere conversation about what Wyatt is into and what this other guy is into, and Wyatt finds himself eager to hold up his end of the conversation, and he curses himself afterward for being so craven, for responding in such an almost pathetically eager way, for — yes — wanting Denise's lover to know what a hip, cool guy he, Wyatt, is in his own way.

Well, what's sauce for the goose... one night, Wyatt gets his own back by sleeping with a girl he happens to know. All quite accidental, nothing calculated. Just a friend, you understand, and — well, no use in pretending they were carried away by passion either, because they had been drinking beer all afternoon in a public house, sitting together and talking about how depressed they both felt, while around them, old men in greasy raincoats sat watching "Hollywood Squares" on the overhead TV set.

Wyatt looked at the girl with her stringy hair, and pale blue eyes, and pale skin, like piecrust before you set it in the oven . . . not one of your passionate, longing gazes, exactly. Wyatt does not feel passion. A little lust perhaps. She is wearing a T-shirt, and of course, no bra, and this happenstance is enough to set aside piecrust complexion, stringy hair, and the plain, un-adorned little-girl face — the loins are stirred. It's completely weird. Twenty years ago, this girl would be wearing a dress with a filigree collar and buttons down the front, and her bosom would be entirely concealed and modest, and Wyatt's loins would be stone-cold sitting across the table from her. But this thin T-shirt is too much.

Anyway, they end up in the girl's flat, and Wyatt realizes, almost from the first instant, that it is going to be a disaster. For one thing, the girl is almost completely plastered, and so Wyatt finds himself with this restless spirit on his hands, a girl who can hardly lie still, who is under him one minute, on top the next, then sideways, backways, all sorts of exotic positions, like those violet-hued gymnasts coupling in erotic Hindu tableaux, and through it all, Wyatt finds himself sweating like a galley slave. Needless to say, the girl does not end up fainting on her pillow in ecstasy. No, after they finish, she is still restless, and goes over to her record collection and puts on her earphones, and sits there naked on the floor nodding her head abstractedly to the music of rubbery, perverted Mick Jagger, while she smokes a cigarette. Wyatt lies there trying to work himself up to saying his farewell. *This is one of the most miserable evenings I have ever experienced*, he tells himself, lying there on this bed of spent desire.

Soon after that, he and Denise split for good. It wasn't the guy with the guitar and the moustache. It was . . . too many days of trying not to be aware of each other when they were together in their flat. Wyatt, to be honest, had mixed feelings about the end of their relationship. On the one hand, he seemed to experience all those childish, those infantile feelings like . . . *I'll show you, Denise, you bitch. You'll be sorry when I'm gone. I'll get a better chick, and one day, you'll see the two of us sitting at a sidewalk café, waiting for the* Harper's Bazaar *photographer to come and do a spread on us, and you'll be sorry.* And he has about a thousand variations of this fantasy going. He knows he is going to miss her badly, and it hurts. But on the other hand, he tells himself that maybe he's one of those men who are destined to move from woman to woman, becoming more worldly, more experienced with each relationship, an artist savouring the unique drama of each love affair and then moving on when the savour is gone.

Ah, Wyatt. No matter that certain politically minded women are now ready to say to any such Byronesque character — *you, buster, before you go on to savour another fragrant blossom of love, you've got a few dues to pay. You've got certain obligations like changing diapers too, and cleaning toilet bowls, and if you don't want to, we fragrant blossoms have certain other options like masturbation, lesbianism, chastity, etc., before we are obliged to turn to you.* No matter that, on the other side, certain voices of reaction are also piping up, like Gilder's: "When the man submits his limited sexual impulse to the woman's (i.e., when he marries her), he is adopting a higher, more extended mode of sexual life. He is submitting, that is, to the values of maternal morality and futurity." Maternal morality and futurity. That means a family, life insurance, quaking in your boots every time the boss, the old plantation master, looks at you cross-eyed, because you have those invisible leg irons marked Family Man clamped on your two sturdy ankles. Wyatt can't stand it. There have got to be better prospects than these.

So, Wyatt goes to parties, and mingles, and exudes the fatal scent of the young man on the make: it's so obvious from the way he holds his body talking to this or that girl, the shoulders hunched just a trifle, the head tilted forward just two or three degrees off the vertical of his spinal column, standing in the middle of a conversation, abjectly grateful for each opportunity to deliver a few *trenchant* remarks to the lady (witticisms are too much to hope for). Each halfway attractive girl becomes a . . . *possibility.* Yeah! Wyatt is going nuts. The girls he most fancies are all attached, taken, occupied, possessed by other men. Perhaps he is just too anxious, not relaxed, not letting it flow . . . all things come to him who waits, after all; and when the karma is right, nothing is easier than getting a girl. However, Wyatt has "man on the make" written all over him—perhaps even "I'm just out of one relationship and dying to get into another one right away so I can forget that bitch" written all over him, and nothing is less conducive to making it with girls than that.

Whatever the case, Wyatt soon finds himself directing his attentions to girls he has, deep down, not a great deal of affection for, much less burning desire, because they are, well, good to talk to, and they're not bad-looking, and there's the old mutual-interest thing going—not like in high school, when the guy and the girl are sitting in the back seat, and the girl is dying because she can't get him to say two sentences in a row unless it's about the basketball team, and—thank God, this is the big city, and there are thousands of girls who are into the same things as Wyatt, who can discourse knowledgeably on tarot cards, Bauhaus architecture, cross-country skiing, the music of John Cale. . . .

I met Wyatt one night with one of those girls he had taken up with, sitting in her apartment. She lived in a crypt-like flat with linoleum on the floor and water stains on the plaster, and a few avocado and spider plants here and there wilting from lack of sunlight. You could tell the place belonged to someone who did not scorn arts and crafts, however, because it was full of mac- ramé hangings, lattice-like designs made of viscose and jute. The girl was a weaver. That was her main interest, anyway, and she was saving her money to buy a real loom. One of these days, you could tell, she would announce her intention to take her loom and her macramé and her few surviving avocado plants, and move into some southern Ontario farmhouse off a conces- sion road, where she could weave in a sitting room with all kinds of sunlight and fresh air coming through the windows. In the meantime, she was doing the best she could, working in a library, doing the macramé, trying to get in and out of the place every day without coming across the fifty-year-old drunk who liked to stop her and talk to her about the latest outrages of that ——, Trudeau.

Do you really like her, I asked Wyatt afterward. Wyatt hemmed and hawed, and started on this elaborate explanation of how *interesting* she could be, and sensitive to certain things, and he wasn't, you know, into some great, lasting permanent relationship with her or anything like that, it was just a friendship. . . . Later, the two of them are sitting on the couch after coming back from a night on the town, and Wyatt is starting to get passionate like your horny teen-ager making out with his girl on the sofa of her parents' living room. They exchange kisses, and Wyatt . . . well, it's embarrassing to talk about, Wyatt says, but his hands are getting a little active, and the concupiscence is building up by the minute, and he is asking himself — *is tonight the night!* — and telling himself, for God's sake, to stop behaving like that high-school basketball player, eager to score. Hell, Wyatt is *mature*. The girl is mature. They are not teen-agers. So, why aren't they looking at each other over glasses of some rich aromatic burgundy, with ironic smiles on their faces and eyes glinting with wickedness and desire, informing each other with a meaning clearer than words that, *yes, darling, it would be such fun to sleep together tonight*. Instead, they are grappling on a couch.

The girl puts a stop to it after a few minutes, however. She disengages herself and looks at Wyatt with a troubled expression, and starts telling him about this guy she's involved with right now, who's visiting with some friends on a farm near Collingwood at the moment, but, really, she is into this particular relationship, and she doesn't want to, uh, lead Wyatt on or get into unnecessary complications. Wyatt feels like someone is pouring barium down the convolutions of his stomach, listening to her explain. But what can he do? He is nowhere near being able to offer her a sitting room with a southern exposure and a loom, in some Ontario farmhouse. Perhaps her friend with the connections in Collingwood is a step closer to it than Wyatt.

Perhaps her friend is more country-robust, more artsy-craftsy, more . . . well, anyway, Wyatt tells her he understands. Understands perfectly. Unnecessary complications are not desirable. There are a great many other women in the world, thank God.

Wyatt's next girlfriend is absolutely unattached, no rivals lurking in the woodwork, no torch carried for someone in Collingwood. You might even say that she is somewhat devoted to Wyatt. But here again, Wyatt is ambivalent. He doesn't feel as if this girl is really the object for which he has been searching so restlessly, that this is the relationship that can satisfy body and soul and fevered psyche even for a short while. She is not the girl Wyatt can fantasize going to parties with, where she will say just enough so that people (i.e., other men) will be intrigued with her but not so much that they can do the mental classification thing with her, like deciding what category of New Woman she belongs to, militant libber, earth mother, etc. She does not have the kind of tender, misty-eyed, yet self-confident reserve— the reserve captured by those models who pose in a field of daisies for feminine hygiene ads — that suggests to men that here is a mixture of womanly innocence and experience, a woman who knows more than she lets on.

To tell the truth, this girl of Wyatt's is a bit of a bore at times. Some inner compulsion forces her to relate long stories of love and hate, pain and pleasure, friends long since left behind, political manoeuvres in the office where she works, the whole tempestuous range of her life, in a breathless tone of voice like a seven-year-old girl telling her mother about this dream she had. Wyatt sometimes wonders, in the middle of one of her narratives, if she is really talking to *him*. If the mailman or the bus driver or the building superintendent were to show a sympathetic ear, would she talk to them in exactly the same way? Would she take them in hand the same way she sometimes takes Wyatt, and laugh at their silly mistakes, like the time Wyatt drove his Datsun through a STOP sign and she said to him gaily, "Oh, Wyatt, how you ever got a licence is beyond me — you can't drive *at all*." Talk about your gall and wormwood.

But then again, you can't deny she's attractive — slender and lithe the way Wyatt prefers his women. Of course, Wyatt has his conscience too, and wonders, from time to time, if it is right that he sleeps with her, since, really, he doesn't love her. I mean, Wyatt is hip to the sexual revolution, and so is she, presumably, and sleeping with a woman is not like kissing a woman in the Victorian era, a sign that you had practically plighted your troth right then and there, and it had better be true love or else. Still, these things can get messy ... and to tell the truth, the occasions when Wyatt sleeps with her are infrequent and always preceded by one of those long, heated, indecisive, agonizing grapplings on the bed, as if neither really wanted sex but neither wanted to stop the groping and the heavy breathing and Wyatt taking liberties with his hands like that damned basketball player again — where in hell are the burgundy glasses and two adults in evening dress eyeing each other with the glint of wickedness, etc., and the ironic smiles, mutual consent in a flash! Not this grappling for hours, peeling down to your unmentionables before you finally give in and pull back the sheets, and have sex — with this regret, this reluctance, as if Wyatt here, the male brute, has really just forced the woman to submit to his rutting urge. If this is a sexual relationship, Wyatt thinks, then there might be more to chastity than he has previously suspected.

His latest girl, he told me, is indeed unique. Her name is Vivien, and she is quite openly, unashamedly, uninterested in sex. Wyatt likes her just the same. No more grappling on the sofa. This Vivien is a cool number, wearing a batik-print headband wrapped around her glossy raven tresses and usually something like a simple, matching tan skirt and blouse. Actually, she is someone you could wait with at the outdoor café for the *Harper's Bazaar* man. But, of course, she is not really Wyatt's "girl". She is, as I say, quite bored with things like sex and sexual relationships. "I just want to be friendly with men," she tells Wyatt. "I don't want to have to choose between absolutely withdrawing from them, or becoming their sweethearts" —

pronouncing that last word with a simper—*sweethearts*—like it doesn't matter if you're a high school basketball player or some smoothie pouring Le Corton into the lady's glass and flashing the jaded, ironic smile which says, yes, I am weary of life, but you, my dear, make me want to savour love once again —it's all the same, the fevered rutting, the restless, aimless, vaguely humiliated feeling one has lying there on the bed after desire is spent. Yes, sex is boring.

So, Wyatt and Vivien spend evenings lying around in her apartment, listening to Cleo Laine on the stereo, sipping mint tea, conversing ... and often, with a few other men there, wearing mellow-yellow high-waisted slacks and soft milky-white sweaters and large, round Elton John glasses and short cropped hair styled at the House of Lords ... no circle of stags ready to do battle for possession of Vivien but rather a coterie of fellow spirits whose most threatening equipment is their sharp tongues. Yes, Vivien likes the company of men, all right, but make them harmless please, or if not completely harmless, able to take disappointment gracefully, like Wyatt.

Of course, for Wyatt himself, this is not quite what he had in mind. But then, he is not exactly sure what he did have in mind. The life of the swinging single? The man of the world? The jaded bachelor? The artist-genius with no scruples — like Richard Wagner, who is said to have had an endless procession of women marching through his life? But we've already gone through that number, haven't we, and we know it just won't play.

What else then? Your liberated man, cleaning toilet bowls, changing diapers, pouring a drink for his woman coming home from a hard day at the office? Or George Gilder's traditional monogamous breadwinner, forsaking the shallows of the singles life, providing for and protecting his thriving social unit, his happy nuclear family? Wyatt knows some married men. Married men who no longer do anything except work, come home on the subway, play basketball in the driveway, watch "Columbo" on Sunday nights. Married men of the liberated variety who push the baby carriage while the wife walks alongside, all three, hubby, wife, infant, with sour looks of regret on their faces. No — spare Wyatt any of these visions. There are worse things than being a naked nomad, if that's what you want to call it. Worse things than waiting, hoping, searching for that soul-satisfying lover. Worse things, indeed. Wyatt will insist on that. It is a legitimate comfort when the searching promises to become endless.

BACK TO THE BUSH

If you're hanging out in the Gateway to the North, Edmonton, Alta., you can descend no lower than the tavern of the York Hotel. It's a steamy pool in the middle of a neighbourhood which is already a fen. Other skid row taverns, of course, have their individual flavours — the Alberta Hotel where fifteen- and sixteen-year-old hookers hang out, and the Cecil Hotel where patrons will express their displeasure from time to time by throwing the TV set out the window, and women with tattoos on their biceps will show a drunken young telephone lineman back to his seat after he's gotten up to shout threats at the three-piece country band playing "Ghost Riders in the Sky". But the York Hotel is definitely the toughest. It's more than the festering, grey-undershirt, *lumpenproletariat* atmosphere; more than the old men sitting there with faces the colour and texture of automobile rust, and noses inflamed and crusted over with hard rubber skin because of the burst blood vessels underneath; more even than the old women turning to fat once they hit the age of twenty-three, the eighteen-year-old girls already developing bad teeth and beer bellies so that in five years they will be rounded out like turnips. This is the human residue you can find in any tavern in the vicinity of 97th Street.

The neighbourhood heavies are what give the York Hotel its distinctive menace. A black man with a polo shirt and a golf cap sits drinking at a table with some friends. He is one of 97th Street's chief dealers, and he carries an authority that you don't notice until some little incident erupts, like two girls screeching at each other at a nearby table. The screeching, of course, is perfectly all right, nothing unusual here—but one girl stands up and throws her glass of beer in the other's face, and that is a definite mistake. Whatever else you do, you don't throw beer around in this tavern. Everybody turns to look at her, and her companion in the beer-soaked T-shirt, and the girl who threw the beer has tears of frustration running down her face, like a three-year-old who has just gotten her mother's attention by deliberately smashing a bowl full of guppies. A hefty woman (with charcoal rings of eyeliner around two eyes lifeless as moon rocks) moves in and grabs her by the arm. It is not for nothing that the dealer has hired this woman to carry and sell some of the goods — he will not have to be worried about her being attacked, molested, or bushwhacked. "You've had it, sister. You don't do that kind of stuff here," she informs the girl. But it is the dealer who gets up and throws the two girls out, without fuss or muss. He does not like his tranquillity disturbed by two young brain-damaged chicks acting up next to his table.

Pimps, hustlers, dealers, B&E men — yes, and young Indian women who came off the bus, fleeing from the terminal boredom of life on some reserve near Edmonton, and were met by friendly strangers, men who gave them new clothes, a room, and a lifetime supply of Tuenols — they're all here at the York. My friend Robert points them out to me, along with some of the more harmless characters. "You see that guy over there," he says to me. He is referring to an old man wearing green work clothes and an orange phosphorescent cap like the kind highway construction crews wear. "They call him Holy Smokes. He'll take a fistful of quarters and go down to a school playground, or some place where there's a lot of kids, and he throws these quarters in the air. The kids all run and grab for 'em, and he stands back and says 'Ho-oly Smokes!'"

There are three of us, actually, sitting at a table — my friend Robert, who is a Cree Indian, his friend Louise, a girl from the Nishga tribe of British Columbia, and myself, a stranger being shown the sights. We have a vague idea of heading tomorrow for the foothills of the Rockies, where a mixed band of Stony, Cree, and Blood Indians are camping out with tents and pick-up trucks, living a kind of back-to-the-bush existence, away from the reserve and the white man's poisonous city. Now, as an instructive contrast, Robert is also showing me what life is often like for Indians who decide to stay in Edmonton.

Nobody knows exactly how many Indians there are in skid row here in Edmonton, but they certainly make up a sizeable minority. They are sizeable enough that the subject of Indian drunks has become extremely touchy around these parts. Indians and alcohol! Benjamin Franklin said it all two hundred years ago when he remarked, with that businesslike American ability to come straight to the heart of the matter, "If it be the design of Providence to extirpate these savages in order to make room for the cultivators of the earth, it seems not improbable that rum may be the appointed means." Yes, it was alcohol that decimated the Indians and won the West, not the Seventh Cavalry or the RCMP. White men doubtless inoculated themselves against the toxin of alcohol over the millennia, but among the Indians it hit like an unknown plague bacillus. Many of them still haven't built up adequate defences against it — particularly in the city, which frequently has nothing to offer the Indian except its grime, dirt, traffic lights, and beer parlours.

So they come to the city, and some of them never get off 97th Street. It's a kind of life. You can sleep till one p.m. and then shuffle out of your room where the cockroaches are mating in the sink, go on over to the Dreamland Theatre, maybe, to kill the afternoon. The Dreamland Theatre is a movie house with an ancient tongue-and-groove hardwood floor and an unforgettable scent like the inside of an abandoned '52 De Soto with rotting upholstery. You can go there to watch a double feature for fifty cents — perhaps some old Tarzan flicks, or soft-core pornography, like *Night Call Nurses*. The audience is filled with old men in cracked Adidas running-shoes and windbreakers, pensioners wearing topcoats shapeless as tarpaulins and maybe a green felt Tyrolean hat without the brush dingus in the hatband, and young men, too, white and Indian, walking down the aisles looking for their buddies, tapping people on the shoulder in the dark to see which band of four or five guys is the one they belong to. Here and there a severely retarded adolescent wanders down the aisle with his arms held stiffly, as if his humerus bones had been soldered tight to the shoulder sockets. They're all watching some movie where girls are stripping and exhibiting themselves in a kind of low-camp parody of southern California encounter groups.

And of course after the Dreamland matinée is over, there is the Alberta, or the Cecil, or the York. Or perhaps just the stretch of turf beside the Dreamland, between the street and the long, steep embankment covered with bushes that descends to the North Saskatchewan River. On a summer day you can sleep on the grass there, or—on a very hot day—fight for a patch of shade beneath the Colonnade Motors billboard. A few even venture into the bushes once evening comes, stumbling through a maze of paths that lead, now and again, into some little hollow in the bushes where you can sit down amidst unspeakable litter and share a bottle of Bright's Hermitage Sherry with a couple of buddies, safe from the eyes of the Edmonton police. Sherry and beer and Acadian 400 rye whiskey and Seconals and MDA and every diabolical pill, powder, or juice invented by man to distract him from the pain of living—Robert knows this score. He was a walking juicehead, a full-fledged drunk with rotting liver and pancreas, before he decided it was time to switch over to some other scene, and spent seven days doing cold turkey in his room, alone with a sack of lemons. The lemons, you see, with their sharp acidity can fend off the sharp edge of the craving. When you're lying there shaking, covered with sweat, stripped naked except for maybe a pair of boxer shorts and they're soaked with sweat, too, and you can't stand it any more, you grab a lemon and devour it, peel and all, and then sleep for maybe five or ten minutes before you wake up again and watch your limp body try to expel its poisons. Well, Robert lived to tell the tale.

He still drinks heavily, but it's "controlled", as they say.

Now he sits teasing the Nishga girl. "When are you gonna sleep with me?" he asks. The Nishga girl doesn't say anything but takes a drag on her cigarette and gives him the aw-cut-it-out look. She knows this character pretty well. "On second thoughts," Robert continues, "you better not sleep with me. You sleep with me and you won't want to sleep with any other man. You'll be after me all the time. I don't need another problem like that." Again the girl doesn't reply, but looks at him out of the corner of her eye with cool detachment—*Robert*, her detached eye is saying, *for a guy in your forties, you're pretty robust, you're indestructible, in fact —but would you please stop bullshitting me like this?*

In the background some country-and-western singer is pouring out his bitterness from the depths of the jukebox: "You should'a known country feet weren't meant for city streets," he sings. "You're just a country girl trackin' dirt." Well, Louise will take care of herself anyway, city streets or no. Except for one or two missing teeth, she looks pretty well intact. Of course, there's more than a hint of toughness, of knowingness, in her eyes, but that's all right — you don't survive on 97th Street walking around like Goldie Hawn. Another song starts winding up on the jukebox: "They fixed up his lungs and his fever, but they didn't fix up his mind." Ah, the down-home flavour of country-and-western music! It's the perfect background music when you're deep into the suds, getting a little glaze over your corneas. Its lack of subtlety reaches out to people who cherish their age-old misery, finger it tenderly, like a sore that never heals — but that's another story, of course, and meanwhile Robert and Louise and I keep drinking until some old guy being carried out to a waiting ambulance reminds Robert that we'll be doing some travelling tomorrow and maybe it's time to leave.

Yes, by all means — let us get away from this squalid urban scene. To the bush, and the natural Indian way of living. The next day three of us, Robert and his brother and myself, climb into his '69 Ford, and it's off to Louis ——'s camp, nestled in the foothills of the Rockies. Robert is not sure, actually, where the camp is located, but he hopes to meet up with Louis's brother somewhere in the town of ——, which is near the camp anyway. This brother, supposedly, will be able to tell us how to get there. For now we're content to drive westward through the Alberta countryside with a twelve-pack in the front seat. Robert, who is driving, takes his hands off the wheel for a moment or two to open a couple of bottles, using the old hooking-the-caps-together-and-pulling-the-bottles-apart method. It's a skill that requires both strength and *savoir-faire*, and it reminds Robert of a story. "I used to be a powerful man," he says. Seems that years ago, in Grande Prairie, he had a reputation as a pretty sturdy fellow, a mean mother to tangle with, in fact, and a huge white man built like a granite obelisk had challenged him to fight in the bar of this hotel — had acted like Ernest Borgnine trying to bully Spencer Tracy in *Bad Day at Black Rock*, sticking his fingers into Robert's draught glasses, and saying something like, "I guess these beers are mine, eh?" Well, Robert was cool, he had no intention of fighting, so he just left and went to another hotel bar, but the white guy followed and went through the exact same routine again. "I wasn't gonna run any more," Robert says. "So we went outside and started fighting. Geez, we must've gone down a block and a half of city street, fighting all the way. There was a whole crowd of people just watching. You'd've thought one of them would've tried to stop it. I guess they were gonna wait and see who came out on top, though. Anyway, I kept going for his face, and by the time I was through it looked like a hamburger patty, but damned if he didn't keep comin'. Nothin' would stop him. Finally I got him in the kidneys, and he fell over, flat on his back. But this guy—I couldn't believe it, he started to jump back on his feet right away. So I aimed a kick at his face, one of his cheeks, you know, and that knocked him over again, and he started comin' up again, and this time I landed my boot on his jaw, and I smashed it. Smashed it to hell. He didn't come up after that. The goddam magistrate gave me sixty days in Peace River for that one."

Oops — speaking of magistrates and jail sentences, there ahead of us are two police cruisers parked on the side of the road, and a police officer standing there in the middle of the road, and — yes, folks, he's waving us over. It's a spot liquor check, of course. Robert's brother takes the bottle out of Robert's hand. "Hide it!" Robert says, which is a somewhat obvious suggestion under the circumstances, and also quite futile. Robert's brother puts the bottle back in the case, along with his own, and kind of shuffles the case into a corner of the floor, under his ankles. The cop walks over, and asks, "Any open liquor in this car?" Robert and his brother say "no". It is a denial about as convincing as the ones you used to hand your public school principal, when you were sent to his office for throwing spitballs. Needless to say, the cop looks around, and in one-half of a second spots the twelve-pack and the two opened bottles. "Tsk, tsk," he says with delightful cop humour. "You know you go to hell if you tell lies. Whose is this?" Robert's brother, of course, takes the rap. It will mean fifty dollars, or a day in the slammer, when he comes up in court, but—what the hell. This is just one of the hazards of driving on the white man's highway. On to the foothills.

By evening we roll into the town where Robert is going to find Louis's brother somehow. Our first stop is the beverage room of the local hotel, one of those rural Alberta beer parlours that has little round tables covered with pink terry cloth, and a few pool tables at the side, and an elk's head looking down on you from a wooden plaque on the wall, and up on the two-foot-high stage a couple of fellows in cowboy shirts playing some hurtin' music for the boys out there meditating over their eleventh glass of beer and fourth bag of beer nuts. Louis's brother is nowhere in sight. As we start to leave, however, an Indian comes up to us— not too firm on his feet, mind you, but the old gyroscope between the ears is working all right, he seems to know where he's going, and all of a sudden starts talking a flood of Cree to Robert, and the two of them get into this intense conversation. Robert looks like he can't believe what he's hearing. We all sit down over the pink terry cloth, and a few rounds of draught are ordered, and this fellow, his hair tied in the back with a rawhide thong, and his skin almost the classic copper colour of the classic American Indian, sounds like he's pouring out his soul to Robert.

After a while Robert explains to me. This man, Charlie ——, is a medicine man with Chief Small Boy's band of Cree, which is encamped further south along the foothills. This weekend, though, he is staying with Louis and his band. Somehow he had known Robert was coming for the weekend, known this for a certainty even though Robert himself was undecided whether he was coming or not, and had never so much as hinted to anybody except myself and a couple other people in Edmonton that he was even considering the idea. Well, Charlie had decided to come into town today to find him and lead him to the camp. He knew, I mean he just *knew*, that Robert would be there some time today. Of course, he had never laid eyes on Robert before, but when we walked in Charlie went right for him. Subtle knowledge of the medicine man. "Have one on him," Robert says to me, almost in a tone of voice like a curate telling the altar boy to go up and shake hands with the archbishop, so I gratefully accept a cigarette paper and a clump of Macdonald's Export A tobacco from Charlie.

After a few minutes we finish our beers and our smokes and pile into the Ford. It is dark now, and as we barrel along a gravel road through the hills I am beginning to have this eerie feeling of being totally out of it, a feeling which is encouraged by Charlie asking, somewhat facetiously I hope, "Hey, white man, what you doing? . . . Are you lost?" Nope, I reply. At least I don't . . . think so. "I think you are," Charlie laughs, in a kind of hoarse, tobacco-stained, semi-inebriated guffaw. Well, nobody's arguing. I just keep looking out the window, curious to see the sights here, as we get off the gravel road on to a dirt track sufficiently rugged to remove the muffler on Robert's Ford, and wind up in the middle of a cluster of tents and Cree medicine lodges.

This is certainly a distance from the York Hotel — above us the snow-capped Rockies, and below us some breast of elk smoking over a camp fire, along with the lower mandible of a moose, looking like one of those jaw bones cartoonists put in the middle of a desert scene, with the vultures circling above. Ahead of us stands a tent, with smoke coming out of a galvanized sheet-metal elbow-joint sticking up from the canvas. Inside this tent there are half a dozen people lying about on quilts and blankets, gathered around a fire which burns inside an up-ended galvanized washbasin with a sheet-metal flue attached. It is not easy to pick out details at first, because of the gloom, and the smoke seeping from the flue hurting your eyes, but eventually you can see faces all right, and supplies like vitamin-enriched bread and a pound of butter stowed away in cardboard boxes in a corner, and a four-year-old suddenly materializing out of some hollow in the quilts and blankets like a young pup springing out of her hiding place in the woods. I am introduced to Louis's wife, an old woman who, when she sits cross-legged in her purple dress, looks like a Buddha with rickets. She—it is discouraging to report all the marks of ill-health on her person, she looks as uncared for as one of those burned and blistered Vietnamese war orphans—is covered with scabs, and her lips are crusted over with a ruby-coloured grit, and the aqueous whites of her eyes have spilled over and discoloured her pupils. But she is certainly lively enough. We shake hands, and she laughs and says something in Cree, and Robert grabs my wrist and explains. "She says you're too skinny." My wrist should be more the size of French bread, apparently. But I smile back at her anyway, and start chewing on a hunk of warm moose tongue which has just been hospitably stuck in my hand. No hostility here. There is much conversation in Cree, and Robert explains once more. "Listen, don't get the wrong idea. They want to tell you that you're as welcome as the flowers in May. But they're having a sun dance tonight in one of the medicine lodges, and you can't come in. They don't know you yet. Believe me, it's not a rejection. It's just—the lodge is kind of sacred. Maybe tomorrow you can go."

Well, that's all right with me. Later, I follow them up to the medicine lodge and wait outside. There are about ten of these wooden lodges in the camp, actually, made of the long, thin trunks of the white poplar. Before they go in, Robert stops for a moment with his brother. He senses that his brother, who is a crack fisherman, mechanic, oil-rig installer, and doubtless several other skilled things — basically one of your native people who is well-integrated into contemporary urban society—is not at all comfortable with these campground Indians. And tonight is shaping up like some hairy ritual out of the primordial beginnings, when all those proud and free Red Men danced around the camp fire, centuries, aeons, light-years ago. So he puts his hand on his brother's shoulder and says, "You've always trusted me, haven't you?"

"I trust you now. I got no choice."

"You're a little bit scared now, aren't you?"

"I'm not scared of nobody."

"I know, but you're a little scared right now, aren't you? Well, just follow right behind me."

So the two of them walk in, and I lean against a tree a few yards from the lodge and as the evening goes on, with the sounds of singing and dancing and the drumbeat, which is about as primordial as you can get, and then silence and a man's voice raised like an orator's—I can see being inside a lodge with a fire blazing, and an opening at the top so that you're always aware of the night and the hills around you even darker than the night, and I can understand, for the first time, how deadly serious oratory really is. We live, of course, in the age of the shrinking globe, but in the days when the land was huge and man was small, especially at night-time when he sat around the fire, huddled beside almost every human being he knew on this earth, then oratory was as intimate and moving as a hand caressing you or shaking you violently by the arm. So I'm perfectly respectful of the place, standing outside it listening to a man's voice rising and falling under the foothills. If they say it's sacred, I'm not the one to argue with them.

The sun dance, or the powwow, or the assembly, lasts perhaps for two hours, and then everyone heads back to their tents for the night. They are not the most comfortable places in the world to sleep, if your ideal is the Holiday Inn with the maids coming in to vacuum every morning. In fact, even if your ideal is not the Holiday Inn, even if you like sleeping on a mattress in the front hallway of your hippy commune, they're still uncomfortable to sleep in. In my tent there are perhaps seven or eight people stretched out in a space which is about eight-by-six-feet square, covered with blankets and quilts which have been walked on and eaten on, except for a clear space around the fiery washbasin which is often spat upon, due to a fondness for tins of Copenhagen chewing tobacco among some of the men. This is not to mention your fantasies of perishing in the middle of the night from smoke inhalation. When the fire starts roaring under the washbasin, the atmosphere in the tent becomes quite, uh, dense. But no matter. One sleeps anyway. In the morning you get up and there's a whole day ahead of you of doing nothing but being an Indian in the bush. Of course you want to sneak off to the stream in back of the tents with your toothbrush and your tube of Crest toothpaste. It's not that your teeth will decay significantly if you don't brush them this time, it's just you can't stand, as a white man drilled in the white man's rituals, to start off the day with jungle-mouth. The Indians can, but you can't. So you slip off, as I say, hoping that nobody is going to see you going through this ridiculous performance by the bank of the stream.

But that's the last concession to the white man's way of doing things. We have our elk and our moose meat here, several cases of beer and a few twenty-sixers of Branvin Sherry, no need to worry for the morrow ... so the men start horsing around, arm wrestling, leg wrestling, finger wrestling, and engaging in this one contest of physical strength which is painful to watch, where two men get down on all fours and press the tops of their skulls together, pushing against each other. (Pushing, not butting. They're not mountain rams.) This particular exercise is supposed to use all the muscles of your body, from the trapezius muscle on your shoulders to the iliacus muscle in your thigh, but mostly it looks like it gives the occipatal bone in the cranium a hell of a workout. Anyway, it's all very friendly, with a lot of competitiveness but none of that slack-lipped, acid-edged taunting that teenagers get into when they're hanging around, working off their excess libido by whacking each other on the arm and trying to tip over each other's chair in the high school cafeteria. Two guys will be lying on the ground arm wrestling, say, and another guy will have this little springy branch from a red willow tree, and he'll be giving one of the contestants a swat on the backside with it from time to time— like a boxer's trainer who keeps slapping the big lummox on the face between rounds, to work him up, only this swatting on the backside is a form of teasing, like saying to the guy, you're lying flat on your belly, boy, like when your mother was wiping you clean, and let this be a reminder. Then there will be guessing games, in which one person will take a cap from a beer bottle and keep switching it around from hand to hand, chanting in a kind of medicine man wheeze *haaayyaaaaaloooowahahah-laaaayyaaa*, moving his hands over the top of his head (where he might slip the cap down his shirt collar) or around his back and chanting like crazy, and finally, after about half an hour of more or less co-ordinated arm and hand movements, he will present his two closed fists and somebody has to guess which one has the bottle cap.

But mostly it's sitting around the camp fire talking. Robert tells the story about the time he killed a moose, a jackfish, and twelve ducks with one shot. He shot this moose standing in a lake, see, and as it fell dead it kicked, and as it kicked it managed to punt a jackfish out of the lake and the jackfish landed on twelve duck eggs. Another tall tale from the North Country, land of fresh flapjacks, spruce pine, stubble on the chin, and gristle in the gut, and of moose-killing Indians. . . . Robert can be quite serious, actually, on the subject of hunting moose, the same way people can be reverential Catholics while still telling jokes about the Pope. Years ago, he tells me, he wounded a moose, shot him in the lungs (he could tell it was a lung wound from the orange-foamy blood the moose trailed behind him). As Robert shot him, the moose bellowed, or roared, or transmitted a curse in some vocal fashion. I mean a curse. Robert is quite serious about this. It was a moose curse. This is no shuck, put-on, or Indian jive, white man. It was a *curse*. The way it worked, a little while afterwards Robert developed some trouble with his own lungs, he was operated on, he had a hole cut in his back, and for a while, a long while when his very life was in the balance, he practically breathed through that raw, bleeding aperture. I saw the hole. It looked like a huge O-shaped mouth with raw sirloin gums. I don't know if the revenge of the wounded moose caused that hole, but it seems artistically probable anyway.

In the same way, one would not necessarily believe that some of these men are hunters, with their eyes clogged with rheum and their knees wobbling from the Branvin, but one has the evidence of the fresh moose hide and breast of elk. Jim, for instance, is pointed out to me as their ace hunter. When that elk jumps, he jumps right with him, haunch to haunch with the elusive beast, they tell me. Old Jim looks like he can hardly make it to the door of his Chevrolet Custom Ten pick-up, he looks like he can hardly put one toe of his pointed boots in front of the other without lurching ten degrees to the horizon. Jim, to be truthful, is not an impressive figure, with his rheumy eyes buried deep in his face and his gums streaked with chewing tobacco so that his mouth seems to be filled with deposits of black fungus. To a faithful Crest user the mouths of these Indians are almost uniformly painful to behold, actually. Their remaining teeth look like headstones in an abandoned cemetery. Partly it's their diet, of course. Poor diet, and too much booze, sweet wine, and cigarettes—but still they can hunt, and they have surprising physical strength, and they are clinging to a lifestyle, a lifestyle which is a shadow of its former self, with a kind of desperate, fitful tenacity.

I thought of this when we were lying around the camp fire

talking, and suddenly out of nowhere came this troop of young army cadets or paramilitary Boy Scouts or whatever, headed for an afternoon in the great Canadian wilds. They were all marching in formation past the camp, two dozen pre-adolescent boys in army uniforms led by an older boy about sixteen years old. This older boy was playing at being drill sergeant, yelling at the kids lagging behind, "C'mon you slackers back there!", running back and grabbing them and forcing them to jog alongside of him. It was a sight to make H. R. Haldeman smile. No candy-asses in this platoon, no sir. Robert's brother turned to me and said, "What are these army dudes doing here?" but no one else in the camp so much as turned his head. God knows what was going through the minds of the white kids — marching all spruced up in their military duds through a camp where the people probably didn't change their underwear regularly or wash their hands after going to the bathroom.

The teenaged cadet with the rigid sphincter attitude and his marching playmates do raise a point, however, which goes beyond the mere odium of their presence. It is impossible, except perhaps in the very northern stretches of the country, for an Indian to try to live his own Indian lifestyle without bumping into a white man wherever he goes.

I was reminded of this on the last night I was in camp, when I was invited to another sun dance. Apparently, they had had enough time to look me over by now, and had decided that, well, for a *moniao*, he's not so bad. *Moniao* is Cree for white man probably with the connotation of "goddam white man". One of the ways you can gauge the feeling of an Indian for you is to notice the tone of voice in which he says *moniao*, when you're the only white present. This evening the *moniaos* were sounding pretty jovial. Anyway, Robert gave me a couple of beers, and told me to present one to Louis's wife. To Louis's wife, he emphasized — not to anyone else who might come up real friendly-like and ask what I was doing with that extra beer. This was a gift from the *moniao* to the head man's woman. A token of gratitude for the hospitality and the moose meat.

So I went up to Louis's wife, who was sitting cross-legged outside the tent with two of the camp hunters beside her, and presented her with the beer, and the four of us sat there for a few minutes, each of us with our own beer, each of us savouring a bit of its sudsy goodness from time to time, feeling part of the land ... and then watching this ... RCMP car come bumping up the trail. It pulled up by our tent, and the officer got out, a young man with light, curly, brown hair and a serious expression—but more like the serious vice president of the Student Council than some thoroughly wised-up, hardened, corrugated, old veteran of the force. I started to get to my feet—the middle-class, honours-student part of my brain was signalling furiously. But one of the guys put his hand on my wrist to stop me and gave me a look that said, *what are you letting this chickenshit merit-badge type get to you for — we've been dealing with his kind since before you were born*. Robert came out of the tent and intercepted him as he walked toward us.

"What's the problem here?"

"Who are you?"

"Me? I'm an Indian."

"I guessed that."

Another cop with a sense of humour. Robert decides to let him know he's not dealing with just another bush Cree, but a heavy political type ... a *militant*.

"I'm Robert———. I work for Native Outreach in Edmonton, and I'm a member of the Alberta Métis Society and the Alberta Human Rights Council."

"I got a call tonight there's a lot of liquor here."

"We're just having a sun dance. Nobody's getting drunk."

"Right. Okay. I'm here to see nobody does. Your own people called— they don't want liquor at this dance."

"Look, if there's any trouble, *we'll* call *you*, right?"

Once again, the RCMP makes its presence felt, as it has throughout this long century past. Robert must argue for about twenty minutes before the officer leaves. He wasn't about to stay the night here anyway, but he can't leave until he lets

Robert know that nobody intimidates and hassles an officer in the performance of his duty, and furthermore he's no bigoted, racist mountie, but *reasonable*, a fair man, and . . . oh God, let us get on with the sun dance. The sun dance is practically the only thing these people have left, this all-night ceremony held inside a medicine lodge where no beer or wine is allowed, and no curly-haired earnest young mountie dares to enter. . . . I am asked not to write anything about it, and I promise I will not. As I say, it's one of the few things they have left, and it's not necessarily the white man's business to know about it. Print, of course, tends to kill the sacred, and they are perfectly sincere when they describe it as sacred. If they lose this, they are that much closer to getting totally bleached out into some kind of non-white, non-Indian limbo.

Of course, the profane world still lies outside the lodge and from time to time some of us slip out to have a few swigs of Branvin or Pilsener, and talk about the girl sitting there, who is married to the old guy who came down tonight from the Hobbema Reserve to do some of the singing and chanting for the sun dance, and, yes, one does hope she might come out of the lodge for a few minutes before the night is over . . . and Charlie tells me, now that I am practically blood Cree myself, that tomorrow he will demonstrate his marksmanship by lighting a match which I will hold upright in the air, with one shot from his trusty twenty-two. The only thing is, he tells me, when I'm holding that match in the air, I must not *move.* Not a fraction of an inch. Of course, I reassure Charlie, who is now wobbling in front of me like some person who has been forced to stand on his toes for sixteen hours, that I will not, under any circumstance, move when I have that match in my hand.

Actually, at that moment I am looking forward to standing there with a match in my hand while some dead-eye redskin stands in front of me aiming his twenty-two at it. I am definitely feeling good. The Rockies looming up out of the west look beneficent, the night sky and the stars look beneficent, the medicine lodge with a reddish glow and the sound of chanting and drumbeats coming through the canvas looks beneficent, the clusters of willow saplings, the dark, unrecognizable figures drifting here and there, muttering to each other, stopping once in a while to piss on the good Alberta grass—everything looks beneficent. All the signs are right. I will be protected from evil for at least the following twenty-four hours.

And I was. Charlie didn't follow through with his promise of a marksmanship demonstration, but the next day I had every need of the good karma offered by the sun dance. Driving back in Robert's Ford to Edmonton, I kept nodding at the wheel—I had had perhaps two or three hours' sleep, and there was all that Pilsener to be absorbed by the mucous coats of my stomach—but I managed to fight off total unconsciousness long enough to get almost to Edmonton. Later Robert took the wheel, and drove too fast around a curve, with the result that the car went off the highway and flipped completely over. I was sitting next to him in the front without a seatbelt and found myself bouncing up against the car roof—a sensation which instantly restored me to wakefulness. No one was hurt, however. We were still under our twenty-four-hour protection.

The rest of the people in the camp packed up and left at the same time we did. Back to their reservations, or to other camps, or to their semi-permanent residences. Unlike Chief Small Boy's people, they weren't completely into the "back-to-the-bush, live-the-old-way" existence. They're still testing the waters. They're still going off to the bush on weekends like middle-class whites going off to the cottage, white people heading for the great outdoors with a couple of twelve-packs in the cooler, and a hankering to "unwind". But perhaps eventually a full-time "live-in-the-old-way" existence — even if it is still locked into the white man's world and in constant danger of being destroyed by it—will prove more attractive to the native people in Alberta, perhaps in the West as a whole. The reservation life is probably doomed, and that will leave only this as an alternative to complete integration into the white man's society, the nine-to-five, social-insurance, Canada-Pension-Plan route, perhaps even with bowling nights and car pools — what native leaders term "cultural genocide."

Yes, and one other alternative. There will always be the York Hotel and the Dreamland Theatre, and afternoons of sitting on the grass under the shadow of the Château Lacombe gazing out on to the North Saskatchewan River while taking periodic nips from the bottle of sherry in a brown-paper bag. There will always be this kind of Indian, acting out on a personal level the destruction of the world which began two hundred years ago when the white man first came here.

THAT OLD FAMILY FEELING

Debate about the future of the North American nuclear family revolves around very simple questions, such as: *is this heavy aggravation trip necessary? Is all this family togetherness, this sharing the same tube of toothpaste, and having to hear your mother's "Good morning! Time to get up" trill through the bedroom door every day, and fighting and arguing, and watching TV while your father complains about a torrid scene involving Tony Franciosa and some babe with Varathane lips necking in a convertible — is all this really necessary? Is this family scene going to be a permanent fixture of one's life, like tooth decay or the February slush?* Please, God, answer no. Take away your North American nuclear family, and give me something like the nineteenth-century Shaker communes, where members celebrated their release from mother and father and all the little aggravating siblings by singing homespun lyrics around the butter churn, like:

Of all the relations that I ever see
My old fleshly kindred are furthest from me.
Oh how ugly they look, how hateful they feel!
To see them and hate them increases my zeal.

Well, that's sort of the idea. One doesn't have to hate necessarily, but still . . . alternative lifestyles, communes, group marriages, all these radical experiments in living that have cropped up in the late 1960s and early 1970s, stem mainly from the simple desire to avoid the chronic in-fighting and pressure-cooker atmosphere of that single-family bungalow life where mother and dad and the three kids are sitting around the dinner table, and dad initiates conversation by saying something like, "If you kids didn't have time to mow the lawn this afternoon, I don't see how you have enough time to go to the shopping centre tonight." Terrific, dad — everybody's stomach is fizzing and gurgling with the tension acids while you pass around the lamb chops and launch the first verbal floating mine shell of the evening.

For people desperate to get out of that trap, to break the cycle by not settling down and marrying some girl and living together in a high-rise heaven, in total isolation and with almost an infinity of time to explore each other's psychic pressure points, living by themselves until the moment when they can afford to have a baby or two to share the heavy aggravation trip with — well, as I say, for such people, who also did not want to live like medieval anchorites or one of those urban lost souls sitting in front of the TV set trying to get up the courage to call Dial-a-Date, the idea of communal living is definitely not bad.

Religious communes, political communes, back-to-the-earth communes, shared-minds-and-bodies communes — the variety over the past few years has been fairly stimulating. And each one of these serious-minded communes has had at least a slight tinge of the old Shaker spirit which proclaims: we have cast aside our old flesh-and-blood nuclear families, and all their works, for a totally new way of living. No more family roles. No more daddy coming home from a hard day of work to see just who has stepped out of line in his absence. No more mommy sitting around bored and fidgety. No more squabbles, tensions, competing for favours, or feeling left out. We are all in this together — in sharp contradistinction, need we say, to most people living on the outside.

Groovy. This is exactly what a person like Joanne was looking for when she moved into a commune in the city a year and a half ago, a nice old Edwardian brick house with a front porch and seven people living inside. Joanne heard about the house from a girl she worked with in the university library. One day they're carting around books to the shelves and Joanne starts going on about how much she dislikes the city—I mean, there's a guy in the boardinghouse where she lives who always walks around in a T-shirt and American army pants with these huge pockets with flaps over the top on each thigh, making eyes at her and saying humorous things like, "Any time you want to come up and borrow a cup of sugar, honey. . . . " But other than that she has hardly made any human contacts in the city since she came down to escape her dreary family in Sudbury, Ont. And this other girl, listening to her complaints, suddenly has a secretive smile on her face, as if she is just about to spring a pleasant surprise on old Joanne, as if she is dying to say, you don't know it, Joanne, but your troubles are almost over. But she doesn't say anything, actually, she just has this smile on. A few days later, after consulting with the other members of the commune, she sits down with Joanne at coffee break and explains to her about this house she lives in, with some very together people, and she asks if she'd like to meet them and talk things over, because they just might have, I mean, if she's really interested and all, space for her to move in, too.

Yes, well, it sounds—interesting. A house with seven people, you say. Joanne is not 100 per cent certain that this is what she truly desires. However, she would like to visit and talk with the people, definitely. And one night that very week she does go and visit, but under rather distressing circumstances. She had accepted an offer of some golden hashish from her pal in the T-shirt and the army pants, a very foolish thing, of course, because he assumed her acceptance was practically a guarantee of a little badly needed sexual gratification, and it ended up with him grabbing her arm and trying to pull her on to his spongy mattress—she thinking, *I am not really experiencing this tacky rape scene, I can't be*—and she barely managed to scream at him loud enough to frighten him into letting her go. Anyway, she got to her girlfriend's house, and was sitting in the living room with these curious faces looking her over and she started to feel paranoia moving inside her, like a brew swilling up from the intestinal regions — she didn't know what, exactly, they were going to do to her, but the way they were looking at her!

And she sat there, not saying a word until one of the men asked her what was wrong and — don't ask her to explain it — perhaps there was something soothing in his voice, a genuine note of concern to penetrate the paranoia shield. Anyway, she just burst into tears, and covered her face with her hands and sobbed like a madwoman, and she didn't have to say a word, everybody seemed to accept and understand. When she had finished crying she looked around her and these faces — well, she was high all right, her head was practically floating through the heavenly ether in this room, but it wasn't from the dope. Everyone else seemed to her to be floating, too, but in an inexpressibly nice way, and then somebody touched her and asked her if she would like to sleep there, and she nodded yes, and the next thing she knew she was lying alone in somebody's room and dropping off almost instantly.

The next day she moved into the house, and that was that. A new kind of family, with the warmth and companionship traditionally advertised as part of family life, but without the heavy aggravation trip, without the roles. Bob sat up with her the first night and explained what they were trying to do. His theory was that almost everybody is convinced, deep down unconsciously, that he or she won't get all the warmth they need, and therefore everybody turns off and tries to compensate by putting something over on the next fellow, taking away *his* bowl of porridge, and so forth, and by getting into sexual relationships which exclude everyone else in the whole world except the two people involved.

Here at this commune they tried to overcome this unconscious negative thinking, and turn the old kinetic warmth rays back on. Everybody has infinite resources of warmth and generosity, after all, and we should never fear either drawing on these resources in ourselves to give to others, or asking others for some of their resources. Of course, this was an extremely difficult task, overcoming the unconscious barriers to warmth and generosity, but everybody there was trying, and some deep relationships were being developed. Now Bob and Rachel were in a sexual relationship, actually, the only real couple in the house, and while Bob realized that it was very dangerous, they didn't really want to be exclusive, and they felt they still could be very open to everybody else in the house despite the fact that they were, well, lovers.

He was almost apologetic about this fact of life in Joanne's new commune, that he and Rachel had this thing going. Joanne was not exactly shocked or anything, not having expected a house full of celibates and not seeing why anybody shouldn't have any kind of sexual relationship they wanted, whether it was exclusive or all-inclusive, or whether it involved two people or the whole house or just strangers passing by on the sidewalk. Anyway, there was Bob and Rachel.

Bob seemed like a conscientious tour guide through a Mind Resort under construction, always asking after people and drawing them out and pointing with pride to future plans for the place. Dark-haired Rachel, his old lady, cool sexy yin to his hyper-energetic yang, was perfectly nice as well, perfectly nice but perhaps just a trifle ... *hasty* with the barbed comments. Joanne never felt that waves of warmth and generosity were washing over the two of them with the irresistible force of a great pounding ocean, precisely, but she thought it might come someday, or Rachel would eventually leave, or something. In the meantime, she would certainly be gracious and civil and— no use kicking a sleeping dog in the ribs, as they say, by getting into some ridiculous fight over a sarcastic remark Rachel might occasionally deliver, like the one about Joanne wearing her cuticles down every night washing the dishes, or something like that. Well—so she doesn't help with the dishes every night, or even very many nights, but let's keep our sense of cool about this, there's no need to get uptight, as if we were back in that single-family-bungalow, pressure-cooking atmosphere.

After a month, or two, however, one does notice that Joanne

has a certain propensity, a certain *knack*, one might say, for attracting attention to herself in negative ways. There was the day when people came home to find the second floor bathroom painted in flaming cherry red, and there was Joanne with the roller dripping cherry paint clutched in her very hand, and flaming cherry splotches all over her work shirt and jeans and ... people who had to use the second floor bathroom, including Rachel, stared at her handiwork and thought of all the mornings they would be groping their way into the bathroom and staring into the mirror for a few seconds while hanging onto the sink, and having to absorb those four walls around them, four walls of rich, gleaming cerise tint, like the inside of a cherry tart. Rachel, for one, couldn't stand it and burst into tears, which was freaking unusual for her. There was a big scene then, with Rachel going on about how Joanne was driving her up the wall, this brat who couldn't take care of herself, or clean up after herself, or stay out of trouble, even. Joanne just stood looking slightly dazed—*I am not experiencing this ludicrous, laughable, absurd blow-up, I can't be* — and almost unconsciously she turned to Bob, as if Bob might be able to say something or do something. Calm down the woman, for God's sake, she's your old lady.

Bob did his best as mediator, trying to soothe both Joanne and Rachel, and being matter-of-fact about the damage done. Yes, uh, I know it might take about fifteen coats of white latex to cover over the flaming cherry, but if we all pitch in a bit. . . . And Joanne cried a bit herself, and said she was sorry, she hadn't thought people would be so upset, and she would help re-paint the bathroom, and try to be more responsible, in general. Okay, Joanne, forget it. And you forget it, too, Rachel, let's try to go on from here.

Only there's this thing that Joanne undoubtedly has, of getting into little scrapes like this, and over the next few months tension between Joanne and Rachel keeps circulating like sulphurous vapour, Joanne leaving a mess behind her in the kitchen, Joanne inviting these kids into the house, adolescent boys with puffs and wisps of hair on their faces and groovy patches with designs of cannabis leaves on them sewn on to the backs of their fatigue jackets, and loud, shrieky voices, laughing and shrieking the whole night in their goddamn living room, and Joanne keeps *doing* things like this. Not intentionally to annoy Rachel, or anybody, of course, but still — they keep happening.

Obviously something has to be done, because the old reciprocated-warmth theory of communal living isn't working too well in this particular case. Is it just a spat between two women who rub each other the wrong way, as our pre-encounter-group, pre-Gestalt-therapy ancestors would say? Surely, we can go a bit deeper than that. It's not, of course, that Joanne is acting like a child who gets attention by upsetting her parents, or more specifically, her mother. One would never go so far as to say things like that, or that she occasionally inclines her eye towards Bob, old Bob, who is basically a very together person, but who sleeps every night in the arms of his Rachel, tantalizingly out of Joanne's reach.

One night Joanne is talking about things in the house with Ken, a fellow commune member, and Ken tells her he's thinking of moving out of the house, but in a tone like there's a real grievance somewhere behind there. So Joanne starts prying and prodding and Ken goes through a fit of mumbling and head scratching, and saying things like, "I just need more space, that's all," and "I can't do my own thing around here, there's too many other things coming at me." After about ten minutes he finally mumbles Bob's name, and goes into a story about how Bob has been asking him to work around the house, painting the halls, and putting down plywood flooring where some of the old oak tongue-and-groove has been slowly decomposing, and how Bob had suggested that since Ken was living off welfare payments anyway, and didn't seem to be into too much besides practising his guitar, he should have lots of time to do these things.

Well, Ken got a little pissed off, and stomped off in a huge sulk, until finally the two of them had it out, but Ken didn't end up feeling a whole lot better. Instead of patting Ken on the back and saying it was all right, he understood, Bob seemed to be rather annoyed himself that he was always the one who had to think of these things, and get other people to help him. The only thing Ken could think of to reply was that the old flooring had probably been rotten for the past forty years and it could stay that way for at least a little longer.

Even Ken had to see that wasn't exactly the keenest logic anybody in the house had ever employed. When you thought about it, Bob really was the only man in the house who seemed to initiate these home-improvement schemes, as well as sharing with Rachel the responsibility for collecting rent and food money. The attitude of the other people in the house seemed to range from indifference, punctuated with little bursts of enthusiasm for cleaning up and doing the handyman thing, to outright resentment at being asked to do anything.

Talking with Ken that night, Joanne opened up to a dim realization that there was a phenomenon occurring here no one had yet dared to acknowledge openly. It sure did seem, now that one looked at it, that in this non-role-playing house, two people, at least, had assumed the two most primordial roles of all, the hulking primordial roles of mother and father—Bob and Rachel.

It wasn't long after this talk, in fact, that Joanne did leave the house. She didn't really like Rachel, after all, and why be hypocritical about it and pretend otherwise? She really did like Bob, liked him not in a sexual way, exactly, but in a possessive way, wanted his attention, and—well, of course, she knew she would never get it because it just wasn't in the cards. According to theory, she should have gotten everything she wanted from him. He himself would have tried to give her what she wanted, in his conscientious way. But that was half the problem, his being such a deep-dyed conscientious type. There was a missing piece there, despite all those conscientious ways, and all that sincerity ringing true as plate glass in a supermarket. And besides, you couldn't convince Joanne that in a communal-living situation little blow-ups weren't bound to occur, all those unpleasant scenes of tears and shouting. They were just bound to occur, and who needs them?

Blow-ups, and raging snits, and sulking marathons... symptoms of unhappiness among commune-dwellers as common as Frisbees in the summertime. Hunting down a commune which is really "together" can be a frustrating experience, indeed. It's like hunting down the Indian rope trick. Someone always knows somebody else who's seen it. Of course, when you get a hold of that somebody else, it turns out he hasn't seen it either, but he *did* use to know somebody. . . . In the same way one hears, in Vancouver, of communes which are "really together", but they just recently moved off to the Kootenays, or communes in Toronto which packed up and moved to Killaloe where everybody is now happily throwing clay pots or doing Arapaho beadwork. But for actual, existing communes in the city—they, many of them, just seem to be in a state of subdued agitation. They just seem to have fallen short of the concept of togetherness.

If it isn't because one couple is beginning to act like mom and dad for the rest of the house, or because somebody's woman is taking up with another man in the house, it is because of something like...children. You'd be surprised what commune-breakers these energetic little creatures are. Almost inevitably they take over a house, with their twenty-four-hour-a-day demand for attention and their refusal to fit into the grooves older people have laid out for them, consciously or unconsciously. In this one house a group of people moved in who were all more or less committed to the ideas of sharing, co-operation, ecology, complete human equality. They were refugees from boarding-houses where they had to cope with speed freaks and old men terminally ill with cancer trying to push Demerol on them, and had all been searching separately for a communal living arrangement, had investigated everything from your hippie crash pad at one end of the scale—chocolate-brown walls, mauve baseboards, vanilla-fudge window trim, grey wooden floors encrusted with layers of old wax—to houses inhabited by photography freaks or macramé freaks, with arty furniture and five hundred house plants, at the other end of the scale. They had all been searching separately, as I say, and had then gotten together through the agency of a housing co-op and taken a good look at each other and decided that, hell, these people here were all right. So they moved in. One of them was a mother with a five-year-old boy . . . cute, curly-haired, a nice kid, but a bit . . . *aggressive*, in the opinion of some.

But only some. What's "aggressive", after all? Depends on your definition. His own mother did not necessarily regard him as "aggressive". Active, inquisitive, determined, forthright perhaps—but not "aggressive". In any case, everyone there was prepared to give this thing a go on the basis of sharing, co-operation, equality, and not getting too upset about things like this boy Lannie and the case of the Thorens turntable in the living room. The Thorens turntable, if we must go into details, was part of a sound system somebody had set up in the living room for the general use of the house. When Lannie and his mother Stella had moved in, Stella gave Lannie very firm instructions not to play with the turntable. Too delicate a mechanism for five-year-old boys. Unfortunately someone else, who was not aware of these instructions, showed Lannie how to work the thing. Soon, of course, Lannie was putting records on when no one else was around and grooving on the sounds of Led Zeppelin and Jefferson Starship, and then, growing bolder by the day, he would even put records on when people were there. Most of the people didn't really want to get into the hassle of telling him not to do it, so he usually got away with it, but one guy really became irritated when he saw Lannie with the turntable. It wasn't even his turntable—the person who did own it seemed perfectly oblivious to the fact that the kid was fooling with it—but he was annoyed just the same. It wasn't *right* for the kid to play with it. It wasn't right that he shouldn't respect this boundary, this piece of someone else's grown-up property.

So this fellow, Carl, started confronting Lannie every time he walked into the living room and saw Lannie working the turntable. He didn't sweet talk the kid either. He laid it right on the line. *Don't play with that turntable, Lannie, you're going to wreck it.* And Lannie, who was indeed a determined young soul, would pull out his lower lip and come right back, *I'm not gonna wreck it,* and the two of them would have an argument there and then, which ended when Carl grabbed the record albums away from Lannie and said, *I don't want to see you playing with this again.* Well. This did not go over very big with the child's mother. It was true she had originally forbidden Lannie to use the machine ... but what right had Carl to lean so heavily on her little boy? *I'm just trying to restrain him, that's all,* Carl would say. *Somebody has to do it.* And Stella would say, *Look, it's my child, and I'll decide myself when he should be restrained.*

Yeah! Carl, of course, came back immediately with, *not when it comes to house property you don't!* and the argument continued. The first long argument in a continuing series. After that it was practically a war of nerves. Carl would not back down. Every time he saw Lannie playing with the machine he would confront him. Not at the top of his voice, but not in the "soft-spoken, gentle-but-firm" manner prescribed by the parenting textbooks, either. And every time Stella was present she would tell Carl to lay off. Lannie there, he just took it all in. His eyes got wider and wider looking at his mother and this other man fighting, like the eyes of Brandon de Wilde watching Alan Ladd shoot Jack Palance in *Shane.* But these scenes also had their effect on the adults in the house. In a very subtle way they soon began to line up and *take sides.* It seemed you either approved of how Carl handled the situation, or you didn't, and among the people who didn't were those who discovered that it was a perfect issue to raise every time Carl irritated them for one reason or another.

One girl had just about had it with Carl. She hadn't left her lovely Burnaby home five or six years ago, and her father who had nothing better to do than to find fault with her at least twice daily, and to insult her boyfriends when they called her and he answered the phone — she didn't leave all that to live in the same house as a guy who also found fault with her and got on her back about things like paying her staples on time and helping to clean up the kitchen and God knows what, and here he was telling Stella how to raise her kid — this girl used to play with Lannie all the time because she was "into relating to children". That's what she told her friends in the house. Children were very important to her. She supported Stella one hundred per cent. Stella — my God — to think of someone actually undertaking the terrifying responsibility of being a mother. It boggled her mind. In the meantime, she wouldn't have Lannie pushed around if *she* had anything to say about it, either.

Half the people in the house, it seemed, were lining up beside Stella. They wouldn't *say* anything to Carl — they'd just exhale their breath loudly when Carl started talking to Lannie or arguing back to Stella — or they would exchange disgusted glances with each other which said things like: *there he goes again, laying a heavy on Stella.* It was weird. You'd walk into the house on any given day of the week and not know whether the latest dramatic scene in this unfolding conflict might be taking place right then and there in the living room. There hadn't been this much excitement in the house since the two girls who were into the Primal Scream had left. Now *there* had been excitement . . . suspense . . . dramatic unfolding of conflicts . . . you'd take a long-distance call in your room after answering the phone in the kitchen, and in the middle of the conversation you'd hear a rich, pulsating scream because one of those girls was lying on the kitchen floor doing a Primal and the phone down there was still off the receiver . . . but Stella put an end to it one day by announcing she and Lannie were moving out of the house because her kid's mind was getting hopelessly bent out of shape.

Before she left they all had a meeting — mostly at the instigation of Stella's allies. Some people had decided they wanted to vote Carl out of the house. It had come to that. Of course, Carl wouldn't take this lying down, either, and the meeting became fairly memorable before it was through — tears, shouting, the boyfriend of the girl who identified with Lannie telling Carl he would punch him out if he laid a finger on her.... They finally took a vote, and Carl lost out by one vote, six to five or something, but this, too, he refused to take—Stella had been given a vote, for instance, even though she was moving out, which was not fair at all, and his girlfriend had abstained from voting—now she wanted to change her mind and cast a vote in his favour, but they wouldn't allow it—and so the whole voting procedure was moot, to say the least. The official result was still that Carl was voted out of the house but, as it turned out, he wasn't moving at all. Nobody was about to throw him out. I mean, he did own the radial saw in the basement, and he *was* the only one who offered any leadership in doing the renovations in the house, and so Stella left, and the girl and her boyfriend who had insisted on defending her, and the house settled down a bit....

Yes, the departure of that mother and child did, in fact, help a good deal — amazing how a child could bring out such contentious feelings in the grown-ups he lived with, such raw and difficult emotions! But children do this to communes, as I say. They sort of aggravate things, especially when there is already a covert family structure emerging within the commune—when there are people, in other words, who are relating to other commune members like the feckless brat, or the bossy elder sister, or the mother's favourite they were in their original flesh-and-blood families, the thankless parts they had to play in the beginning which they will be helpless ever after to discard, helpless to change. Unless some ways are found to deal with these re-emergent family roles, communes in the future may become as rare as rock festivals.

THE OFFICE AFFAIR

A h, the breath of scandal: even the girls in the typing pool are now talking about Susan and Murray's new, full-blown love affair. Not that the two of them are flaunting it, by any means. They hardly say ten words to each other in the course of a working day. Except at lunch, when they rendezvous somewhere behind the potted plants and the burlap office dividers and kind of disappear for lunch. Very unobtrusive.

With Susan and Murray, however, you're talking about two intelligent young people. Susan is not one of your girls who gets curvature of the spine from sinking into her chair and working her nails over with a file for about three hours non-stop while throwing out remarks to the other girls like, "Well, Joanne, you can tell your boyfriend for me he's fulla crap." She sits straight up in her chair behind the office switchboard, with a copy of *Dear and Glorious Physician* by Taylor Caldwell on her lap, which she reads between incoming phone calls. She is soft-spoken and sensible. Just last month, for instance, she moved out of the antique white surburban bungalow owned by her parents into an apartment with a girlfriend. Her parents reminded her that this was a very important decision for any young person to make, that it was "nothing you should do on a whim." No indeed, Susan. So she reassured them her budget could take care of her rent as well as the payments on her 1971 Valiant. She told them she could break her lease if anything drastic or unpleasant happened. She insisted there would be no problems with Vicki, her apartment mate. At twenty years of age, mother, she was mature enough to handle a thing like this. Of course, it was not very long after she moved into this apartment that she started to stay overnight at Murray's, but that had nothing to do with it. At the time she moved in, she only thought of Murray as that boy in the office who knew how to dress really well.

Murray, actually, is the one in this particular relationship who tends to stand out in a crowd. For one thing, he does have a wardrobe, though it's not your $300-a-suit variety. Let's face it, a junior data systems analyst does not make enough to dress like a successful stock broker, but he feels there's no excuse to come in like some of the guys, like his friend George there, who sometimes chooses as his workaday ensemble a pair of slate-blue slacks and some incredible grey-and-red-check sports jacket with shoulders an inch too wide so that it looks like he's wearing epaulettes underneath them. On a good day Murray will appear in a nice bow tie, shirt and sleeveless sweater combination, like a scaled-down plaid in a crinkly knit or something.

George has overheard two secretaries making some joke about Susan and Murray, but the way he found out, ultimately, was through the businessman's lunch. This was a lunch he and Murray and a couple of the guys used to have every Friday noon at a downtown bar, with these intimate booths decorated with English hunting prints, and a waiter in a little starched wine-coloured jacket to bring the Export Ales and the shrimp salad. Ten minutes before noon one Friday George heads for Murray's office, which he shares with two or three fellow data systems analysts, and Murray is nowhere to be seen. This is upsetting to George. Friday noon businessman's lunch is as much a part of the semi-permanent order of things, the reassuring daily office routine, as the line-up at the coffee machine in the cafeteria at ten a.m. George thinks of it as a nice touch of extravagance, a little highlight of the week that (along with after-hours pub-crawling) binds three or four guys together. When people discuss the boredom and alienation of late-twentieth-century corporate clerical and semi-managerial personnel, George replies, "Well, I don't know, at my office I've gotten to know a pretty good bunch of guys," and he is referring to these Friday noon businessman's lunches. So Murray's absence is definitely threatening, and also George really likes the guy. Murray, besides being a distinguished dresser, is a lively talker and helps keep the conversation going over the late stretches of the businessman's lunch.

Next Friday George comes over twenty minutes early and there is Murray working away at a calculator. "Say, Murray, you goin' out to lunch today?" Well, Murray suddenly gets this blank look on his face, as if George has just asked him if he wanted to play basketball at the Y. "Uh, not today, George, I've, uh ... I've made plans to, uh, see somebody today at lunchtime." You've *what*? Murray, you prevaricator. George bloody well knows what you're up to. You've got somebody on the line, is what you've got. What else can this hemming and hawing mean?

But George just mumbles an "okay" and walks off in total dejection, as if he has really discovered something terribly disillusioning about his best friend. As if Murray has betrayed him, in fact. But even if Murray *has* got somebody on the line, Susan the switchboard lady to be precise, what is the big deal? Who wouldn't choose a little romance at noontime over lunch with the gang? Haven't they all discussed girls at the office from time to time, in more or less lascivious terms — as if these boys weren't well-behaved office workers at all, faithful users of Scope mouthwash and Old Spice underarm deodorant, but a bunch of horny, smelly barnyard goats barely restrained by social convention from mounting the nearest wearer of pantyhose?

Two weeks later George has all his suspicions confirmed — funny how these things work out — when he and his buddies decide on a different restaurant for a change and walk into a downtown tavern done in a Castilian Manor motif with a waiter in a little starched wine-coloured jacket bringing a bottle of Casal Mendes and a shrimp salad to ... Susan and Murray, holding hands at a corner table. George and his friends are ushered into another part of the room, but not before George has had time to stare at this couple and for Murray to look up, spot George, and as quickly look down again to resume gazing at his right hand locked in an embrace with Susan's left. I mean, George looked at Murray as if he were sitting there with George's wife, which is absurd because George isn't married, and what is this weird jealousy, anyway?

George, however, does not tell Murray he is jealous, or in any way bothered by this new development in their little office society. Next Monday at coffee break he is sitting with Murray alone and figures that now is as good a time as any to sort of bring it out in the open. He struggles to work a little jocularity into his tone of voice, as befits one guy asking another about his girlfriend. "Well, Murray, what's this with you and Susan?" And Murray doesn't know whether he should be jocular in return, as if he can't believe he's just picked such a ripe, rounded morsel off the office vine, or blasé, like this is just something for him to fill in the time, or — hardest of all — serious, like she's really a terrific girl and he cares about her.

Murray decides his safety, for the moment, lies in jocularity. "Not bad, eh? Let me tell you, those quiet types can really surprise you."

"What do you mean?"

"I mean she surprised me, even though I'm such an evil-minded person, as you know, George." Murray is trying to fend off George, partially because he suspects that if he lets on that he is in any way serious about Susan, George and his other friends will drop all these subtle hints that they think Susan is a wash-out. She's certainly not bad-looking, but she will never be the life of the party — any party, no matter how moribund to begin with. Murray would rather have the guys think Susan is what his mother would call a "good-time girl" than hear any of these subtle hints.

However, George is not really satisfied with Murray's answer. He leers at Murray, all right, and arches his eyebrows, and he repeats after him, "Not bad, eh?" But he can't really believe that there's a lot of high-voltage desire buzzing around behind Susan's rather mousy exterior, and besides, even if she is just an insatiable creature driven by lust, George doesn't see why he shouldn't be reaping the benefits instead of Murray. But George's resentment is deeper than that, in a way. George has a feeling that these two are a genuine couple, immersed in each other, and likely to stay that way for quite a while. It's an honest-to-God relationship, blooming right there in the office, and no mistake about it. Why can't Murray go out and get involved with somebody who doesn't work in the same bloody office?

The difficulty in understanding George's problem is that we've all been brainwashed by *Playboy* magazine and certain advertisers into seeing the modern, urban, middle-class, under-thirty male as some guy who has nothing better to do than go from one party to the next impressing women with his witty conversation and a kind of hip rootlessness, hip urban middle-class post-existentialist detachment from all those things that have traditionally kept humanity down to earth, like a brood of kids running in and out of the house and the remorseless necessity to go out and plough the fields every day. There is no such thing, in this fantasy, as a sense of belonging to a family or a community or a tribe, or that fulfilment comes in any other way than picking up some broad at a dinner party who reads Marcel Proust in French.

To be honest, however, neither George nor Murray is like that. Nobody in their office is like that. George comes from a farm in southern Ontario where on Saturdays his parents always packed him and his sisters — all of them well-scrubbed and wearing laundry-fresh clothes — into their car and drove into town and did their shopping and had dinner at the hotel where the manager would come over and ask them what the dry spell was doing to their lettuce crop. After dinner they went in the car and parked right in the middle of the downtown section, near the Post Office where there was angle parking by the curb, and they sat in that car for most of the evening listening to the Salvation Army band in front of the Post Office playing old favourites like "Hail to the Lord's Anointed" and "How Sweet the Name of Jesus Sounds". And while they listened to the band, they watched people walk along the sidewalks and every ten minutes or so they saw someone they recognized and sometimes they invited that person — perhaps a cousin or uncle — into the car and they all chewed the fat for a while, while the strains of the Salvation Army band drifted in their rolled-down windows. There were more than a dozen of such cars, filled with families like George's, parked alongside the street on a warm Saturday night. It was practically a ritual, like the Sunday afternoon marathon *pétanc* matches carried on by men in the central squares of sunny Mediterranean villages, or the dance of the Iroquois women at the Green Corn ceremony.

It was a ritual, no doubt extinct by now, light years away from the hip-rootless, witty-detached scene of the *Playboy* male, but George remembers it vividly because he lived it, and he is only twenty-three! That ritual, and the times he spent stomping June bugs to death under street lamps at the height of the triennial June bug invasion, or whatever, were at one point in his life his idea of how people truly enjoyed themselves. And—moreover— a social organization where people could park their cars on the main street of a town and spend an entire evening just sitting and watching people walk by that they were personally well-acquainted with was at one point his conception of how the world in general was set up.

Now a person like George who ends up living and working in a modern metropolis may take on every attitude of the people he works with, the notion, for instance, that recreation is watching the Pittsburgh Steelers on TV, and work is sitting attentive at a desk from 8:30 a.m. to 4:30 p.m. with fifteen-minute coffee breaks and an hour off for lunch. (Back home a fourteen-hour day of work was not considered unusual, but here people think that 4:30 or 5:00 p.m. is the absolute limit, and then the day is over except for "unwinding".) But somewhere in the recesses of his brain, there is the old homing instinct that will not die.

According to this instinct, there must always be brothers and sisters and cousins in the world, and a mother and a father to rule that world, because a man without a family is the exact equivalent of a dead man—ridiculous though it may sound. But it's the instinct! Unconquerable and unavoidable, like a recurring dream. The stranger who mixes well at parties and poses for the What-Sort-of-Man-Reads-*Playboy* ads has no family—but he does not have instincts either, and perhaps he doesn't even exist. In the meantime, George, and hundreds of thousands of people like him living in our cities, have to satisfy the homing instinct in some fashion.

It's not easy, believe me. Without the old structure of parish and school, blood kin and next-door neighbours, where the chief contact one has with humanity around one's "home" is the apartment building super who spends half the day dozing off in front of his TV set with a bottle of Johnny Walker anyway, there is only one group of people in the city who can stand in for family and community—the gang at work. The boss there, who tries to be a good fellow, who never scolds an employee without trying to mix in some awkward compliment to sweeten the criticism — who else but dear old dad, worrying half to death over bills and never feeling very comfortable with his children? The secretary there who makes faces at you when you hand her some work—who else but Sis, or cousin Jane, who used to sit on your chest and rub your scalp with her knuckles when you were eight? Let us not say that any of this is necessarily conscious— murky and mysterious are the ways of the homing instinct. But it will be satisfied.

Nobody in the office has very many friends, or even casual acquaintances, outside work, especially if, like George, they have not grown up in the city. Even for simple fellowship they have to stick together. Almost the only time George goes out, in fact, it is with the guys at work, drinking beer. Such beer they consume! Three nights a week, not counting the weekend, sometimes. Already the wasteland of their atrophied stomach muscles, the roll of fatty tissue hanging inside there like a batch of wet Polyfilla, protrudes over their belt buckles exactly like the flabby stomachs of men twenty years their senior. The sad truth indeed is that they are all deteriorating physical specimens. And yet what else can be done—George knows he could probably be married like some of the guys, but then his beer drinking would merely be replaced by evenings of TV watching. Or, at best, YMCA courses in leather-working, or adult-education French classes, or God knows what. Somewhere George knows that this isn't the most enriching extended family he could have stumbled on, but it's certainly the only one he's got.

And as such, it does not really provide a salutary setting for a love affair. The Miwok Indians of California managed things better. They spent their whole lives in bands no larger than a single family headed by the Old Man and the Old Lady, but they would travel miles to find another Miwok band, a band of complete strangers, when the mating season came around, rather than break the incest taboo. "The violation of the [incest] prohibition . . . is most energetically avenged by the whole tribe as if it were a question of warding off a danger that threatens the community as a whole or a guilt that weighs upon all." This according to Freud. Primitive groups dealt with violators of the taboo by killing or driving away one of the incestuous pair. Modern-day employers often fire one of the people involved in an office "relationship" for the sake of removing a "potentially embarrassing and emotionally difficult situation".

George looks at Susan at work: reading her Taylor Caldwell in her Sunset-Over-the-Pacific Cerise nylon jersey designer dress she made from a Butterick pattern. How plainly, simply—yet carefully—she dresses, like all the rest of the girls in the office. Not one of them comes in, say, with a blouse creeping in tiny billows over the top edge of a skirt or with legs free of nylons or with nylons bagging at the knees in folds like a contour map or hair that hasn't been tortured into submission with hot curlers, electric warm air driers, stale beer rinses, etc. Of course, they're all single, and like the men they have this problem: they don't know many people outside of work. Susan can think of a cousin her age who attends university—now *she* goes off in the morning in jeans and a U.S. Army fatigue jacket, and spends half her day in the Student Centre with a Styrofoam cup full of lukewarm coffee just talking to her fellow students. Aimless chatter, but at least she *sees* people. Wasn't it only a few years ago they were solemnly proclaiming how dehumanizing the university was? Dehumanizing? Come in and work in Susan's office for a while, where the highlight of the day is the euchre game at coffee breaks and lunch, and you're lucky if you can get a hold of some guy like ... well, like Murray, who is really sweet.

And George looking at Susan thinks angrily to himself, that Susan is quiet, but underneath it all she is a silly, stupid bitch who never should have gotten involved with Murray. Silly, stupid girl! This is just going to end after a few months when the two of them get tired of each other. A veritable mockery of love. Let me tell you, if and when Susan and Murray break up and decide they hate each other, Susan will have two bitter enemies in the office, and one of them will be George. George who, actually, was quite fond of her before all this, who always asked her how things were going when he came into work in the morning, and stayed to listen to her answer. See if he asks her now how things are going!

In the meantime, Susan has to explain to her girlfriends this new involvement. "How are you and Murray getting along these days?" is the way Marilyn phrases it when the two of them are alone in the Ladies' Room after the 3:00 p.m. euchre session. Marilyn looks at Susan with wide-open eyes, and no trace of spite—not only no spite, but a genuine note of concern in her voice, as befits one girl asking another about her boyfriend. And Susan doesn't know quite how to reply, whether she should give Marilyn this knowing look, as if to say, listen, honey, he's no better than he should be, but I can tell you he's not gonna take me for granted, or, on the contrary, a look of innocence that says, we always talk to each other, and I don't know, we just seem to *understand* each other.

Susan decides that neither is quite appropriate. She tries to find the words that will give Marilyn an idea, kind of, of their relationship without necessarily telling her *everything*. "We're doing all right. He's really a sweet person. I don't know, I think he just needs somebody to take care of him. He likes to think he's very mature for his age and independent, but you know — underneath he's just a little boy. Don't tell him that, though."

Ah, there it is: the Maternal Instinct. Susan has an inkling that Marilyn and a lot of the other girls in the office don't really think that Murray rates as Mr. Suave. Not precisely. In fact, he's more of a klutz, in some girls' opinions, with his corny jokes for the secretaries and his brisk and snappy walk around the office, like he's always on his way to the boss with this month's battle plan for the big push on profits and productivity. On his way to the john for a smoke and a good look at the morning paper is more like it.

Consequently, Susan would rather have them think she is merely taking Murray under her wing, supplying a little warmth and shelter, as it were, to this outsized twelve-year-old, than let on that their relationship is in any way a serious, passionate affair. No, not that. Such affairs are too easily mocked, misunderstood . . . but everyone, from the boy who picks up the office mail to the boss in the front office can surely understand motherly, protective love in action, must surely understand and even sympathize? It's not really an "affair", after all, with all the ridiculous connotations of that word — surely everyone will be able to see that?

THE GREENING OF THE TOWNSHIPS

Driving up to Quebec from New England is always a treat. You leave behind you a wintry, woodsy country where the farmhouses, the old decaying kind with pointed gables and shutters that actually close, suggest stingy temperaments, hot cocoa, and the occasional ax murder. You enter a wintry, woodsy country where the farmhouses, with lots of filigree on the railings and the eaves, suggest starchy meals, a snifter of brandy behind the glass cabinet, and an invalid child somewhere in a back room.

Of course, since the Second World War we've all been heading towards the same Arborite-kitchen and garburator universe. Only the farmhouses built before the war remind you of what was distinctive about these regions. The people who live in these farmhouses, on both sides of the border, now have jobs twenty, thirty, forty miles away, in factories or mills around decent-sized towns. They commute on the interstate, or on the autoroute, and at work they make bets on the Super Bowl and talk about Sonny and Cher getting together again for a new TV series. The old villages, townships, hamlets are awash and dissolving in the flood tide of late-twentieth-century-finance capitalism, corporate, global-village technology. The old-style community is obviously dead, whether it was the Quebec township, centred around the church, or the New England village undergoing various mutations on its evolutionary journey from Grover's Corners to Peyton Place. Dead or dying—except that recently kids who were born and raised in the big city and couldn't tell you which end of the harrow you put in the ground are starting to move into these old rural communities and re-shape them.

I was driving through the Eastern Townships not really expecting to come across any of these new communities of young refugees from the city—for some reason I had the notion that the kids in this country who were into that all ended up in B.C., where they built themselves teepees and chewed the amanoetis mushroom for spirit visions. I was merely going to interview a young family who had lived in Montreal and then moved to the village of St. ——, where they were renovating an old farmhouse. I was mainly interested in them because I wanted to meet a couple where the husband was English and the wife was French and they had both decided to be assimilated into the French-Canadian solitude, instead of the other one, for a change. When I finally did meet them I realized that this aspect of their lives was less important than the fact they were part of this unofficial rural resettlement program, but, as I say, it never entered my mind that anything significant like this was going on in this part of the country.

I had only the vaguest notion of where St. —— was, when I drove up from Vermont; certainly no one whom I asked had ever heard of it until I got to within ten miles of it, and as I drove deeper and deeper into one of the far corners of the Eastern Townships, I found that I was truly *en provence*, as they say. Country stores where *les gars* sit around the soft-drinks cooler, wearing green-checked heavy flannel coats, and caps with earflaps, and trousers with paint and silicone caulk stains on them . . . lonely farmhouses where you ask for directions and then spend half an hour trying to back out of the ice-covered driveway while their ever-vigilant watchdog, a huge Labrador retriever, follows alongside, snapping at your door handle . . . the real French Canada. Country stores and lonely farmhouses, and a grateful feeling that you're no longer in Montreal, and that no matter how clumsy your French gets, how often your past participles and auxiliary verbs inflict mortal wounds on each other, no one will interrupt you and say, "If you can't speak French, buddy, why don't you try a little English?"

No, nobody would say anything like that to you in these regions. Nobody *could* say anything like that, because their English is even poorer than your French. But besides that, nobody would be rude enough to say it, in this country of gravel roads and delivery trucks from grocery stores which serve half a dozen towns and settlements, and circuit priests, and old men who deliver eggs to your door once a week, old men bent over, with the flaps of their cap down good and snug over their ears in wintertime, and walking as if their joints had indeed crusted over, with all the fluid dried up like hard resin. I mean, you know they'll be delivering eggs to your door once a week until about twenty minutes before they have to die — because the spirit of the old small-town farming community lingers yet.

I admit to a feeling of *nostalgie de la campagne* as I continue driving past nightfall, and the condition of the road gets more interesting, and the houses get fewer and fewer . . . is it possible, I ask myself (despite my certainty that it is *not* possible) . . . is it possible that I am at last getting away from the great North American interstate/autoroute nexus, the universe of Arborite kitchens, and getting into some of that genuine, old-time rural culture? Could it be that I am actually entering a different world here, where they haven't yet sold all of their hand-carved duck decoys and hand-made oak chests to proprietors of antique shops on Avenue Road, where they all go to mass on Sunday and perform their Easter duty, and get together in somebody's barn every Saturday night for hoedowns and square dances (local varieties, of course, dating back to *passepieds* danced in medieval Brittany)? And these aren't the only visions conjured up in the darkening twilight. There is the matter of that . . . geodesic dome standing behind the ancient farmhouse up on that hill. Very interesting. A few lonely pioneers of the counter culture, perhaps, setting up camp in the heart of this nineteenth-century filigreed world.

Well, not to worry. Tomorrow, in the cold light of day, I will stop by a country store where a girl from Minnesota sits behind the counter in her peasant smock and watches other young men and women come in shopping for walnuts, rice, lentils, flour, wheat germ, dates, raisins, and other staples of the Consciousness III diet. English-speaking kids from all over North America have established their beachhead here. They even have their own newspaper, *The Townships Sun*, which gives you advice on how to press apples, and build your own home out of bent maple tree trunks. They gather at this country store to talk and socialize just like other folks in other townships, but not around the cooler full of soft drinks because there isn't one here — just the flour, lentils, etc., in clear plastic bags.

One is aware, of course, that this is not a real country store, because the sign hanging out front is a hand-carved wooden sign instead of a big red and white Enjoy-Coca-Cola quadrangle. One is also aware that these are not real rural folk. They have beards and wire-framed spectacles and long stringy hair. They look like they put in time writing a thesis on Schopenhauer in graduate school, or living off social assistance in some hippie crash-pad in downtown Toronto or Montreal, or working as lab technicians and fooling around with pyramids and orgone boxes in their workshop at night. Unlikely reinforcements for the dwindling number of real villagers, but there you have it.

"When the sad, sad tale of the gradual disappearance and eventual extinction of the small farmer is finally told, we'll all be the poorer," says *The Townships Sun*. When the last farmer sells his last suckling calf to Canada Packers and hires on at the shipping and receiving department of the nearby furniture factory, it will certainly be a melancholy day . . . except that it will never happen if they continue to pour in from the city, all these postwar babies grown up in bungalows on Oak Lane and Maple Lane and Beech Lane and Willow Lane, all these kids who never noticed any real oaks and maples and beeches and willows when they were growing up because they were too busy absorbing "I Love Lucy" in the dark confines of their family rec rooms.

In a way, it was disheartening for me to come across this store because it was evidence that I hadn't come very far from that autoroute nexus. Not much filigree in these parts. No traces of medieval Brittany. Just my friends in the counter culture settling in. The counter culture! No one could deny it was admirable, all these young people committing themselves to a life of hard work and simplicity, farming without chemicals and so on, using kerosene and garlic juice instead of DDT to keep the potato bugs out of the potato patch, but how familiar it had all come to sound by now, how routine, like Frisbee tournaments and glitter rock. This is the clean-living wing of the counter culture, basically. Spiritual ideals, whether articulated or not, are a big influence on their lifestyle. It is not an exciting lifestyle. One will have to wait for their children to grow up on these farms and form their own communities, which will hopefully bloom with gossip, vendettas, primitive blood rites, and other enlivening folkways.

The couple I am visiting are not really part of this beachhead. For one thing, they live around St. ——, which is totally French, and they and all their friends rarely speak English. For another, they do not really seem to be interested in farming. They are all sort of artists and craftsmen. But they do share some interesting characteristics with the English kids. They are refugees from the city (in this case, Montreal) and they are interested in resuscitating many features of the old rural culture which the rural folks themselves have long since abandoned. The farmhouses around here may be decaying but they have kitchen tables with Formica tops and tubular steel legs, after all, instead of oak tables with three hundred years of gouges and scratches filled in with hard shellac. And the rustics go in for things like snowmobiles and dune buggies, which, of course, the young people from the city despise.

Another interesting characteristic that this couple, and their St. —— friends, share with the English kids is a rejection of the commune as a vehicle for getting back to the earth. Which is a start, anyway. An indication that they're at least ready to claim their adulthood. (Communes, for some reason, breed infantilism like hot-houses nourish orchids.) No, John and Yvette and their year-old daughter, a modern nuclear family, have taken over this ancient farmhouse for their own, an unpromising old house where the old ceiling and floor have had to be ripped out so that the ceiling joists are now exposed, with cobwebs hanging down between them and clumps of fibrous dust and grime spun together like cocoons — colonies of them spreading out and multiplying over the long passage of years. And the walls — as far as the walls are concerned, one is not sure about the walls, no, but one fears the frame of the house may have become imperceptibly rhomboid instead of rectangular since it was built, rhomboid or even trapezoid....

Nevertheless! They are redoing this farmhouse, having an electrician come in for the wiring, and perhaps a plumber one day for the pipes so they won't have to continue flushing the toilet by pouring a basin of water down it each time they use it. But in the meantime John is putting in new insulation, Ten/Test, Gyproc, and so forth, jacking up the out-of-kilter floor joists, and his wife is trying to bring a little order into the chaos, cooking the meals over their wood stove, which is one of those sprawling iron stoves with chrome finishing and baked-on enamel and a hinged mirror at the back that grandpère used when he was a young man before the Boer War, shaving over the water he had heating up on that stove....

It is not easy to keep house under these circumstances, especially when your daughter has resources of energy you never dreamed possible in a year-old infant. I mean, this baby is indefatigable. Loose, delicate objects, liquid substances, any kind of food, human or cat, building supplies, notions, wood scraps, things that rattle or bump inside containers, are all calling out to her and saying touch me! fondle me! shake me! see if I am edible! She can be trusted to discover the box of Graham Crackers and be eating them off the floor before you have finished shooing away the cat with the dead mouse in his jaws. *Maudit cochon*, the mother says, wiping her daughter's mouth — but still patiently, like a castaway who spies another leak in the lifeboat and just goes ahead and fills it up with a little emulsified silicone — this is the kind of life they have chosen, making a home and everything in the middle of a construction site.

Slowly they are starting to get to know their neighbours. Some of their friends from the big city are gaining an entrée into St. —— society by teaching their neighbours some back-to-the-earth skills like pottery and macramé. Macramé the village women like because it has associations with big-city sophistication, *Better Homes and Gardens* décor, smart apartments done up with ivy plants on glass-topped tables, fig trees growing in a corner of the living room, under the skylight. Weaving, on the other hand, still stirs too many ancestral memories of lonely nights in the farmhouse, working away at a rug which would all too soon become a home and nest for cockroaches. No, the St. —— women consider weaving a useless skill now that they can buy carpets with miracle rayon fibre for the pile, rayon with a water-repellent and crease-resistant finish — they haven't yet learned to associate it with multi-coloured ponchos they could wear in the springtime with their shades and blue jeans and leather purses to the country store.

John and his wife had no skills like this to teach, but they were able to become involved in village life through their participation in Sunday mass, John with his fiddle working with his musician friends on a few variations on some well-known liturgical themes, the Kyrie, the Sanctus, etc. And not only the mass, but weddings and baptisms — they played jigs and reels and led *chansons à répondre*, and tried to do something with the church choir, which was truly in a primitive state, one male soloist, and with no idea, really, of what you could do with harmony....

An odd twist of fate, when you thought about it. Back in Montreal, John and his wife would no more have thought of darkening a church door at mass time than they would have applied for membership in the Kiwanis, or volunteered to lead a troop of Boy Scouts. John has never even been a Catholic. Occasionally, when they are preparing for a mass, John will ask the woman who heads the choir, okay now, where does the *agnus dei* go, and the woman will stare at him for a second and say, "You're not a Catholic, are you?" and she'll be wondering—why is this lad with the moustache and the hair like some wild man coming back from a buffalo hunt spending time here? Why *is* he? I mean, he's very nice, and everything, very handy with the fiddle, but—how do you explain to this woman who heads the choir something like the Desire for the Authentic Life which comes over people of John's generation, and the English-speaking kids over at the country store? How do you explain to her about the City, which for years over-stimulated their intellects and nervous systems and adrenal glands and, in the process, created a spiritual hunger, a *craving*, for rest, peace, surcease — how, after a while, their very nervous systems start exerting silent pressure for this rest, and their brain starts formulating fantasies about living in the country and following *le beat de la campagne*, rising with the sunrise, resting with the sunset, etc., and being part of a *community*—even if that means going to mass on Sunday.

Yes, being part of a community. Neighbours who are really neighbours, and not strange voices on the other side of the duplex wall, rumbling and shrieking over a bottle of suds on a Saturday night. At St. ——, John is finding that it is not a one-way street as far as teaching the neighbours and offering a little culture is concerned—the neighbours have their lore, too, and are willing to share it even with a stranger from Montreal, if he's not weird or threatening. Little tips like cut the wood for your stove in the winter and let it dry over the summer so it will split more easily when you want to use it *next* winter. And, when that next winter rolls around, don't take your car into the city for one of those commercial rust-proofing jobs, let Uncle Zotique apply his home-made mixture of oil and grease to the undersides of your car, because that commercial rust-proof coat will just harden and crack and let water in between it and the car, and keep it there sloshing away all winter so that your car will rust twice as fast as it would if you hadn't done anything to it.

It's a cultural exchange, more or less. The effect of this exchange on some of the younger people in the village is particularly interesting. Young TiPaul, for example, has become very friendly with John and his wife ... a droll young fellow, this TiPaul. At seventeen or eighteen he walks around with a slight stoop in his shoulder, and he already has one or two teeth missing and his voice is high pitched, particularly in moments of excitement, when it seems his vocal cords just tense up so completely that they vibrate helplessly in the larynx like brass prongs. This tensing up occurs frequently to him, because he is one of those people who go through life expecting to be mildly ridiculed or, at best, shrugged off. He realizes he comes across as a little odd ... stooped shoulders, missing teeth, high-pitched, uncontrollable voice ... and he has a father who rides him pretty hard, anyway, in case he's ever in danger of relaxing too much, so naturally his shoulder muscles become even more stiff, locked into place, and the stoop becomes semi-permanent, and the vocal cords are down there quivering....

But when TiPaul got to know John and his wife another side of him emerged. He would tell them about the time he found a bear cub in the woods and took it home and cared for it, and he would show them this photograph of himself standing by this ... well, yes, it had to be a bear cub, all right, it had brown shaggy fur and it was kind of roly-poly ... and John looks at the photograph and asks what happened to the cub, and TiPaul practically breaks up. That shaggy critter in the photograph is TiPaul's faithful dog, of course, who happened to look particularly ursine on the day it was taken, or at least ursine enough to fool one of these kids from Montreal or Toronto who has never actually seen a bear except to throw popcorn at, in a zoo.

Later, TiPaul began hanging around after John and his friends had finished showing movies which they had gotten from the NFB (where John worked occasionally on a freelance basis in the schoolhouse), and someone introduced him to beadwork, and damned if he didn't have a cunning eye and hand for the work, like some village Memling....John looks at his work and thinks, this kid will probably grow up and work at a service station, or something, pumping gas for station wagons passing through from Utica, N.Y., or Niagara Falls, Ont., and he will ask their drivers if they want their windshields done and they will stare back at him and be vaguely reminded of those Appalachian characters in the movie *Deliverance*, the ones who look like they've just come from a cabin where their mammy is slowly dying of pellagra on the corn-husk mattress.

Well, let 'em head back to the autoroute, and stick to their sightseeing. Let 'em just keep passing through. John himself is in the village to stay ... a young man from southern Ontario, from a family as Anglo-Saxon and Upper Canadian as one could ask for, and here he's beginning to melt into this absurd, weather-beaten, fast-fading-away society of small-town francophones. His French is now as fluent as if he were born here — he had to master a few little peculiarities of the local idiom and pronunciation (when he's telling somebody about nailing up the Ten/Test, for example, he uses the St. —— verb *coluer* instead of *clouer*) but that was easy enough. He's so good, as a matter of fact, you can forget about him back in St. Catharines. This man has gone French. His parents should have known when he and Yvette were leaving after a visit one time and they asked him a question, and John, a little preoccupied with packing the car and saying something to Yvette, absent-mindedly replied to them in French, a language which his parents understand about as well as they understand Magyar. It was a signal that the linguistic reflexes in John's brain had been reconditioned past the point of no return — he really was changing his identity, in the most serious way possible, i.e., by immersing himself in another language and another culture.

John's parents, actually, were surprisingly tolerant. The only thing his father said, when John informed him he was going to marry Yvette, this French girl from Montreal, was, "Well, uh, you know Yvette is a Catholic." No sweat, Dad! Even for a boy like me raised in the bosom of the Anglican Church. . . . John was also aware that both his parents were dubious about their moving to Montreal because of a lingering picture they had in the back of their minds of Montreal as Sin City, a picture, of course, which at one time was an essential component of the world-view held by southern Ontario citizens who owned their own homes and belonged to a Protestant church—Montreal as a haven for greasy mobsters, girls with silicone hair and Bakelite fingernails, creatures who roam by night, and so on.

And that was it as far as their racial or ethnic feelings went. English Canadians really have no strong racial bias against French Canadians any more. I mean, they get annoyed at Trudeau and Montreal and official bilingual programs and airport controllers using French, but they save their real gut-level hatred and bigotry for West Indians or Pakistanis or black dudes coming up for the weekend from Buffalo or Detroit. On a milder level, they may detest some of the more Mediterranean-looking immigrants from Europe. There's not much ill feeling left by the time you get to French Canadians as a group, except perhaps politically, as I say. Only in Montreal are there numbers of English who still like to think of themselves as disinfected Anglo-Saxons, more inherently trustworthy than the crowd of oily francophones they see every day. And that's just Montreal, the city guaranteed to fry your ductless glands in their own hyperactive, hyperstimulated secretions . . . the city which fosters paranoia like a civic resource . . . the city where the cultural mosaic is more like a jungle gym. . . .

No, John and Yvette have the right idea. If one is ever to have a hope of escaping from the prison of one's identity — middle-class, Ontario anglophone, product of the counter culture, whatever—then that hope will have to be realized in a place like St. —— instead of Montreal. A village community, a rural lifestyle, a slow infiltration of a dying culture by numbers of young people who have been spinning for years in the vortex of Technology City, and are now looking for a place to batten on and root into . . . a place where they don't have to be instantly identified and pigeon-holed by waiters and cab drivers, where they don't have to apologize for who they are, or go through that excuse-my-French routine, or anything like that, because everybody in this place is following the same beat, basically, and everybody will at least see who you are before they decide whether or not they can stand you.

JUST A LITTLE LOVE
BETWEEN TWO SWINGING
SINGLES

It's Friday night at the Singles Bar, Toronto's after-hours de-compression chamber for all those white-collar scuba workers from the office depths, and the eyeballing man-oeuvres have already begun. The idea behind this type of manoeuvre, of course, is to get a message across to someone without having to spell it out for her. On a good night at the Singles Bar two dozen or so pairs of eyes, a little glazed after a hard day of speed-reading inter-office memoranda, will be there warming up in the darkness, transmitting tiny signals all over the place. The more sophisticated of these signals contain complex thought sequences such as: *despite the fact company policy allows my hair to curl only three-quarters of an inch over either ear, I am still pretty cool: if I asked you to dance, baby, would you put me down?* At this stage the transmitter doesn't have to worry about a refusal. If the girl stares him back in the face for more than two full seconds, he can safely feel encouraged.

These preliminary manoeuvres are entirely necessary, of course, even in a "singles bar". There are girls here who can make hash of all these junior-executive-trainee-assistant-sales-manager egos, if given a fair enough chance. The blonde one there, blonde and slim enough to belong in a commercial, in her tight Levi's and steel-grey blazer and boots such as Fred-erick William of Prussia might have worn, actually deliberates for a while when this one office stud asks her to dance —

presumably without having first eyeballed her. You can see the corners of his smile slowly cave in as she thinks it over, as if she has to calculate whether it's really worth getting up there on the dance floor with this guy who probably dances like Joe Frazier moving out of a clinch, and then finally she says "I guess so," which is as much as to say, "Sure, mister, I'm not proud, I'll dance with anybody." And then she spends her time on the dance floor exchanging mysterious little half-smiles and hand waves with her girl friend who is also dancing with some unfortunate, so that by the time the five-minute number is up the guy figures he has done the equivalent of half a year's solid penance and mortification for his sins of pride.

That is not the way John handles it, obviously. John is from a higher sphere of socio-economic life than all these wrinkle-free striped shirts here from the Toronto-Dominion Centre. In fact, one might almost say he is slumming. Certainly he doesn't brag to his friends at The 22 that this is where he gets his girls — but that's beside the point. You can only take so much of the girls one naturally, casually, invites to The 22, anyway, with their Holt Renfrew accounts and "creative" flats redone in solid three-tone super-graphic designs and Robert Rauschenberg prints. Give John your typical, unspoiled Prudential Life Insurance secretary stuck up in the eightieth floor of one of those outer suburban plaster-cast high-rises, in an apartment with a Formica coffee table and an honest-to-God TV set in the living room. No status competition, no heavy rapping, no life-and-death struggle for the final serve in the match of wits with your dinner partner — just sheer unblinking admiration, please, blind adoration of the life available to successful lawyers like John and so elusive for the poor Prudential Life Insurance working girl.

Anyway, John knows that the Singles Bar is the place where such girls often go, in search of people precisely like himself — so naturally they are girls he asks to dance, and forget Blondie over there with the Prussian jackboots. It is no accident, by the way, that the Singles Bar is located near the Toronto-Dominion Centre, where so many of them work, because the two establishments enjoy a kind of symbiotic relationship, the one supplying the other with exactly what it needs and can't produce by itself. The T-D Centre supplies the Singles Bar with customers, and the Singles Bar supplies the T-D Centre with ... well, take a look at the Toronto-Dominion Centre. It was designed, for one thing, by Mies van der Rohe, an insane architect born in Germany, who practised his art as if he had sworn a fanatic's oath somewhere along the line to uphold forever the Dutch Cleanser image of his native land, and so never conceived of a building which was not, by the purity, simplicity, and coldness of its glass-and-steel construction, an abiding reproach to the messiness of the human body, with its fat, hair, glands, glandular secretions, and tumescences.

Well, that's the T-D Centre, exactly. You can lust there after your favourite nineteen-year-old in the office typing pool. By all means, eat your heart out. But how can the spark of serious romance, so to speak, be struck and kindled in such a climate, where the temperature is always controlled, the air forever conditioned, all shadows banished under the tyranny of indirect lighting, and where the most exotic scent is from the electro-staticized sheets fresh off the photocopy machine? It can be done, of course (doubtless there are astronauts who have been troubled by sexual fantasies on their way to the moon), but the total effect of the building is to make any such wickedness, any flirtation or even desires, yearnings for orgasmic embraces in the bush, or a tumble under bedcovers of plush whorehouse velvet, seem as welcome and appropriate as a bit of truly pungent body odour. Of course, this is apart from the psychic toll exacted daily by the status rituals and office management techniques of modern corporate capitalism, but that's another story. Suffice it that at five o'clock every weekday, and especially on Fridays, there are numbers of these muzhiks of the IBM electric typewriter, deodorized office mules, male and female, who are ready for something else entirely different, a refresher for mind and spirit.

Where else, then, if not at a place like the Singles Bar, where the visibility is always low, the lighting is primitive, the ceiling is constructed of wooden joists and has lead 33 BX cables exposed, such as you can pick up at any big Canadian Tire store for your own basement wiring, yes, and where you can buy a beer for your nineteen-year-old, and dance. You don't even have to look good on the floor, nobody else does. And the whole yassuh-boss, look-at-me-sitting-up-straight-in-my-chair-keeping-my-eyes-on-my-calculating-machine syndrome is turned upside down. Have another beer, and watch the office manager, the bald head over there with the serviettes sticking out of his ears and a wife waiting home for him with his two fine children, hold up his arms and snap his fingers as if a marvellous transformation is about to occur.

All wonderfully liberating, never doubt it. But the number of "serious romances", or even one-night stands, which are successfully realized among these disheartened people in such an atmosphere remains doubtful. It is enough that the dreams can be warmed up, the illusion of sensuality encouraged—it takes a truly serious swinger like John to act out what others keep safely confined in their fantasies. John realizes that, while many men might desire to sleep with a great many women, to accomplish this goal requires as much single-minded dedication and perseverance as, say, skiing the slalom at Innsbruck, or doing mayoorasan poses in Hatha Yoga. You really have to *want* to do it. Now, John is in his late twenties, and not bad looking: more to the point, he wears a three-piece, rust-coloured herringbone, with a vest with two rows of leather buttons down the front, a two-tone white shirt, and Italian leather boots with raised heels. Any girl there from the office would think twice before refusing to dance with this customer—a little too well dressed to be into the yassuh-boss routine, obviously, or to have to account for his sartorial tastes to a superior with a fine eye for "appropriate wear" during the office hours.

From the initial step of dancing with the girl, John moves with true swinger self-confidence, born of a lot of practice. It's almost easy, actually: he can count on the girl asking him after the dance what he does for a living, and then on her eyes widening to take in a little more of him, there in a corner of the dance floor, when he tells her he's a lawyer, and then, "Oh? What kind of law do you practise?" After another dance or two she returns to her own table, hoping he'll ask her again, and he does, and, really, he doesn't have to tell her much more after that — not about his office with its teak panelling, shag rug in flecked gold, desk a good seven feet wide, and prints of Renaissance cartography on the wall; or about his address on Bloor Street, the Colonnade Apartments, which is not bad, either.

If he does not leave with her that night (few girls still care to be *that* easy), he'll leave with her number. A few days later, she gets the call. "What'll your pleasure be?" Smooth, John, very smooth! Might as well get a few things straight with her, right off the bat. There are a few unspoken messages, a few hints to be subtly repeated throughout the evening, even in this relatively simple opener. First, there is no idea of pleasure she, in her most abandoned moments, could ever conceive of which would possibly exceed what you can afford to offer her. Second, she must be, obviously, the type of sophisticated woman a sophisticated man like you would call up — a woman who would never worry about such niggling questions as, how much is this costing me? Or, more ridiculous yet, whatever will happen to my reputation? Girls in their second year of high school worry about their reputations. Poor maids who go from thatched huts to work in Edwardian mansions as serving wenches worry about their reputations. No, it's too ridiculous. Life nowadays is a novel by Gore Vidal, not by that dear old weeper Thomas Hardy.

It is the second message which John will take considerable pains to reinforce throughout the course of an evening with his date. After the girl has stood there on the phone for a second or two, figuring out all the nuances of his first question, he casually suggests dinner at a place like Noodles, which today happens to be a pretty cool place in Toronto to have dinner with your girl, a nice bit of seventies Bauhaus to eat your scampi in. Of course, conversation over dinner tends to be a bit difficult for two people who have nothing in common, and have really only met for the first time, but leave that to John. Again he's had a lot of practice. A good topic to bring up in the circumstances is vacation time — an almost infallible topic, in fact. You could bone up on it, if you wanted, by going through back issues of *Holiday*, but that's hardly necessary for John because he's actually gone to a lot of these places; he can serve you, in his apartment, 155 proof rum from the Bahamas, killer ouzo from Greece, etc. No date — certainly not your life insurance lady chained from nine to five to the Prudential rock — can possibly *not* be interested in this subject. It's good for five straight evenings of dinner-time chit-chat with the same total stranger, and God knows, John doesn't need five evenings.

And that's really the hardest part, actually. No need to inquire where the lady plans to spend *her* three weeks . . . visiting Uncle Fred and Aunt Mary in Tillsonburg, Ont., perhaps. But for the purposes of this night she is a lady who would not be surprised to find herself whiling away a few weeks in the Aegean, though normally, you understand, she's the type who reads stories in *Good Housekeeping* about girls like herself who go to places like Tillsonburg, Ont., for their vacations and — surprise! — discover Mr. Right making the scene there instead of some goaty old Aegean island where you'd expect him to be.

But that's a bit of reality it's nicer to forget, when you've just been treated to a meal at Noodles by a guy who, if his eyes are just a trifle beady for Mr. Right's, is plainly in his league, and who's driving you home right now in his — hey, wait, he's not going back to Don Mills, he's driving you just around the corner to . . . the Colonnade Apartments, the underground parking lot to be specific! And now he's actually parked the car and opened the door for you to step out and into the elevator.

Sorry miss! You didn't actually think he'd *ask* you to come back to his apartment, so you'd have a chance to act surprised, and say, well, John, I had a marvellous time, but . . . but Sally Jane, or whatever your name is, that's not how a swinger operates! It's all an unspoken thing, you see! Because right now he's bombarding you with silent messages to the effect of: are you about to tell me that you didn't actually *know* we were going back to my place? Are you about to tell me you aren't sophisticated at all, that this is an act you've been putting on, and in reality you're some kind of dog who reads *Good Housekeeping* and secretly envies the estate of the married woman! Because if you are, this is it, baby, I'm not interested.

John's eyes are practically overheated now, with all these furious little signals they're trying to beam on the poor girl, who's sitting there trying to figure out what her next move is going to be. She hardly deserves this. Life is hard enough as it is for girls who come from the old home town to live and work in Toronto, when every passing month the old circle of friends from Uxbridge, or whatever, shrinks a little, as various couples get together, and the next thing you know they're getting married, and that's two more people you can scratch off your list. (And as for the gang from the office—it took about two months to go through *that* list.)

Unfair! Sally Jane knows this one girl from their home town who's got a dozen men hanging around her every weekend, and she doesn't do a thing except dispense good cheer and a little wholesome affection now and then, as if the whole dumb male world needs nothing more than a pat on the head to keep it warm and contented. She treats them all as if they're her adorable baby brothers. And they eat it up! They propose marriage to her! It's incredible. It's as if all those smarmy high school sermonettes about how boys value a "warm, outgoing personality" more than a willingness to put out are true, after all. Unfortunately, Sally Jane gave up trying to fake warmth and outgoingness a long time ago. If anybody needs cheering up, it's got to be her. And, besides, it's too late to start being warm and outgoing now, not here in the Colonnade underground parking lot with this guy who's just laid out a lot of bread for a high-class meal silently asking her if she's going to get uptight and make a fool of herself, or if she's simply going to do what's expected of her. Just what's expected, ma'am, that's all, just a little love between two swinging singles.

MANITOBA JOIE DE VIVRE

It is impossible to hang around the *Festival du Voyageur* in St. Boniface or read any of its literature without coming across the phrase "joie de vivre", a quality which is said to belong to the French there in a big way, as alcoholism belongs to the Irish and shrewdness to the Lebanese. It's a very joie-de-vivre Festival, this whole *Festival du Voyageur*. Much drinking, singing, dancing, conviviality, and so on. Of course, there are other official reasons for the festival, having to do with preserving the Franco-Manitobain culture and reminding everyone of their voyageur heritage—of indestructible types like Jean-Baptiste Lagimodière, for example, who walked on snowshoes for six months from the Red River to Montreal in the winter of 1815–16 so he could warn Lord Selkirk that his colony was in danger. Lagimodière's feat reminds one of how accidental fame really is, and how fortunate, say, Paul Revere was for having Henry Wadsworth Longfellow publicize *his* feat, and also for having a name, "Paul Revere", that could fit nicely into Longfellow's dactyls. "Jean-Baptiste Lagimodière" just does not fit into dactyls like that. Anyway, there is a definite lack of proportion when you compare how famous Revere is, and how obscure Lagimodière is, and if the festival helps to perpetuate Lagimodière's memory, I say more power to it.

"Joie de vivre", however, is the key phrase. Not many people care deep in their hearts about Lagimodière, or the French language in St. Boniface, but they really want some of that joie de vivre. So the soul of the festival is in the beer halls and casinos they set up for the occasion. There are several of these, and each has its own sort of atmosphere, but perhaps the most remarkable was one particular beer hall which had been set up in the gymnasium of the Centre Culturel Franco-Manitobain by the Chevaliers de Colombe. Every night of the festival there was a dance for the kids in this gymnasium. Now, you've got to imagine a fair-sized gym where the floor space might be, oh, equivalent to an official NHL hockey rink, and the walls are ordinary cement block, and there's a stage at one end of it. For the occasion this gym had been decorated with long strips cut off from logs, those semi-circular strips with the bark on the curved side, nailed vertically in rows along the cement block walls to provide the correct rustic, voyageur note. Long wooden tables with tubular steel legs, a little battered with age, like the kind you sat at for a church supper of scalloped potatoes and chicken à la king in the basement of the parish hall, thirty years ago, had also been set up along the walls.

The remarkable sight I saw there was this dance, which drew hundreds of teenagers. It was remarkable because — well, it's hard to pin down the unique components of the scene because one has, of course, seen many gym dances where impacted human bodies are writhing and stomping, and everybody is drinking lots of beer, and the air is about as healthy for your lungs as the air in the Lincoln Tunnel at rush hour — re-cycled cigarette smoke in incredible quantities is circulating down there and corroding the pulmonary membranes, and there's no way you can escape unless you're game to fight your way to the exit through this madhouse, this mob flailing away to the music, which would be like Baptiste desperately trying to get through the crowds dancing in the streets of Paris, in the last scene of *Children of Paradise*. I guess I would have to say I was impressed, not by the concentration of bodies or the foulness of the air, but by the sight of so many absolutely drunken, soused adolescents in one spot, throngs, hordes of them, responding now, out of brain centres that were somehow still functioning, to the musical stimulus of a rock ensemble playing *Chanson du Voyageur—Bearing tales oui! oui! oui!/ Bearing tales non! non! non!* — while the "security" men in their maroon C de C T-shirts stood around and told little girls with shiny pouting lips to get down off the chair where they were standing and screaming to get the attention of their boyfriends who were standing about six feet away.

A very heavy scene for an organization to sponsor whose motto is "Youth is our business. We make it our business", since most of these kids should have been home working on their logarithms for math class tomorrow morning. I had heard lots of stories, too, that these dances always ended up in fist fights, melees and so on, with the old C de C security boys sort of jumping in and swinging with it because they always had a few beers themselves by the time these things started, and they weren't exactly your super-cool bouncers, but I must say I never saw any evidence of trouble while I was there, although with hundreds of bombed-out, blasted, hyperkinetic teenagers on the scene, there was certainly potential for trouble.

And this was as good an example of joie de vivre among the teenage set as one could find that night. It was a madhouse, as I say, but in the afternoon, anyway, things are calmer. That's when the adults and the smaller children are there in the gym, and the tables are only about one-third occupied, and you can breathe in air that actually feels like there might be some oxygen floating around there somewhere. Of course, another musical group is up on the stage doing *Chanson du Voyageur — Bearing tales non! non! non!/ Bearing tales of the voyageur-eur-eurs!*—and that can certainly drive you insane, or at least to the point where your eyes lose their ability to focus, every time you hear a few bars of that song. Also, the adults are drinking lots of beer, too, and you have a few old guys doing improvised jigs on the dance floor between the tables, with a glass of beer in their hand so that pretty soon they're jigging around sizeable puddles of beer they have created, but on the whole this is where you're going to find joie de vivre, if you're going to find it at all.

At least you can tell the whole thing is supposed to be about voyageurs, anyway, because some of the men are walking around in chamois and buckskin jackets they got from Mallabar's, and coonskin caps and occasionally moccasins with heavy woollen socks. A group of students from Northland College in Wisconsin, who have formed a choir for the express purpose of doing *Chanson du voyageur* and other songs of that genre at festivals like this, know how to do it — they walk around carrying canoe paddles, hunting knives strapped to their ankles, long toques on their heads and with wooden lattice-work backpacks that look like old-fashioned laundry hampers hoisted on their shoulders, I mean big, round, commodious backpacks for carrying their dried pemmican over the long portages. These outfits, and the maroon T-shirts, are what first catch your eye when you walk in, but basically the harsh truth is that what we have here is nothing more than a community beer hall, with a few Franco-Manitobain voyageur overtones.

And why not? The fact that men and women are drinking together in the afternoon with no feelings of guilt or shame, in this country where the Mountie is still an accepted symbol of nationhood, is pleasant enough, and I don't see how the ghost of Lagimodière can be offended. No one is going off snowshoeing through the wilderness right now. The fur traders in the North West Company no longer threaten to wipe out the city of Winnipeg or St. Boniface sitting across the river to the east. There's no reason everybody shouldn't unbend a little and stalk the elusive joie de vivre for the afternoon.

So stop worrying there, Raymond. Don't worry about your wife. She won't get out of hand. Don't worry about your kids. That is not your three-year-old daughter who is standing on the dance floor howling, while the nice man with the grey and yellow beard, speckled with beer foam, tries to get her to dance a jig with him. Your kids are right by your side, looking bored and inert as usual. So join in the conversation . . . mingle, bend an ear, listen . . . that's your friend Georges on the other side of the table, talking about his wife's precarious health, his favourite subject. "My wife had an operation last October," he is saying to your wife, Elaine. "For three years she was going to a doctor, you know — we all thought it was her change of life. Well, he was giving her medication for migraines and every damn thing, and then this other doctor took a look at her and — geez, she went into the hospital and inside a week, he took out — it wasn't gall stones, it was ... *sand*. You could've filled a *glass* with it — not one of these beer glasses here but a shot glass like we had a minute ago, *this* full. Anyway, now she's gotta exercise and diet...."

"Oh yes, bran, a lot of roughage ... "

"...and, you know, use will-power."

Raymond looks at his wife for a second. Bran. Roughage. Good for cleaning out the old system. That's what Elaine keeps telling him. Your old clogged system needs that bran and roughage, boy. Sometimes it disgusts Raymond the way Elaine goes on about keeping healthy and eating right. Raymond just does not care to be "cleaned out", thank you, as if his colon and intestines were like those transparent pipes under the kitchen sink, in the old Drano commercial, collecting stagnant water and hair balls and a big dark-coloured mass of God knows what before the Drano comes along. But Raymond realizes, at the same time, that Elaine is keenly interested in this type of thing and he must be patient with her. Seven years ago, after all, she was pretty sick herself, and now she is brimming with health and so has a right to comment frequently on anything pertaining to one's physical well-being. Physical *or* spiritual, actually, because the two are one, Elaine says, and again she should know — seven years ago there she was, suffering migraines herself, backaches, even palpitations of the heart, or something a lot like palpitations of the heart — her appetite did not fail her, she kept on her feed, so to speak, and thank God for that, but otherwise she was a mess and that was the truth. That was the time of her "nervous breakdown". Don't ask Raymond to go into all the reasons why his wife was having a nervous breakdown. She just had one. Her doctor became worried enough to send her to a hospital for tests of various kinds, and she stayed there for a few days, actually, undergoing tests, reading a few magazines listlessly, talking with other patients listlessly, staring at the ceiling . . . until the day she got a hold of a book by T. Lobsang Rampa.

The book *You—Forever* did not start out on a very promising note. "I am Tuesday Lobsang Rampa. That is my only name, it is now my legal name, and I answer to no other. Many letters come to me with a weird conglomeration of names attached; they go straight into the waste paper basket, for, as I say, my only name is Tuesday Lobsang Rampa." Elaine read this listlessly. So his only name is Tuesday Lobsang Rampa — that's terrific, she thought, that's just great. If she wants to send him a post card now, she'll know how to address it. But she kept reading the book almost compulsively, because T. Lobsang Rampa, who-ever he was, had a certain tone, an authority, in his writing that suggested you were doing yourself a large favour by reading him, and it was really a very sincere authority, a very sincere tone. Before she knew it, Elaine was hooked. Here was a man who had figured out how you escape from your petty concerns, and your depressions, and your bouts of temper, how you can communi-cate with the Oversoul via the Silver Cord, and get in touch with the etherics and auras that surround every human body, and the vibrations of the cosmos, in general, the Fourth Dimension, God, and so on—how, when Christ said He had come so that we may have more abundant life, that was no lie—we just have to understand what He really meant, understand how we can get some more of that abundant life, and that was not necessarily by memorizing the Baltimore Catechism. No, it was by other means. . . . Shortly after Elaine came home from the hospital and really got into Lobsang Rampa, Raymond would want to go to the bathroom and find the door locked and wonder why Elaine had been in there for about forty minutes after he had definitely heard her draining her bath water and, of course, he had no *idea* that she had taken that bath in the first place to cleanse her aura of any influences from her clothing and was now standing naked in front of their mirror in an attempt to see that selfsame aura ... or the blue flame of her etheric anyway, which was the first step to seeing the aura.

Well, Raymond wasn't complaining. He didn't even give her an argument when she started talking to *him* about the Fourth Dimension, and auras, and feeling love for people, and so on. Let her read all that Lobsang Rampa shit, he reasoned silently, it was doing her good. Really, she was improving day by day. She wasn't feeling any *warmer* towards him — Lobsang Rampa never promised any miracles — but she was a hell of a lot more *pleasant*. Day by day her temperament seemed to improve. One time her little niece even piped up right in the kitchen, "Gee, Aunt Elaine, you're not so *crabby* any more," in honest, open-mouthed wonderment—the outspoken little tyke! Elaine could have kissed her. She *wasn't* crabby anymore. Now she practised yoga daily, and meditation—letting the mind go blank, breathing deeply, relaxing muscles and nerves — and she got lots of exercise and ate healthy foods, including bran and roughage, of course.

She even became active in the Church again, going to mass on Sunday, attending parish socials, seeing it all in a new Lobsang-inspired light. She was following the Christ of love, not the Christ of law. She was looking forward to His Second Coming as the triumph of the Fourth Dimension. The triumph of the Fourth Dimension meant that a lot of things were going to change, you could be sure of that. At the table where we are sitting she asks me, after she has found out that I am a writer, "Do you write what you want, or what people demand?"

"Well, uh ... I try to keep my finger on the public pulse."

"In ten years, believe me, you'll break out and write whatever you want. Now everybody's in a period of transition. Just wait and see.... Don't you feel people are coming closer together? It's the Fourth Dimension."

Yes, the Fourth Dimension. Something definitely to look forward to. In the meantime, now that we have discovered this new religion of love, and know for a fact that things are going to turn out all right, why not celebrate? Why not work up some authentic joie de vivre? *Vive le festival du voyageur! Vive le Conseil Goulet des Chevaliers de Colombe!* ... Raymond, in the meantime, takes another swallow of beer. From the looks of it, his wife is getting into the spirit of things, all right. He should be happy for her. Why is he feeling so sour, instead? Why do all these occasions give him such a pain in the ass? Why does he detest the whole *Festival du Voyageur*? Raymond is not exactly sure, to tell the truth. He looks around and takes in all the C de C boys cleaning up, serving the beer, just standing around. Those maroon T-shirts sure don't do anything for the old paunch, the old gut. He takes a look at the man sitting a little to his right, M. ——, a big, hearty guy in a business suit and paisley tie and silver-plated cuff links. M. —— used to be active in the C de C, and, in fact, is still officially a member, Raymond believes, but you'll never catch him walking around in a maroon T-shirt stretched over his distended belly, picking up those plastic beer glasses. M. —— is becoming an important man in the community, important even in the city. You can tell that by the way he lays his powerful meaty hand on your collarbone and hollers, in a voice like a plane going over a rough piece of board, "Chug-a-lug like a buffalo, *garçons!*" You can tell by the way he keeps glancing at his watch, even in moments of heartiest conviviality — a subtle message for the *garçons* that it's not every day he takes this much time to mingle with the folks.

Raymond feels a twinge of guilt for this cynicism. But, damn it, he knew M. —— in the C de C in the days when he, Raymond, was a member himself. M. —— was always coming out, in those days, with earnest exhortations to the fellow members like, "Meetings are not enough! Meetings are not enough, *garçons!*" No, we should all be out thinking of new ways we can translate our Christian faith, you know, in an active way, into something of positive benefit for the whole community here in St. Boniface. What a pain. That was exactly the way he talked. Of course, he had a point there, since that *was* the purpose of their organization. Not just getting together once in a while for a few drinks, you guys. They were all supposed to be thinking of good causes to raise money for. When the earthquake in Guatemala hit, the Conseil de Goulet was right there, for example, raising money. And *Le Festival du Voyageur* . . . well, maybe it's better not to use the Festival as an example of anything. This beer hall and the nightly dances are not exactly one hundred per cent within the strict guidelines of proper C de C activities . . . not exactly the best example of translating Christian faith into something of benefit for the community, I mean, not like helping crippled children or cerebral palsy victims or teenage junkies sweating through withdrawal agonies. . . .

But then all of the Christian underpinnings of this organization are not what they used to be. To join you just have to say you're a believing Catholic, and that's it. They don't all go to mass and communion together, or go on retreats, or anything like that. I mean, there are no religious fanatics around these days, right? Nobody except tarot card readers, Jesus freaks, Hare Krishna devotees, and the like. So the boys in the C de C accept this fact. Raymond thinks of his own family, of his own devoutly Catholic mother and father who had eleven children. Well, you can go down the list of those of the eleven children who married and see a neat arithmetical progression, or regression . . . the eldest child, now in his fifties, with seven children, the next two with five each, the next eldest with four, Raymond himself in the middle (he is now in his mid-forties) with two children, and so on. The grip of Holy Mother Church (or is it just the old rural-Manitoba-pioneer-Lagimodière spirit?) lessening with each succeeding generation, the faith weakening as you work down the age groups, until you have your nineteen-year-olds looking around for an abortionist for their girlfriends. . . . It is a common story in St. Boniface and Windsor Park. Well, Raymond just asked himself at one point, if we're really not that keen on translating our Christian faith, etc., what is the point, and he left the C de C.

But that does not really explain the sourness in Raymond's stomach here this afternoon. He is not a religious fanatic himself. He is not offended by all this worldliness. He is not even sure what he believes in, or what he's supposed to be doing with his life. Maybe his wife Elaine is right. Maybe he should be reading T. Lobsang Rampa. Going to mass on Sunday, and the rest of the week meditating and torturing his brittle, aching ligaments into various yoga postures, and keeping an eye out for the etheric flame, and waiting for the triumph of the Fourth Dimension. On the other hand, maybe his sister Gaby is right, Sister Gaby, who went into a cloistered convent when she was twenty-five, sealing herself forever from this world, and the temptations of this world, so that, for example, she never saw a television in her life until she watched the Pope saying mass at Yankee Stadium on the TV screen.

Or maybe his father is right. His father, who is still going strong in his late seventies, a restless little man who takes out the garbage and shovels the snow and is as tough and knobby as those octogenarians who run five miles daily at the YMCA gym. His father once told Raymond, "Son, if you've got your health, you've got everything." He practically nagged at Raymond about his health the way parents of Raymond's own generation nagged at *their* kids to study hard and get their degrees so they wouldn't have to spend their life selling bedroom suites at the furniture department of Woodward's. Maybe Raymond should stop worrying about things and just be grateful he's got all his organs working reasonably well.

After all, his father seems to be a lot sturdier than Raymond. The old man just won't stop going. Right now he is holding the fort, so to speak, back in downtown St. Boniface, in a two-storey house not far from the Centre Culturel. Raymond is part of that generation of St. Boniface-born-and-bred French who left to settle in Windsor Park, a "suburb" of St. Boniface, when Windsor Park began to develop in the late fifties. "Windsor Park", of course, sounds like a hunting preserve of the Royal Family, like a place where E.P. Taylor would feel right at home. To go from "St. Boniface" to "Windsor Park" is like going from *bocce* ball to tennis. Anyway the downtown core of St. Boniface was practically left to old-timers of his father's generation, those battered but still durable men and women in their late sixties, and seventies, and eighties, who are all that are left, really, of the French community around streets like Provencher Boulevard. With their children grown and living in Windsor Park they are now subdividing their houses into apartments for students attending St. Boniface College or for people who have jobs as orderlies and Licensed Practical Nurses at the St. Boniface Hospital or the Taché Convalescent Home—people who are sort of the equivalent of Winnipeg Okies, living with their hotplates and radios and framed pictures of The Last Supper on the wall and mattresses and box springs on the floor, with the sheets that have a sour smell if the family has small children.

By a curious sociological twist of fate, old St. Boniface, bastion of the French in Manitoba, is now being filled with English-speaking losers. Old and proud St. Boniface families who still have children going to school in St. Boniface schools are discovering lice in their children's hair when they come home from school. *Lice* for God's sake — those flat, squashy little insects that root around between your hairs and the sweat gland ducts on your scalp, and suck. They see them in their children's hair, and they think of the house next door where two noisy little girls live in a flat with their noisy parents—one of them is out on the sidewalk right now, kicking around the head of a dismembered doll with vicious enthusiasm. Poor thing, she's caked with mud after her bigger sister shoved her backwards on the "lawn" in front of their house.

Well, what can one expect? That house where those two girls live—when it was built in 1920 it was truly lovely, with high-ceilinged rooms, oak panelling, stained glass in the front vestibule, acanthus-leaf plaster friezes on some of the walls. Of course, M. and Mme —— haven't been able to do any repairs on it for twenty years. Sometimes it's as sad to see a house like that go to seed as it is to see a human body deteriorate. Rainwater seeps through the wooden shingles and the rag-paper barrier on the roof. The feed pipes begin rusting out and you get a spurt of rust-coloured water every time you turn on the bath water. The lead drain pipes start leaking and the moisture and rot in your bathroom floor spreads over the years so that you close your eyes whenever you turn on the bathroom light at night because you don't want to see how many cockroaches have been breeding under those floor boards lately.

It is to these decaying houses that Raymond and his fellow Windsor Park residents repair on Sundays for the family dinner. It's like a little pilgrimage across the generation gap, from the stucco paradise of Windsor Park back to the old country. The real centre of gravity for Winnipeg Franco-Manitobains has definitely switched to that clean new stucco settlement, however, and there's nothing that can be done about it.

Windsor Park, actually, is worth a few words. At its north end it borders the Winnipeg stockyards and from there spreads south for about two miles, past the Trans-Canada highway. The suburb as a whole conforms to the rigid traditional social law of Winnipeg geography which has always stated that the further south you go, the wealthier and more prestigious will be your neighbourhoods. True to this law, the north end of Windsor Park—north of Elizabeth Road, say—is filled with duplexes and row housing, and its residents, generally speaking, are not really your authentic Windsor Parkites. If Windsor Park is a country of the mind, they are its landed immigrants. Anyway, the social landscape gets more scenic as you go south, until you hit the Trans-Canada, and below that, of course, are the newer developments, the more expensive houses, and a social set-up not essentially different from some 1950s Vance Packard horror story—privileged middle-class delinquents with no place to go and nothing to do except hang around the 7-11 store, arson at the local school, with at least one daddy using his influence to keep his arsonist boy from suffering the consequences, other kids getting hate messages from their parents along the lines of: if you think you're going to enjoy yourself like a happy feckless teenager, while we've got the hairy claws and fingers of the mortgage around our throats, and its monkey feet on our shoulder blades, while we're practically selling pints of our blood to keep it from strangling, biting, and chewing us into financial ruin, you're crazy. Anything you want to do that costs money is gonna *cost* you, kiddo, believe us.

Well, that's Windsor Park, a suburb like any other ... except of course that the people there, some of them, anyway, speak French along with English and force the kids to watch some French TV programs to balance their English viewing, and at Christmas time you don't serve the roast beef and Yorkshire pudding, you put out those tourtières. And, yes, at parties you'll gather around the piano and sing *Chanson du voyageur* lustily, with maybe Aunt Lise doing the solo parts in the soprano voice that is the admiration of the church choir ... we may be indistinguishable in most ways from the folks who live in the better parts of Indianapolis, runs the common thought, but by Christ we've still got a little of that joie de vivre, we're still French. ...

And Raymond thinks maybe this is what is really bothering him, here in the C de C beer hall, at the festive height of the *Festival du Voyageur* — all this emphasis on Frenchness and voyageur heritage and the sacred historical soil of St. Boniface. If his old man talked like that he might believe him, or any of his father's neighbours in rotting downtown St. Boniface—but not us folks from Windsor Park who have our own used-car dealerships, and service stations, and jewellery stores, and printing shops, and whatever. Not us, because at heart we're all like this guy M. ——, who always kept saying to the boys at the Conseil du Goulet, "Meetings are not enough!" and now that he's hit the big time, now that he's putting big real estate deals together with some of those Jews from Tuxedo Park, you see him around here about once a year, renewing his ethnic and cultural heritage at the *Festival du Voyageur*. Not us, because at heart we're all like those businessmen who can't get it together to start a mall on Provencher Boulevard in the summertime, with all sorts of outdoor cafés and other attractions, because they don't even have the confidence in their French heritage to believe that American visitors will spend money over in Provencher

Boulevard for a kind of New Orleans, Vieux Montréal, Disney World version of St. Boniface at its Gallic best.

Yes, his old man is the real thing, definitely, but let's face it, he's going to die pretty soon, along with his friends and neighbours. They'll die, and we'll be that much further removed from whatever real links we have to the world of Lagimodière. Raymond's father and Lagimodière would probably have understood one another, for that matter, if fighting against the harsh Canadian wilderness and enduring privations gives you a unique vision of the world, because his father's family spent years up in northern Manitoba trying to farm a few acres of muskeg and that gave them all the wilderness and privations anybody could ask for — mosquito heaven! land that shook when you stomped on it! — Raymond's father watched his own father work himself to death because he had this ancient unspoken Franco-Manitobain idea that a man was only a man if he worked his own land, was dependent on nobody, and did not have to take orders from some foreman in a warehouse or a foundry.

Of course, that was an extreme case, but even for non-farmers back in the city of St. Boniface, in those days when every home had an outhouse in the backyard and a few chickens running around, there was always something that could be called a real French community, people growing up with each other, entertaining each other — maybe it was just nostalgia, of course, idealizing the past and so on, but when Raymond looks at a photograph of his father with his old band, the Fanfare de la Cité, standing there beside the drummer in the leopardskin, Raymond definitely thinks there was something more in a group like that band than in all the good works of the C de C, and all the St. Boniface and Windsor Park community clubs. I mean, this band went all over the province, playing at picnics in every little Franco-Manitobain town, because the leader of the band knew the priests in these towns, he carved inscriptions on gravestones for a living and so cultivated their acquaintance in hopes they would let him know about the latest funeral, and consequently his band became sought after as well—it was a real Franco-Manitobain network they had going there. A network of communities that has been slowly deteriorating over the years, St. Boniface included.

Of course, Winnipeg itself is not what it used to be, so this decay around it is not surprising, in a way. Winnipeg in the first part of this century could see itself as one of the most vital centres in Canada, a haven for immigrants from almost every part of Europe, the clean Prairie city, standing, really, for the future of Canada as opposed to the old moneyed cities of Montreal and Toronto, Bay Street and James Street, the old Orange Lodge, United Empire Loyalist, *habitant* societies of the East, either priest-ridden or incurably colonial—it was possible to think of Winnipeg as becoming a truly great North American city, more cultured than Chicago, say, but just as populous and lively and full of those earthy Carl Sandburg qualities.

Somehow it has not worked out that way, however, and much of Winnipeg's best talent has been sucked into the great megapolitan vortices of Montreal and Toronto—Winnipeg has become known as a city where people come from, instead of a city to which people gravitate, like Calgary or Toronto (the scarcity of native Calgarians and native Torontonians has become a joke in both these cities). Winnipeg has — well, the suspicion lingers that Winnipeg is a town where, if you're young, you decide to get married and settle down in a nice community like Windsor Park or River Heights, or you decide to get out and go to Toronto or Vancouver or Montreal and taste the life of the *real* big city, pursue an off-beat career, get a job in the media, go through a series of lovers, whatever. A lot of very talented young Winnipeggers, needless to say, have chosen this route, and left Winnipeg behind them—old Winnipeg, plodding and stable, still under the domination of its old families, still a good town to raise kids in, still reasonably prosperous. Of course, one must admit that the city will be there when boom towns like Calgary are as oil-exhausted and empty as Shreveport, Louisiana, but, again, you're not talking about vitality, excitement, heart beat, here. . . .

You're talking about carrying on, and, yes, Winnipeg will carry on, and St. Boniface will carry on, and Raymond and his wife Elaine will carry on, despite the fact that all of them are losing their sparkle. It is understandable, all in all, that Raymond feels a bit sour on the occasion of the *Festival du Voyageur*, and yet — Raymond remembers the time he was talking with his father one evening when they had been having dinner together, and his father had asked him how Elaine was, and Raymond blurted out, "Elaine — hell, Dad, Elaine and me live on two different planets." And Raymond's father just looked at him very seriously, and asked, "What about the kids? Does she take care of the kids?"

"Oh yeah. She does the meals on time, she — you know, they get sick, she always knows what to do. I never know what to do, Christ, I've never even *had* the flu. I haven't missed a day's work in my life."

So Raymond's father took it all in, and didn't say anything, but Raymond could tell from his somewhat puzzled expression what he was thinking — he was thinking that Raymond and his children were all healthy, and what more did Raymond expect? His wife couldn't have been doing all that bad a job. She didn't run around with other men, she didn't get drunk, not that often, she didn't fight with Raymond in public, she had at least kept them all healthy, and maybe Raymond was asking too much from her. He didn't say all these things, but that's what Raymond surmised he was thinking. And Raymond thought, well, maybe he's right. I mean, that's what it all comes down to, doesn't it? Not joie de vivre, or preserving your heritage, or even keeping up a living community, but simply keeping well yourself, carrying on.

Yes, his father was right. His father had watched his own father die one winter when things were going particularly badly on the farm. First, his father started coughing, then he contracted fever and chills, then he began bringing up this thick, brown sputum, thick and brown as molasses — his lungs were burning up inside him with pneumococcal pneumonia, and he didn't last three weeks. It makes a lasting impression on you when you watch your father die like that. Raymond's father himself bears the scars from years of working with heavy machinery, one crushed finger, a back thrown permanently out of whack and constantly in pain — so let's keep things in perspective, eh? Raymond cocks an ear again to his friend Georges, still going on about his wife, " . . . she still felt a bit down, though, and you know what? We discovered she had diabetes. Not a severe case, but there it was, diabetes for God's sake. You know, it's very interesting. One night she can come in here and drink all night and feel *nothing*, and the next night she'll just have one drink and be sick for a whole week — and I mean *sick*. She went to a chiropractor, you know, and he went down her spine like that, and she said 'ouch' right there, and he said — you got diabetes. Just like that. I couldn't believe it."

Well, keep on fighting there, wife of Georges. Keep on battling that diabetes. If Voltaire said that marriage is the only adventure open to the cowardly, he could have added that disease is the only drama open to those living isolated in their Windsor Park stucco bungalows. Disease is a drama, and keeping well is a kind of heroism. Elaine with her ridiculous T. Lobsang Rampa theories and her yoga and her meditation is a real heroine, in a way — she has kept herself well despite so many temptations not to. Raymond can respect her for that. And Raymond himself will carry on without the benefit of illusions. He will carry on, knowing that he is not a true son of the voyageurs — knowing that even his French is like some moth-eaten old woollen coat three sizes too small that he tries to put on from time to time. But at least he will not give up, either. He will remember his father, and be true to his heritage in his own way, and try to forget he ever heard about old Lagimodière, or the Knights of Columbus, or that Manitoba joie de vivrè.

LEARNING TO LOVE
THE BIG CITY

Man does not live by bread alone, but by fantasy and day-dream as well. Young men and women are sitting behind desks in downtown Toronto, Montreal, and Vancouver and thinking, when I get my grubstake I'm going to leave this scene for good. I'm heading for the country. Get a place ten miles from the nearest town and only come in on weekends for supplies, like lentils and Crunchy Granola. Yes. A little homestead far from the Great Urban Maw ... and at the same time as these visions are being entertained, other young men and women are flocking to Toronto and Montreal and Vancouver, from places like Marathon, Ont., and Gypsumville, Man., and Vanderhoof, B.C., for jobs in life-insurance offices and a comfortable nook in some monstrous high-rise. It's not the popular dream, to settle down in the big city, but there you have it—real alternatives are simply too scarce. Small-town life practically doesn't *exist* in Canada anymore. Or rather it exists, but it's fading all the time. We're in a stage roughly analogous to the Late Roman Republic, when poets and politicians were praising the virtues of the simple old Roman country life, sturdy farmers worshipping the household gods and taking cold-water baths, while everybody who had the chance was heading for the city for some fast money and funky entertainment.

For people like Lynda, eighteen years old and fresh into Toronto from a town of 5,000 in the wilds of northern Ontario, all this talk about getting out of the city is definitely puzzling. For a weekend, sure — who doesn't like the peace and quiet? But the city is fascinating. The first few weeks she was here she would spend ten minutes at a time standing on a street corner like the Bloor-Yonge intersection, just watching. She would see, for instance, this young man with a shaved head and a saffron robe dogging passersby on the sidewalk, talking it up for the Lord Krishna. Disgusting! Nobody she had ever known in her whole life would act like such an idiot, but she had to watch. This guy would attack some poor timorous girl going back to work at a reception desk and stick to her like a horsefly, threatening her with his humbleness, his shamelessness, asking for money, asking for her name, her address, silently hinting that if she yielded a little bit he would never let up until she was there in the temple babbling insane praise to Lord Krishna for the rest of her natural life. He did this until he tried it on one guy in a business suit, who just grabbed him by his saffron robes and threw him off the sidewalk, into the traffic.

Well, the things you can see just standing for ten minutes at a big-city intersection. Lynda can't get over it. But, of course, she comes from a town where the main recreation is drinking. It overshadows such country sports as ice-fishing, snowmobiling, backpacking, even hockey. At school dances the Ontario Provincial Police officer is standing by the door watching fourteen- and fifteen-year-old kids reel in, and the only time he interferes is if they start attacking each other. Of course, the booze is cheap up there in the north country — you go to one of the three hotels in the town and get a bottle of beer for 50 cents, or a shot of vodka for 70 cents. It always surprised Lynda when people in Toronto would say they were going out drinking, and then they'd end up having only three shots of rye the whole evening. That was not Lynda's idea of serious drinking. She would be having her sixth or seventh vodka, and calmly watching her boyfriend knocking over chairs as he stumbled back to their table from the men's room — she would be just getting warmed up, you see, and here he was losing control of his basic motor functions after consuming the same quantity of booze.

But after a while Lynda began to grasp the point, which is that you don't really have to get drunk in the big city. Lynda gets drunk in Toronto, and all she wants to do is go home and sleep. That means, really, that she misses all the weird and wonderful action around her, the satin freaks in star-spangled boots, the criminal types with tattoos on their arms, pre-med students wearing sleeveless sweaters and Bulova watches, the whole urban monkey house drinking draught beer out of jugs and having their ear membranes warped from the rock music.

Back home there was a point to getting drunk. You could not conceive, in fact, of having a party or a dance without getting ripped before 10 p.m. You'd end up rolling around on the floor, and the guys would be shouting at each other — "George, get your arms off me, you queer!"—like a class of ten-year-olds who had just been forced to sit a whole half-hour with their feet still and their hands on top of their desks, and the girls would be giggling at the sight of their boyfriends making such utter fools of themselves. And, of course, a few party games. In this one game a person would doodle a few lines on a piece of paper and then another person who didn't know what the game was about would take a strand of hair and try to bend and twist the hair so it covered the lines on the paper, and meanwhile some girl who knew Pitman shorthand would be recording his remarks on the sly. These remarks would then—surprise!—be read back to the guy later as the things he would say on his "wedding night". With half a pint of rye, rum, vodka, gin, or Zing under their belts, the kids would kill themselves laughing at remarks like "Geez, I can't keep hold of this thing." Party night for the young folks in ——, Ont.

But at least it was something to talk about in school on Monday, the number of bottles consumed, and what happened to so and so who was found with his head resting on the toilet, and this other couple who disappeared a little after midnight, under a bed, or some place. A few of the guys, and the girls even, would have arguments about just how much each person drank, it being a point of honour, of course, to hold your liquor and not act too foolish unless the kidneys and the lobes of the brain were actually getting soggy from alcohol. These are all, indeed, lively topics of conversation . . . but after a while it does get tiresome, Monday after Monday, the endless gossip about drinking, and sometimes about sex. Kids couldn't possibly have a little sexual adventure without everybody they met on the street knowing about it within a few days. Sometimes the people on the street even knew about things that never happened. A girl might enter the hospital to have her appendix removed and come out to discover her friends and neighbours all firmly believed she'd had an abortion.

But what else is there to talk about? Lynda is not an intellectual, but sometimes during conversations she tried to discuss topics of wider interest than, say, last night's alcoholic blowout — like what is the future of life in this town, for instance — and her friends started examining their fingernails and clearing their throats and after 30 seconds the conversation slid back into the old, hairy trough of local gossip. Or she used words like "progressive" or "confrontation" in conversation, and they asked, "What's with the vocabulary?" These people are all carrying on like Leo Gorcey and his Bowery Boys. Great for nostalgia, watching Gorcey movies from the forties, but it's not so funny in real life, in 1975.

The guys, for instance, have two alternatives facing them when they leave high school. They can work in the mines or they can work in a garage somewhere. Either way, they will get married and have a family and try to get on the graveyard shift, so they can goof off and sleep for a few hours and brag about it afterwards to their buddies in the beverage room of the hotel. They will actually do things like trade war comics with their co-workers, the kind that feature granite-jawed Marines with five-o'clock shadows, blasting away at Japs on Gizo Island. They will get their greatest excitement from picking fights with guys who come in for the hockey tournament with their team, from some town a hundred miles away, and they will continue to do this until their bellies turn soft from drinking and they can't take the punishment anymore. That will be a sad day for them, incidentally, because they do like picking fights with strangers. The adrenalin wash helps clear up the brainstem and, besides, it's one of the few things they can do that girls can't, with their blue jeans and T-shirts and ability, some of them, to out-gross and out-drink even the hairiest males.

But this is their future, ladies and gentlemen. And their girlfriends do not exactly have it better. They will work in the bank or an insurance office after they leave school, and then they will get married and tend to the kids. Some of them will skip the high school graduation and employment part of it and get married out of Grade 11 or 12. Indeed, it is not uncommon for fourteen-year-old girls to get married in this town. These blossoming children who would prefer scar tissue to wearing something other than their blue-jean-and-T-shirt ensemble — except maybe a short skirt with lime- or raspberry-coloured nylons, for the glamorous occasions.

Lynda recalls that the girl she admired most in this town was a secretary who had her own apartment, her own money, her own definite views on life—she knew definitely where she was going in this world. This was a girl Lynda actually thought stood out from the crowd. This was a girl Lynda thought really had an interesting point of view, some unique statements on life to make, as opposed to the general numbness of intellect around town. If you want to know what a boy you're thinking of marrying is going to be like 20 or 30 years from now, she would say to Lynda, take a look at his father. That's what he's going to be like. Truly a sobering thought . . . and she had more, much more, to say in this vein. Well, when Lynda came back from Toronto for her first homecoming, her first Christmas visit, and met this girl again, somehow she appeared in an entirely different light. Instead of being a person of strongly held views and unique personal vision, she just seemed . . . well, opinionated, and as set in her ways as any middle-aged lady with tortoise-shell glasses and menthol cigarettes whose greatest challenge in life is deciding on what cheese dip to serve for the weekly meeting of her canasta club. Now her discussion of young men centred on whether or not they were "self-starters". That, apparently, is more important than what their fathers are like, because she has just gotten herself engaged to a young engineer at the mines, whose father spends most of his time down in his basement with some ice water and Saltines, going over his stamp collection.

Had this girl changed — or had Lynda changed, in the four months she had spent away from home for the first time in her life, back there in the big city? Lynda suspects that she herself has changed. She suspects that if she had lived in Toronto before, she would never have been taken in by this secretary. One thing she has learned in Toronto is not to take people for granted. They just aren't moulded in those cast-iron, unbreakable reputations that are given to people past the age of five in small towns. In Toronto you have to find out for yourself what they're like; you have to pick up all the subtle little indicators— practically in the first few minutes you meet them.

With guys, for instance, Lynda now can tell how promising they look after two or three minutes. It's all based on the degree of shyness they present to you when they talk to you in your favourite bar, the Nickelodeon, say, or the Generator, or Zodiac I. At one end of this spectrum you find guys who are not shy at all. A guy like this sits down at your table and turns around and leans forward so his face is squarely in front of yours and there's an upbeat, lively tone in his voice as he starts talking about how boring this whole scene is, and what a drag so many of these girls are, they look like they're out on horse tranquillizers, and you know that before the evening's over he'll be suggesting that someone like you is obviously cut out for finer things, like going over to his apartment above an Army-Navy store on Yonge Street and shooting up. Most aren't this extreme, but if there's no *hint* of shyness in the character it often means there is a definite tilt to psychopathic lunacy here.

And at the other end of the spectrum is the guy who is tormented by shyness, but obviously driven, forced, impelled to seek out contact, so he talks to you with his eyes fluttering back and forth between your own two eyes and the little pools of beer on the tabletop, talking with such effort that it is obvious he must have worked himself up to come here tonight by performing unspeakable acts in front of some *Penthouse* nudes.

But Lynda has discovered that it isn't all that difficult to meet reasonable people somewhere in the middle of the shyness spectrum, even in bars. Curiously enough, the fact she was from a small town made it much easier, in a way, because she thought nothing of starting up a conversation with the people sitting next to her in the Nickelodeon or the Generator. Hard-bitten Torontonians do not as a rule do things like this, because they're already sure the person sitting next to them is somebody who will respond to their friendliness by putting a hand on their thigh, or quoting whole passages from the Book of Revelations at them, or shutting them up with their Penetrating Death Stare.

But Lynda, as I say, came from a small town where you speak to people who sit next to you in public places, as a matter of course. And not only does she meet a lot of *nice* guys this way, but she can tell how much other girls sitting around get absolutely burned up at her for it. I mean, she knows they're carrying on as if she were Little Orphan Annie befriending the poor and the outcast, and they're just sitting by doing a pictorial spread for *Vogue*, but—well, that's not her problem. Let them wobble by on their platform shoes, with their slithery satin gowns coming down low under the shoulder blades, let them entice these young men with such obvious displays of themselves; Lynda knows that guys also appreciate a girl who can talk to them, a girl they can approach without feeling they've strayed into a walk-in refrigerator. Good conversations can be sexy, too, as Lynda knows, who comes from a place where they are nonexistent. It kills her, for instance, that Lennox there, who she met at the Nickelodeon two or three months ago and with whom she has been more or less going steadily ever since, was actually interested, in one conversation they had, in the details of how people go about ice-fishing back home in ———. Lennox, who was born in Morocco and has lived in about three different countries in Europe, interested in how Lynda's friends and neighbours ice fish! I mean! Well, Lennox, how you do it is you start cutting a hole in the ice with a pick, and . . . and this is what Lynda came to Toronto for, to meet people and *talk*, to share experiences, to learn, to—oh, Lynda doesn't know, but to—to widen her horizons a bit beyond the world of the mines and incipient alcoholism.

This is what makes it worthwhile for Lynda—her boyfriend Lennox, who is interested in how you go about ice-fishing, and things like the whole variety of clothing stores in the city where you can buy practically anything outrageous or elegant, and you can dress like a lady and put on the nail polish and the green eyeliner without people staring at you in the pub and your friends calling you "green eyes", and you can get your hair cut'n'curled any way you want, and you can get a decent Chinese meal and you can take long walks in the city and admire everything from the skyscrapers to odd little filigreed Victorian houses, and you can even stand at the corner of Yonge and Bloor and watch altercations between secretaries and Hare Krishna mendicants.

Yes, this is what makes it all worthwhile, and at times Lynda actually has to remind herself that for the first two or three months she was here she was often on the verge of packing it in and going home. For those first few months, the fascination of life in Toronto was balanced by certain of its more frightening aspects. It was just all so *unknown*. Before she met Lennox, for instance, she really was dependent on some of the bars in town, the ones with the ear-warping rock music, for meeting people. But it was more than that. It was going into the subway at rush hour, and having people rush by you on the steps in panic, like a scene out of the fall of Berlin. It was the feeling of being a stranger, a foreigner almost, in your own country, riding the elevator in your apartment building every morning and hearing all these different languages, seeing black people for the first time, Sikhs, Chinese . . . I mean, Lynda is no bigot, but she was not quite ready for a lot of the cosmopolitan mix here in the city, the Detroit dudes in the peach-coloured suits, say, with matching fedoras, introducing some of that U.S.-patented pimp-flash to Toronto, looking as if any minute they would approach you on the sidewalk and say something like "Hey, honey, you so *fine.*"

It was the feeling of having to be on your guard all the time, of riding the subway and finding yourself sitting next to some drunk talking to you at the top of his voice, asking you all these questions, like did you know about this here Bermuda Triangle, and everybody else in the car looking at you to see how you're going to handle the situation. It was the feeling of wanting to go for a walk by yourself, late in the evening perhaps, and being afraid to, because guys on the street would be eyeing you, staring hard as if you were swinging a purse and wearing a leopard skin coat and white vinyl boots. One night Lynda was eating by herself in a restaurant and a table full of men in business suits kept *looking* at her the whole time. When Lynda walked by their table on her way out she couldn't take it anymore, she was so annoyed—she said something sarcastic to them like, "Have you fellas had a good look?" and one of them stood up and started yelling at her, calling her names, telling her to get out—it was a thoroughly bad scene. But why can't she eat by herself in a restaurant without being gawked at? And why can't she go out by herself late at night, if that is her wish? It's her right, isn't it? It was certainly her right back home. But then, of course, this is the big city, and we have different rules here, lady.

Most disturbing of all, perhaps, was something more subtle, something Lynda found hard to put her finger on. In its more extreme forms, it was, she guessed, simple big-city rudeness. All those waitresses who never seemed to crack a smile, for instance, and rolled their eyes in exasperation when you pointed out that you ordered your fried eggs done on both sides, not sunny-side up. But even when people in the city were not rude, when they had no intention of being anything other than decent and friendly and sociable, they still seemed curiously indifferent to other people's feelings. At work, for instance, Lynda will be doing these letters, not a rush job but she can't take forever on them. Her boss will ask another typist to do something, and that typist will say, right in front of Lynda, "Oh why can't you give it to Lynda? She never has that much to do." Or at lunch one of the girls will say to another, who is eating a full slice of rich, creamy cheesecake in spite of some obvious weight problems, "Are you sure you should be eating all that?" They don't seem to *care* about what other people think or feel, and they say these things that just cut you, things that people back home would never say.

But at Christmas, when Lynda went back home for the first time, she acquired a little perspective on the whole thing. She found that, yes, people in her town were friendly. Folks had a big smile for her when they met her on the street, and asked her questions — "Have you met anybody in Toronto?" — and seemed just full of concern. But after a while Lynda noticed how they kept giving her these surreptitious stares in the hotel bar when she walked in wearing a pantsuit and all this makeup. She noticed that when she talked about Toronto, especially in an enthusiastic tone of voice, the look on their faces began to get more and more quizzical, as if they couldn't figure her out, as if they were thinking—is this girl turning *strange* on us? And then she remembered all the times she felt she *had* to smile at people on the streets, greet them nicely, be careful of what she said, because, after all, this was a small town and you were going to have to live with these people whether you liked it or not. It was certainly true that she did have a definite place in this town, that her absence from it had been noted, that the merchants here never hesitated to cash one of her cheques. All this was a comfort when you thought about that big-city anonymity ... but it hardly seemed worth it when you considered how hollow much of this recognition, this position in the community, actually was. I mean, Lynda's family happened to live in —— Heights, the most prosperous area of town and her address alone guaranteed that a cheque of hers would be cashed anywhere in town, even if the merchant or clerk didn't know her personally. But there are, of course, other areas in town that aren't so nice, areas closer to the mines where families with eight or ten kids live and the old man works as a gas station attendant. Lynda recalls that a lot of this small-town friendliness begins to evaporate when it comes to dealing with people like this, and you will never find them hanging out with the —— Heights United Church Women, for instance.

So all in all, Lynda finds herself voting for the big city. People who have lived in the city for a long time will no doubt continue to complain about it, and dream of the day they can settle down in the country on a farm perhaps, but for the vast majority of these people it will always be a dream. Economic pressure alone will continue to coerce people into living in the great cities. But there is something else involved. In 1806 John Loudon, in *A Treatise on Forming, Improving and Managing Country Residences*, wrote, "Such is the superiority of rural occupations and pleasures, that commerce, large societies, or crowded cities, may be justly reckoned unnatural. Indeed, the very purpose for which we engage in commerce is, that we may one day be enabled to retire to the country, where alone we picture to ourselves days of solid satisfaction and undisturbed happiness. It is evident that such sentiments are natural to the human mind." Such sentiments may indeed be natural to the human mind, but as long as there are cities there will always be a counter-appeal, expressed in the medieval proverb that city air breeds freedom. For the foreseeable future, the city will continue to draw people like Lynda with this lure—the freedom of lifestyle, the freedom of movement, the freedom of anonymity itself.

NOT A CANADIAN—A CALGARIAN

After he'd been sworn in as a Canadian citizen, the Texas oilman met his friend, the American consul, and said with that hearty drawl, that deep Texas, range-rider voice smoked and cured over the years with eight-inch cigars, "Well, Ed, I guess I won't be needing you any more." Now, Ed was no fool. He knew that his friend had been operating his company in Calgary for a dozen or more years now, paying income tax to two countries, and losing a hefty chunk of the old earnings, and so he said, "Why, ——, does that mean you're a Canadian now?" Well. His friend took a long, satisfying draw on his cigar and thought it over for a minute while the smoke massaged his salivary glands and finally replied, "Hell no, Ed, I'm not a Canadian. I'm a Calgarian."

Of course. What else did one expect him to say? The man liked Calgary. It was just as much an up-beat town as Houston or Denver, only smaller, cleaner, a little more relaxed, and you didn't have to worry that your kid would be attacked on the schoolbus and robbed of his lunch money by some twelve-year-old hophead collecting funds for his daily hit. You just didn't have a lot of minori—well, there's no need to go into all that, except maybe to say that the only big group of misfits seemed to be the Indians, and they were so busy falling over themselves and collapsing on the sidewalk from too much firewater that they didn't really pose a threat to decent folks. They were just sort of civic eyesores. So Calgary was all right. He was proud to be a Calgarian, proud of the Calgary Stampede, proud of the clean Alberta foothills and Rocky Mountains off in the distance. . . .

But Canada was another matter. A fellow didn't necessarily want to swallow NDP governments, the Liberal Party in Ottawa, Montreal, Papa Jean Drapeau — about as charming as a bald Hitler with horn-rimmed glasses—and a lot of provinces down east that were good for scenery and grizzled old picturesque fishermen but not much else. Definitely not. The Texas oilman would have lunch at the Petroleum Club or the Professional Club and listen in to a few of the latest Trudeau jokes making the rounds, and it would occur to him that if the rest of Canada would just shape up and think like Calgary, this country might amount to something, after all. But then the whole continent was plain divided in the wrong way, when you considered it. Instead of the 49th parallel — this north-south division — they should have divided it up the Mississippi River or someplace where the easterners could stick to their part and the westerners could stick to theirs, and no hard feelings. Trudeau and Teddy Kennedy could represent the teeming masses of the eastern seaboard, say, and Jack Horner and Ronald Reagan could do the same for the hardier spirits of the West.

Speaking of Trudeau, he'd heard a good one the other day. Trudeau walks into a bar, takes off his hat, and there's a frog sitting on top of his head. So the bartender says, "Where'd you get *that*?" and the frog replies, "I dunno. It just started off a few months ago as a bump on my ass." Now *that* was a joke. The bit about the frog, for example — you didn't have to sit down and explain it to anybody, of course, unless he was from Albuquerque, but it was *right* that it was a frog instead of a squirrel, piglet, or warthog, even though any of these animals could have been sitting on Trudeau's head without taking away anything essential from the punch line. The frog, of course, suggests a certain language group, concentrated in a certain province, famous for their meatball politicians. *The Roughneck*, a periodical which calls itself "The House Organ of the Industry" (i.e., the oil industry), published in Calgary, put their finger on it when they published in one of their issues recently a "Grade 12 Examination for Quebec", with questions like, "What time is it when the big hand is on the one, and the little hand is on the five?" Of course they shouldn't have done that. It was in bad taste. It might have been offensive to our good Quebec friends. But mercy, they sure do pick some winners back there in *la belle province*, don't they?

Anyway, Calgary is all right for sure. What do they call it — "the city with the largest non-military concentration of Americans outside the U.S."? That common notion may or may not be true. Estimates of the Americans (including Americans who have become Canadian citizens) in this city range from a few thousand to seventy thousand. It is impossible to tell for sure, since there are no useful statistics anywhere. Americans don't congregate in certain areas of town and form their own communities — they don't form the equivalent of Chinatowns and Little Italys where tourists can come and watch the colourful folkways like Little League baseball games and Fourth of July parades. They just fit in wherever they go. In fact, their numbers may well be declining because for years now Canadians have been taking over positions in the oil companies that had been formerly held by Americans.

But they can't deny one thing—American money and, to a lesser extent, American personnel recruited back in the early fifties to work in this hardship post turned Calgary from a kind of Boise, Idaho, into a city where you could actually take your wife out for a drink to a cocktail lounge, or someplace, and not have to go to a beer parlour where she'd sit in the Ladies' Section, and you'd sit in the Men's, and you could spend the evening watching the fist fights and the shuffleboard tournaments. They turned Calgary into a place where, if you wanted some gracious dining, you weren't limited to a couple of Chinese restaurants. Mind you, Calgary is still not your cosmopolitan entertainment centre, jumping and sizzling on a Saturday night— probably never will be — but the damn place is at least *liveable*. Those Americans — a lot of fellows out at the golf club make snide remarks about Americans coming in with their hearty, man-to-man, take-charge, *let's-all-put-our-shoulders-to-the-wheel-and-get-this-thing-done-boys* mentality, so you can't even run a goddamned Heart Fund or Cancer Drive or Muscular Dystrophy Week or Cirrhosis of the Liver telethon without some American organizing the thing sooner or later — yes, and they make jokes about these guys from Tuscaloosa and Waco and Omaha coming in and throwing their money around as if it were fresh from the Parker Brothers' factory, buying stuff from the pro shop without even asking the price, I mean *good* stuff — but the thing that these guys forget is they wouldn't *have* that pro shop, and they wouldn't have that big, gorgeous club house if it weren't for the Americans, and their money, and their ability to put things together and make them fit.

And it's not just a question of those big club houses — the inflow of American capital into this city opened up jobs and career opportunities for a whole generation of Western Canadians who went to university after the war, studied law or whatever, and — well, it's easy to imagine graduating from law in Winnipeg around 1950, say, and being offered, if you were lucky, a job with Great West Life for about $175 a month. It was ridiculous. Why should anyone complain about the Americans spreading money and decent-paying jobs around? It wasn't as if they were just hiring coolies. It wasn't as if there were all these Canadian companies that had the foresight and balls to invest money in the Alberta oil fields when no one else would, and the Americans were just coming in and squeezing them out brutally. . . .

No, if you want to understand Calgary, you have to start with the fact that the Americans really transformed it from a cow town into a real city. Of course, there's not a city in Canada that hasn't been shaped and moulded by American influences. There's not a city whose economic life is not really controlled by American corporations. But Calgary is unique because this American influence is so concentrated and so visible—so direct because the Americans started the only game in town, really, and they're still running it, though anybody's welcome to get in. So if you want to understand Calgary you have to look at a certain style Americans brought with them to the city, and how it set the tone for everyone else, including "old" Alberta families with huge ranches and imported British maids and nannies. It was a style just different enough to be noticeable.

The oilman who became a naturalized Calgarian, for example. He is sitting at the Professional Club one night listening to all his good Canadian friends complain that it's hard to book ice time at the local arena for their kids. He clears his throat and asks, well can't we get together and raise money to build some new arenas so, damn it to hell, those kids can get in their peewee hockey practice? His friends start hemming and hawing and talking about, you know, the Philharmonic Orchestra happens to have a drive on now and the wife has her heart set on reaching their goal for contributions, she being on the Philharmonic Board and all, and they're already supposed to talk it up to all their friends, and somebody else says he's been so damned busy organizing this here junior football league he hardly has a free evening any more, and on and on like that, until the oilman gets a little impatient and says, "Look here, boys, do I hear you right? I thought you were just talking about the fact your kids can't even get on the *ice* to practise a little *hockey*. Are you telling me you just have no time at *all* to do something about that? Are you telling me, Bert, you couldn't talk to your lawyer friends, and you, Sid, you couldn't hit the CPAs, and you, Mel, talk to the doctors, and so on? Hell, I know we could raise the money from my friends in the oil business *alone*—as a matter of fact I could start calling people tonight. . . ."

Get involved, son! That oilman, that night, was demonstrating the slight but significant difference in the intensity of their get-involved drives that the Americans brought with them to Calgary. Now there are probably few successful professional men or successful managers or movers anywhere in the Calgary oil patch who don't feel that part of their success has been due to their "getting involved". It could be the zoo, or the Stampede, or the University of Calgary, or the theatre, or any other fine cause you can think of, but if you don't get involved these days, well hell, there's no particular reason for anybody to respect you, or see you as decent players on their hardball team. I mean, when you come down to who's a real contributing member of this community, and so forth. This way of thinking is common to certain personality types and social groupings all over the world, of course, but the Americans refined and perfected it, and it's because of their particular influence that Calgary is the greatest city in Canada for putting out that old don't-stand-in-our-way-if-you-won't-lend-a-hand philosophy.

The Calgary Stampede is thought of as the manifestation of this philosophy in its highest and purest form. The Stampede is run, after all, by volunteer labour. Three thousand volunteers, in fact, and when you're talking about "volunteer", you're not talking about guys who think they're doing you a big favour by showing up in the first place, so don't expect them to actually work up a sweat or anything. You're talking about guys and girls who know they're expected to perform because if they don't there's plenty of others who want to be Stampede volunteers. And then, too, look at the way Calgary decided they were going to have the Grey Cup game in Calgary for 1975, and so went to the CFL hearings in Toronto to make their presentations, which were printed up in genuine hand-tooled leather-bound copies, and they had records of the weather in Calgary for the month of November going back to buffalo-hunting days, practically, just to show that the football teams wouldn't have to wear snow-shoes at that time of the year, and they got the Grey Cup, and had one of the finest Grey Cup parades ever—a snap to put on, after all their experience with Stampedes—with terrific floats which were all the more terrific when you remembered they couldn't put girls in bathing suits up there like they do in the Rose Bowl parade, you know, to keep your eyeballs focussed and your coffee cup steaming.

Well, that's the American touch, no doubt about it. And it

still operates, even on less glorious levels of civic enterprise. An American family moves in, their little boy wants to join the Cub Scouts, and—surprise—they discover that the local Cub Scout pack is reduced to a weekly meeting of kids who sit around reading super-hero comic books because none of the daddies or mommies who take turns leading the pack have the energy to think of things for them to do. So, of course, Mr. —— decides that if no one else is going to do it, he'll lead that group of boys, by God, and take them out camping and hiking, and organize bottle drives and all the things Cub Scouts are supposed to do, while the other parents stay home and watch "Kojak". And Mrs. —— is not going to be left behind, either. Quite a long time ago she decided that if you want to meet nice people the place to do it is the Church. A quaint notion, in some respects, but she has had a few opportunities to test it out, being the wife of an executive in the oil business who is frequently on the move, and so she promptly joins, among other organizations, the altar guild of the local Anglican Church, which has responsibility for taking care of the flowers, linen, brass, etc., on the altar.

Not all of her American friends choose to be so active, of course. Some descend into that limbo of daily bridge-playing which actually does still exist, in middle-class neighbourhoods, a kind of yawning abyss waiting to swallow up the soul of the bored housewife. Some merely bitch and complain about their frosty and reserved Canadian neighbours, about the winters here—don't hand them that bullshit about chinooks, they still think it's cold enough to freeze your bone marrow and ligaments during those winter months — about the income tax, about the lack (still) of good clothing stores, and so on. The great American healing balm of positive thinking has not yet been poured over their souls. But as she helps to arrange the white chrysanthemums on the altar Mrs. —— thinks, all in all, that no other national group, not Ukrainians or Italians or Greeks who have been in this country for three generations, mingle in this society so easily, put themselves out to meet the natives and to get involved.

And she is absolutely right. Of course, Americans have brought with them other habits besides this instinct for community involvement which has made it easier for them to get out there and make their presence felt. One such habit is the willingness to spend money. Or rather, it's not a habit, it's an unspoken assumption—the assumption that money is a necessary lubricant for all good social and business relationships, a fifth element like air and water, that surrounds these relationships and nurtures them like mist that envelops orchid petals. On a family level it means that you periodically refresh and recreate yourself by going south for vacations — say, to Palm Springs in March, when the flowers are at their loveliest while the Calgary countryside remains the colour of your old broom, or to Baja California, where the deep-sea fishing is great, or used to be before they completed the highway down there so that all sorts of people can now drive down in their Hondas and Winnebagos. This habit of taking vacations in the pleasure capitals far to the South is something, too, that has made its mark on Calgary society as a whole.

But it is on the higher social and business levels that this happy tendency to spend money freely—a tendency only indirectly related in the business world to profit-and-loss bookkeeping—has had its greatest effect. Take the matter of expense accounts. A big-time banker in Winnipeg will have a fraction of the expense account of a big-time banker in Calgary. Winnipeg is far too Canadian in this respect. Bankers there still pick up pennies off the sidewalk. To take a prospective borrower out for a few drinks, or treat him and his wife to dinner at La Vieille Gare on the bank's money, would be considered as base and self-indulgent as masturbating in the office during business hours.

In Calgary, however, this Calvinist rectitude is as out-of-date as starched cravats—in large part because of the influence of the Americans. If you want to keep up with them, you've got to spend money. There's no way around it. If you're a good banker half your homework is done out on that golf course, for goodness' sake, mingling at the clubhouse, meeting new people, sizing them up—you're deciding to give loans, after all, on the basis of your intuitive feeling for borrowers. You're not following a rulebook on sound lending policies written by some Presbyterian choirmaster who ran a bank in 1913. You just take a good look at who's sitting across from the desk, and if you remember how well he handled himself at that dinner at the Ranchman's Club, and, on his part, if he's not hesitant about approaching you because he's seen how straight ahead you are, how naturally you belly up to the bar like—well, hell, like some of those boys from down South who aren't shy about buying rounds, not shy at all about standing drinks for a whole roomful of good buddies — why it's like the chemistry in a love affair.

Of course, sometimes this expense account *largesse* gets a little dicey, because not all of it goes into mere socializing, business lunches, and so on. If money is a lubricant for the wheels of commerce, some of the mechanics who tend those wheels get their hands a little greasier than they should. Some of them end up receiving handsome gifts at Christmastime, for example, from people to whom they have given business over the year. Something a little more impressive than a bottle of Chivas Regal. A new quadraphonic sound system for the family rec room, say. It wouldn't be polite to call this outright bribery, and it wouldn't be fair to say that it is a business practice invented by the Americans. But it is a practice which is more easily accepted in a town like Calgary where the risks and rewards of its main industry—the oil industry—are extremely high, and the style of that industry has been perfected by—well, by the Americans, the people who produced Howard Hughes. It's not bribery, anyway, it's just a way for a grateful entrepreneur to say to somebody, thanks for the business.

And the oil business, if you need reminding, is definitely not for sissies. If you're really into it, you're making deals and acting on them without necessarily waiting for "solid input" from your accountants and your legal advisers. You're contracting out for drilling rigs or farming out parts of land you control to independent explorers, or hustling cash for some wells you've already started, on land that has been farmed out to you, and, as I say, you can't always have the lawyers there on the spot with the contracts drawn up each time you make a move. When the wheels are spinning this fast, they need more than just a little bit of lubricant, and you don't get too finicky about the way you apply it. Again, the Americans are no more unscrupulous than anybody else when it comes to this sort of thing, but they've been at it longer and harder than other people, and as for the oil business — well, don't make them laugh by getting upset, for example, at stories of Lockheed bribing foreign officials, because they know what it's like doing business in those countries; they know what it's like playing golf with the Deputy Minister and he stops you on the fourteenth hole, as you're about to putt, and says something about his government's plan to review oil royalties pretty soon, and foreign companies may have to increase them, one never knows, and you look up at this inscrutable Easterner — about as inscrutable as Lucky Luciano giving a pep talk to his loan sharks — and you figure it's time to start stuffing manila envelopes with crisp thousand-dollar bills again.

Of course, it becomes difficult at this point to distinguish between what is the distinctly American influence and what is the distinctly oil-industry influence — the oil industry having its own multinational flavour about it, its own kinks, oddities, and adrenalin thrills. Certainly the American influence and the style of the oil business coalesce most perfectly in the kind of rugged individualism adopted by almost anyone connected with the Calgary oil patch. Alberta, of course, is the only Canadian province outside the Maritimes which has no social democratic party (i.e., NDP or PQ) of any size or consequence. It is a right-winger's kind of province, especially that species of right-winger who regards liberals and socialists as milquetoasts, misfits, and hot-house plants who just don't want to come out on to the field and play a good hard-nosed game with the big boys. The attitude is perfectly expressed, again, by *The Roughneck*. ("Roughneck" in the oil industry, by the way, is a term referring to the workers who man the rigs out in the field, usually skilled, hearty workers—pumpers, gaugers, and so on—noted for their hard-drinking, hard-working, brawling style. You won't find many of these guys voting socialist, I tell you.) In an editorial entitled "Is Hurtig Hurting? Not Really, Virginia", this magazine takes on Mel Hurtig, the Edmonton publisher and Canadian nationalist, in its roughly jocular way: "Mr. Hurtig has set up the Public Petroleum Association of Canada, and one of the initial actions of the group is to call for the nationalization of the major firms in the Canadian Oil Industry. Again his 'anti-American' feelings show up. Why, Mel? Did some American pull a dirty trick on you, when you were a little boy?"

Yeah, Mel, what about it? Hurtig, who has a sense of humour, would reply in another issue: "Dear Virginia: In view of our long, close and happy relationship I was both surprised and dismayed to see the editor of *The Roughneck* using your name on the cover of the January issue, and then inside in the funny editorial about me. My first inclination was to jump on the next airbus down to Calgary and punch the editor right smack in the middle of the nose." Hurtig, of course, was making a little fun of that I'm-just-a-regular-guy attitude, just a regular, two-fisted, illiterate, straight-thinking, and straight-shooting fellow, etc., put on by *The Roughneck*, and ultimately derived from certain American cultural mainsprings, like John Wayne movies and Daddy Warbucks in the Little Orphan Annie strip. In truth, this receptivity of Calgary rightists to the highly Americanized right-wing style leads to some odd and memorable occasions, like the time Carl McIntire dropped in for a brief talk with Calgarians at the Social Room of the Jubilee Auditorium.

Carl McIntire runs a church in Collingswood, New Jersey, but he has the broad hillbilly accent of some preacher drawing howls and shrieks from his congregation in Rolling Snake, Arkansas, which seems to be standard vocal equipment for American fundamentalists, particularly those specializing in anti-Communism and UFO sightings, as McIntire does. McIntire is a beefy, florid man who minces no words. "Ah am tremendously burdened by Canada," he tells his audience, which consists mostly of old people belonging to the tribe of those who adore John Diefenbaker and Princess Anne and would kill for them, in fact, if the strength had not long since left their desiccated limbs. "Ah've seen the changes since I first came here." Amen! "You people are going on a tuh*bahgg*an slide!" Praise the Lord! "You were the first country to recognize Red China. Your Prime Minister was down in Cuba bein' buddy-buddy with Castro. Planes from Cuba land here regularly — they can't do that in mah country. . . . If you stood by the word of God you wouldn't stand for communism five minutes — you wouldn't be going socialistic like you are up here."

Unfortunately for the cause of anti-communism in Calgary, the listeners here were too few and too old. Some got up later and asked questions which turned out to be uncomfortably long discourses, meandering through several books of the Bible, with Moses smiting this and Joshua smiting that, and they would harp on the necessity of fasting in order to combat the demons, imps, and hellish spirits of communism, and so forth, until it was obvious that, in a few of these speakers, dead brain tissue was starting to weigh a little heavily under the folds of the cerebrum. The lunatic fringe just was not flourishing here. Carl McIntire was just a bit too American, too right-wing, too wild and woolly—"Do you realize," he would ask his audience, "that the people who came here two hundred years ago were *owah* people. They came from England. They were white . . . Anglo-Saxon . . . Protestant . . . *Calvinists*." That was carrying the bicentennial spirit too far. Most Calgarians were not about to be included in any WASP, Calvinist, spirit-of-'76 embrace, no matter *how* Americanized they'd become.

No, the hard essence of the right-wing, rugged-individual stance was more to be found back in the corridors of the Petroleum Club, where the members, from time to time, complain bitterly about government regulations and strangulations and fetters around their beloved oil companies — and, secondarily, about public ignorance of what it all really meant to be in this game, this here oil patch. You wouldn't believe some of the things people out there were saying, ran the common refrain. One oilman turns to another and says, "Why, at the barbershop my own barber was telling me about this cook for one of those arctic drilling rigs who'd been sitting in his chair and telling him about this well they had drilled. The well had struck oil, this cook was saying, and they capped it. This cook was so stupid he kept saying, now why do you think they capped that well? Must have been just to keep the price of oil up. They're capping wells to keep the price of oil up. And this barber says to me, how do you like that? Those oil companies are capping wells to keep the price up. So I said to him, I said, well now just wait a minute. How do you think they're going to get that oil down here? How are they going to do it? There's no pipeline, there's no tankers. How are they going to do it? And my barber is scratching his head, and saying, gee, I dunno, I hadn't thought about that, and I said to him, if you can figure out a way to move that oil, buster, you'll be a millionaire tomorrow."

Well, that's the kind of ignorance you're up against. No wonder people listen to politicians like Trudeau and every cracker-barrel socialist that comes along talking against the oil companies. How many people know about the risks you take every time you decide to sink a well? Not very many, you can bet. This is a genuine sore point with a lot of oilmen who don't necessarily think of themselves as buccaneers or compradors for Nelson Rockefeller. I remember talking to one man who headed his own independent exploration company in Calgary, and I remember thinking that he probably did embody the best of that rugged-individual style in the oil business, that free-wheeling and ingenious way of life which, for good or ill, encourages a right-wing, laissez-faire outlook on government, and may be the finest flower of both the American influence and the oil-industry influence in Calgary. He was, in fact, an American, so he was perfect. He had started out as a geologist for one of the major American oil firms, scraped together a bit of cash (a hundred thousand dollars, actually, which is peanuts in this business), and set up his own outfit. What he did, basically, was study certain geological data and try to determine from them where that oil and gas might be lying around, under those pre-Cambrian rocks. He called it massaging the data. It was a process calling for a great deal of expertise, of course, and also a little luck, because, face it, there's never any way of knowing for sure that gas or oil is down there. You just have to suck up your guts and drill.

If the land where you want to drill is on land already leased by a company you have to go to that company and try to make a deal—sell a piece of your play for fifty per cent, or whatever, in return for their farming this land out to you. If you succeed in getting this farm-out, then you've got to raise the money for the actual drilling. This can be done in a number of ways. You can spin a piece of your deal to private investors. You can go public and issue stock, trying to get those doctors and dentists and CPAs out there to share in the adventure of the oil business, take a flier on a bundle of ten-cent shares which might really take off. Of course, this is where the business sometimes turned wildest and woolliest, because you had a few operators who would start drilling, take a sniff, and then phone their bucket-shop broker in Toronto who, in turn, would sit in a room with fifty phones and call every name on his sucker list.

Sucker lists are worth a chapter to themselves in any study of stocks and their promotion, but suffice it here to say they were lists of fairly affluent people, professionals and so on, who could be milked again and again. Occasionally one of their stocks would pay off, which, of course, merely whetted their appetite for the heady gamble of these stocks, the thrill of being in on what might be a new, major oil discovery from a wildcat well, and so on, and generally ensured they would come back repeatedly for more punishment. Sucker lists were beautiful. They were a bucket-shop operator's most prized possession. Brokers actually had their office safes cracked by rival brokers who were looking for their sucker lists. Some of these brokers exercised a lot of creativity, as well, when it came to working over the lists. They'd sit a particularly juicy mark in their office and make him feel at ease and loved and then have this man walk in, dressed in construction boots, oil-stained work-pants, maybe a hard hat and a heavy-duty parka, and he would be introduced as the toolpush or the drilling superintendent or the geologist who had just flown in from the rig up north at the Wabiskaw River or wherever, and he would turn to the mark and say, well Mr. ——, it's a tight hole we've got, so none of this information has leaked out yet, but we've hit a pay zone up there like you wouldn't believe. No one's ever seen anything like this in Alberta. They've practically chained the crew to the rig so they won't talk to anybody, but we figure a few people like yourself should know about it. . . ." The man, of course, had never been west of Windsor, Ontario, or worn construction boots except to clean out his garage, but one would be surprised how often the technique worked.

As I say, some of these operations became pretty wild and woolly, but serious explorers usually found more straightforward methods of raising money, particularly if they started to acquire a good track record. Of course, raising money for the actual drilling was not their only problem either. If the lands they were drilling on were Crown land, and they had themselves a play and hit gas or oil down there, they then had to petition the Crown to post a sale for the land they were drilling on, so they could actually get the benefit of that gas or oil. The Crown would post the sale and then collect sealed bids on it from whomever. That's when that business of "tight holes" would come in. If you were hitting oil on Crown land you did not necessarily want other companies to know about it before the sale. Other companies, of course, did their best to obtain this information. They would have spies sitting in a pick-up truck on the concession road watching your rig through binoculars or something. A guy like that could tell a lot just from looking at the rig. He could tell how fast you were drilling, he could count the stands on your drill pipe to see how deep you were going, and so on. People like that often ended up stripped naked and locked in the tool shed until the sale was over, but nowadays they don't usually stand for that rough stuff. The only thing you can do is make sure you keep the guy off the lot where you're drilling.

So it was a game, really, and one of the most exciting in Canada. It was also a game, coincidentally, which fitted in perfectly with the American spirit. It was perhaps no accident that the man I talked to who had made such a success of this game, possibly one of the biggest successes in Calgary, still talked with the unmistakeable accent of the great American West. He would sit with his feet on the desk and talk, while the sightless eyes of monstrous stuffed pike and salmon he had caught up North distracted his visitor, and the visitor, who lived back East, after all, could not help but feel that he was in the presence of somebody who was more alive than people he knew who were sitting in offices back home. The game this man played was just more exciting than the games they played, like wearing Gucci loafers because they read in Michael Korda's book that these were "power" shoes and would give them a subtle edge in office politics. Perhaps the free-enterprise, lone-cowboy-on-the-make, anti-government, and anti-socialist underpinnings of this game—perhaps even the fact it was such an *American* game—would eventually doom it, but for the time being it was one reason why Calgary breathed a rawer, more energized air than any other city in the country.

VANCOUVER MEETS THE COMPASSIONATE BUDDHA

"Somebody said the Indians believed that Vancouver is a power spot," Mordie tells me, sitting in his Vancouver kitchen. "I forget who told me, but . . . I'm pretty sure, anyway. All the Indians around here believed it." Well, it certainly makes sense. A lot of Vancouverites are plugging themselves into *some* kind of spiritual energy source these days. It's actually getting difficult to keep track of all the spiritual groups blossoming in this city — groups ranging from Sufi mystics to followers of Tibetan Buddhism of the Kagyur school to your regular non-denominational anarchists with a strong tilt towards vaguely spiritual ideals like "relating to the earth". Of course, people in Vancouver who are not involved in these groups usually insist that it's all just a lingering residue of the sixties, and, besides, Toronto probably has just as many religious cults if you get down to an actual spiritual head-count. They'd love you to believe that Vancouver is no more bizarre than the city of Hamilton, Ontario.

It's not true, however. No other place in Canada is remotely in Vancouver's league when it comes to enthusiastic spirituality.

The power-spot theory is one explanation. This is the theory that certain holy places, Delphi in Greece or Assisi in Italy, for instance, are the result of concentrations of electro-magnetic energy or orgone energy — or *some* kind of terrestrial energy currents, anyway — which unconsciously sharpen the spiritual awareness of people who inhabit that spot. The island of Iona in the Hebrides is definitely a power spot. Iona was sacred to the Druids before Saint Columba founded a monastery there which became the centre of Celtic Christianity for about four centuries. Three hundred and sixty stone crosses were erected on the island, a small granite orchard, before the Protestants came and righteously threw them into the sea after the Reformation. Findhorn, also in Scotland, is another definite power spot, a farming community in the cold north-east where they grow forty-pound cabbages and eight-foot delphiniums, not all that far from the Arctic Circle.

Anyway, you wouldn't surprise Mordie, who is into zhikr (the Sufi chanting which helps one taste the presence of God) and all sorts of counter-cultural, New-Age-Community projects in Vancouver—you wouldn't surprise him at all if you were able to demonstrate scientifically that Vancouver is a power spot. So far Vancouver's power has not yet been made manifest—there are no forty-pound cabbages sprouting on the British Properties in West Van or stone crosses dotting the woodlands around Point Grey—but the hour may not be right. A little time, perhaps, for an earthquake to swallow up the Holiday Inns and Vancouver Hiltons and pricey Gastown boutiques ... leaving untouched only certain humble two-storey frame houses where the spiritual communards dwell. On the other hand, this woman who has just returned from several months in India getting down to some serious Kagyur Mahayana Buddhism tells her friend who lives in a Vancouver Mahayana Buddhist house that a spiritual teacher she met there, she can't remember his name, told her he had been to Vancouver and found it lying under a "black cloud". That's why there are so many spiritual teachers and gurus there, you see, the black static is so fierce that they figure someone has to help these poor devils out. Richard, her friend, leaps at the idea. "Wow, that's right. When I'm in Vancouver I always find I'm back in my own shit." A black cloud— that's definitely Vancouver.

Since no one can clearly settle the issue one way or another— what's a black cloud to one person may be just a refraction in the atmosphere of some supercharged electro-magnetism to another — you have to figure out for yourself what all of this spiritual activity in Vancouver means. You just can't say for sure — whether it is the last gasp of the sixties, or a prophetic movement that will truly herald a New Age ... everybody braincruising on alpha waves, up in the Kootenays or the Kawarthas ... relating to the earth ... cleansing the subconscious of negative images ... or whether Vancouver is just Los Angeles North, after all, a haven for drifters, cranks, and seekers after the Big Rock Candy Mountain. All you really know is there is this tremendous *desire* among a great many people in this city to get their hands on something—to get their hands on it and run with it, hoping that, yes, it's God's own everlasting truth beating and palpitating in their moist hands....

Mordie's friend Leonard, who lives in this house where Mordie sits discussing the power-spot theory, is trying his damnedest to get some of these truth-seekers together. Earlier he had been sitting in that kitchen listening to a Sidney Banks disciple talk about Sidney Banks, whose unearthly smile could be seen beaming from a photograph on a handbill — beaming from the front window of every health-food store and restaurant in Kitsilano as a matter of fact—the smile of the "realized" man, and one more spiritual leader in the already glutted market for spiritual leaders. Anyway, this disciple had been talking about the different paths to the truth, a subject dear to Leonard's heart, only it was difficult to understand precisely what he meant because he didn't speak English all that well, and his syntax tended to be confusing, and on top of that it sounded as if his nasal passages were clogged. Each phrase he uttered was interrupted by these respiratory noises as he tried to talk, eat some cheese and crackers, and breathe through his nose at the same time. "We all speak truth. *(ffffffff)* Why don't we *(ffffffff)* speak truth *(ffffffff)* to each other?" he had asked, and Leonard mistook him to mean ... why aren't we speaking *the truth* to each other ... and he said, in a voice which you know had been honed in many a sensitivity-training T-group session, "Oh? Is there, uh, something here that you're picking up is not true?" Is there? You can lay the truth on *me*, man, I'm ready for it. . . . But the guy just said, "No, no. *(ffffffff)* We all speak truth *(fffff)*, we should speak to *itch udder!*"

"Oh . . . yes. Yes."

Share the truth, you mean. Yes, exactly.

This is precisely Leonard's thing. Leonard wearing his honest denim overalls with the straps over the shoulders — baggy, shapeless overalls for the man who is prepared to shovel horse manure, eschew worldly vanities, and live the simple ecological farmer's life, at a moment's notice — Leonard who had at least nodding aquaintance with just about every spiritual group going, and now was prepared to form a community where people could draw eclectically on the richness of all the various disciplines — practise Kundalini Yoga, transcendental meditation, the Christian beatitudes — Leonard was keen to start talking truth to *anybody*. He figured each spiritual group had to have something to offer — the Christians are really into love, for instance, while the Buddhists are more into clearing away the debris from our polluted minds, and it seems a pity we can't cross-fertilize a bit here. . . .

Leonard's own spiritual mentor, a Mr. R——, was into a blend of Sufiism and his own particular spiritual gleanings. Leonard, writing in one of Vancouver's alternative publications in the fall of 1974, described him as "a cheerful and charming Englishman who talked about a variety of fascinating topics". That same fall Mr. R—— spent a few weeks in Vancouver and gathered some people around him. According to Leonard, "Fifty or more people met and studied with him. We did early-morning exercises, meditated, heard talks, discussed, sang, laughed, and cried together. We felt our love and understanding growing. We felt ourselves beginning to become a group." A year later, however, the only reminder of R——'s presence in Leonard's house is a band of five or six people who meet every Thursday night there, sit back on their heels and do the zhikr: *La Illaha illa 'lla hoo.* There is no God but Allah.

It's the classic Sufi chant. These five or six devotees sit around in a circle, and one person starts it off by first reading a psalm or two from the Hebrew bible (Moslems are no bigots, of course). Or maybe a passage from the Koran, a copy of which they keep lovingly wrapped in black velvet cloth, with a marble pattern on the outside edge of the leaves, like a nineteenth-century edition of Milton. He then closes the holy book, kisses it like a priest kissing the missal after a reading of the Holy Gospel, and explains the chant: Forget everything, your perceptions, your idea of where things are at, all that mental shit which is outside God and His presence. Forget it. It's nothing. Only God is, exists. *Hoo Allah*! And then everyone clasps hands and the chant begins, and afterwards one or two will prostrate themselves on the floor like every photograph you ever saw of Moslems on their prayer rugs praying towards Mecca.

Even an unbeliever can't help being impressed. Of course, when R—— was around, there used to be some pretty wild after-zhikr parties in Leonard's house. Old R—— was definitely a character. "Meeting R—— was like standing in front of a two-hundred-mile-an-hour wind," one of the fellows in the chanting group tells me. He had this freakish ability, for one thing, to hold enormous quantities of liquor. It was as if he had a hollow decanter the size of a washbasin inside his stomach. One night they're all sitting around this table in a Greek restaurant in Kitsilano, and R—— and one of his spiritual pupils decide to have a drinking contest. Cambas and Pendeli and Mavrodaphne and every godawful Greek wine ever invented, they're pouring it down with the single-mindedness of chess players, both of them sitting up straight, both of them keeping their chins up in the air, and the only sign of stress you can see in R——'s opponent is the glaze over his eyeballs getting increasingly moist and thick, until suddenly he topples over like a marble column—just falls sideways off his chair on to the floor. One minute he is sitting up with his spinal column locked in place, and the next minute he's out cold on the floor.

Small wonder that Leonard makes it known he does not want

any alcohol in his house. Leonard is starting from scratch now, putting out handbills announcing a new community to be formed using his house as a base, a community of those dedicated to "overcoming selfishness and self-centredness, developing awareness, freeing our capacity for understanding and love", and leading "a life of simplicity and service". Leonard has a vision of this community. Each morning they will have breakfast together, and then do ten or fifteen minutes of household chores like washing the dishes or sweeping out the front hallways. Once a week they will have a meeting, and everybody will sort of tell everybody else where they're at, and misunderstandings can be cleared up and perhaps a feeling or two can be expressed. And they'll all devote one day a week to some helpful discipline or activity—a day of meditation, or a study session, or even a no-holds-barred encounter group.

Leonard particularly hopes the people in the house will get into neighbourhood service. He sees them going from door to door, offering the neighbours helpful ecological hints. Telling them they can save money on heating their bathrooms, for instance, by not draining their bathwater until it cools in the tub — the heat given off by the water might as well warm up the bathroom as the sewer. Or offering to fix leaky taps. It's not that terrifically difficult.

In this way, of course, they sort of nudge their neighbours into an ecological headspace through the most painless means possible. First you fix their leaky taps—a friendly, neighbourly offer no one can refuse except incurable paranoids — and then you respond to the first glint of curiosity in their eyes as to what is actually happening here by suggesting that this leaky-faucet, hot-bathwater business is just one small aspect of living in harmony with your environment. *Just one small aspect!* They get more interested, and you start pointing out the larger ecological picture, how you have to change your life to get into that picture, and then . . . Leonard may lay the real message on them, which is basically the commandment of Meher Baba's: "Don't worry. Be happy." Meher Baba, with his thick moustache and his infinitely good-natured smile, looks like your fat, comical uncle. He looks like he has had it all worked out for a long time. Don't worry. Be happy. That's it, folks. Nothing more or less — Leonard believes this is really the key. Just forget your anxiety-ridden self for one minute, go with the flow, consider the lilies of the field, and ... don't worry. Things will take care of themselves, love will come, and understanding, and your next-door neighbours will not be far behind you. Like I say, Leonard has a beautiful vision of this community.

Of course, other religious communities in Vancouver have discovered that it's not so easy to get everybody in the commune going with the same flow — unless you're an all-out spiritual paratrooper outfit like the Hare Krishna guys down at the Hare Krishna farm where everybody gets up at four in the morning for a full day of prayer, chanting, meditation, and hauling ass out in the fields. It's like the Marines compared to the Boy Scouts. Leonard's fantasy commune stands right up there with the Boy Scouts — but most real-life spiritual communes, as I say, have found that even Boy Scout discipline is hard to maintain. It's almost a case of Marine Corps esprit or nothing.

In Richard's Mahayana Buddhist house, for example, they started off with everybody getting up at six in the morning and going up to the attic to meditate. Unfortunately this was all happening in December, and it was cold as hell up in that attic. It was a test of endurance sitting up there trying to be still and to clear your mind like you were supposed to. You couldn't do it, anyway, because you'd be distracted by everybody sniffling and rubbing their arms to get the circulation going. So after the honeymoon period ended people stopped getting up at six and going up to meditate in the attic. People practically stopped meditating, period, after they'd been there a month or two. You'd have this wierd schizophrenic split in the house. People who had just come into the house would be ready to join hands in the circle, chant together, meditate together, feel as One with all their brothers and sisters — they were into the whole spirit trip. They were just waiting to have their minds blown. They were the same kind of people who were dying to get into the white cotton leggings and turbans, and bliss-out all day, until you couldn't trust them to cross the street without getting hit by the hydro bus.

In time it became clear that there was a spiritual community only in the loosest sense, and all the sitting and chanting *"Vaitali, Vaitali, life, life/The four-armed Devi riding on a donkey with a white blaze"* in front of the little Buddha statue and the candles and the incense wasn't going to solve the problems that arise whenever people live together.

One day two guys got into a fist-fight over something or other. By the time I had arrived in the Mahayana Buddhist house months afterwards everyone had forgotten the actual reason for the fight, but there was no doubt that the incident made it impossible to ignore the schizophrenic split. More people started to pack up and leave, until nine months after that first frigid December only two out of the original twelve inhabitants were still there. The house was getting to have a higher turnover rate than the personnel of a car wash. It was certainly a far cry, say, from Leonard's fantasy group, going from door to door in the neighbourhood fixing leaky taps.

The curious thing is, the lack of togetherness in spiritual communes like the Mahayana house is rarely due to disagreements on an ideological or doctrinal level. Usually everybody agrees on the basic tenets. Usually everybody allows other people in the commune plenty of space within those tenets . . . so that if George doesn't go on fasts, he just says the Lord doesn't lead him that way, and that's that . . . or if Mary doesn't meditate, she tiptoes around the house and is quiet as a mouse at times when *other* people are meditating . . . or if Sue likes to hit the Johnny Walker every night about ten, one remembers that Mohammed *really* only forbade a certain type of alcohol, and that was because one time he'd been to this wedding party where they were serving that type, and after he left two guests got drunk and got into a fight and killed each other, and that's why he banned it, but it obviously wasn't Johnny Walker they'd been drinking, it must have been home-brewed Kill-Me-Quick or something.

No, the lack of togetherness is not due to heresies or schisms or sectarian deviations. The lack has something to do with the whole commune trip in the first place. Maybe one's chances are better with the wandering-monk trip, or the changing-environment-through-media trip, or even the regular, nine-to-five trip, or . . . any other trip out there in the void at the end of your string. Such trips we have at our disposal! "We should do an organization trip," one of the women moving into Leonard's house says, as she tries to find space in the kitchen shelves for the Heinz ketchup and the carob brownies and the bag of pure salt evaporated from sea water (no chemical additives). An organization trip, she says. No simpleton, this woman here emptying her bag of groceries, and yet she finds herself unable to say something as simple and direct as . . . we should organize this kitchen. She has to make a trip out of it, and—in a way—that's what it's all about.

One never suggests, in one's day-to-day speech, that one is obeying a deeply felt passion, or a spiritual *necessity*, or an iron law of existence. No one is doing a trip. All trips have an ending, of course, and then one finds a new one, because one has lots of time on one's hands. A peasant will never tell you, for example, "I'm into a tilling-the-soil trip," because that is his life, you understand, and St. Francis of Assisi, rolling around naked in the snow, will never sit up and say, "I'm into this poverty trip." Brother Francis will never say that, because he knows that his whole existence, his sanity, the eternal salvation of his soul, are riding on the life he has chosen, and if things get rough he can't just leave it and get into something else, like biofeedback or TM.

Richard, Leonard, all you people chanting the Koran, you spiritual communards getting high in rooms with incense ashes smouldering in delicate brass incense holders—if you could hear yourself talk you'd certainly wonder about yourselves, too, so devoid of feeling is your language. Of course, you're not all as bad as Guru Bawa who, in his column, *Guru's Grace*, has these helpful words of advice to truth seekers . . . *Prayer must come through the light within this Church, and through the awareness and the clarity of that awareness. Prayer must come through the light of that clarity and through the Resonance of that light and through the Meaning of that resonance and through the plenitude of that Meaning — through the completeness of that Plenitude and through the Completeness of the Effulgence of Divine Luminous Wisdom. . . .*

Thank you, Guru Bawa. They're not all this bad, as I say, but still . . . the good Guru is not the only one who balances your head on his index finger and gives it a good spin. In spiritual communes throughout Vancouver, people talk to each other in language that has been stamped on a tray, pre-cooked, and then frozen for instant consumption. In a house where members of the Arica sect live, a young man and a young woman discuss an incident that happened earlier in the day.

"You went all rigid when I tried to cuddle you this morning," he says.

"Well, I felt you were being sort of gushy."

"No, I wasn't being gushy, I — "

"I mean, I thought you were going to come on with the gushy-mushy bit, and I didn't want to consider you."

"Oh . . . I wasn't gushy, I just thought, you know, you looked . . . *cuddly*. Or maybe it was, like, *me* who was feeling cuddly."

"No, actually I was *look*ing cuddly so you'd want to cuddle me and I could be inconsiderate."

Understand? In the language of the Arica sect, "consider" means to respond to another person in the way that person wants you to respond, or you think he wants you to respond. Instead of saying to someone, for example, "Look, I don't want to be cuddled this morning, do you mind?" you can say, "I don't want to consider you," which sort of takes the edge off of things. And you can say about so-and-so, "I'm making a connection with ——," or "I'm having a charge with ——," or "I'm trying to clean up my karma with ——," and so on through the whole Arica phrasebook, until both you and —— feel like cotton batting has been stuffed behind your eye-sockets.

The language is certainly a clue as to why spiritual self-discipline in communes tends to crumble. To maintain such discipline you either have to have it enforced by an institution, or, failing that, by a certain loyalty which people owe to one another when they know they've risked everything on a life they've chosen in common, and they're all in this together, for better or worse. The language quoted above does not suggest such loyalty. It suggests Mrs. Opal Emerson Mudge lecturing the League of the Higher Illumination in Zenith, Ohio. It suggests people who are, basically, not risking anything, and can afford to go on these spiritual trips from time to time.

Not that they aren't sincere. They are always sincere about these trips. But it doesn't matter if one is sitting on a motherlode of hot elecro-magnetism or under a fierce black cloud, the results are the same . . . fairly predictable considering that we do not understand ourselves, and that we do not know what we would, and that we go infinitely far astray from that which we desire, as St. Theresa of Avila used to say. An incontestable bit of spiritual wisdom . . . perhaps ranking even with "Don't worry. Be happy." How dearly, Meher Baba, would we all love to not worry and be happy. To be able to wait, patiently, in the fulness of time, for all of the pieces to fall into place, and the New Age to dawn, when everybody would be sitting on his own power spot and there wouldn't be any talk of black clouds over Georgia Strait and St. Theresa's eternal complaint would not be so painfully appropriate.

MATING DANCES BENEATH THE BASKETBALL HOOP

Whatever images we have of the Drug Culture, derived from the time when that Culture was supposedly flourishing in the land, are now obsolete. Take a look at the girls standing outside a high school in the cosy old stucco-and-brick east end of Toronto, on the night of the school dance. These girls, with their tender-sapling chests, are passing around a joint like it was contraband chewing gum. A few years ago they would have been called "teeny-boppers". The label, however, is now meaningless, like almost all the labels created in the Early Dope Age: "hippie", "greaser", etc. These girls are not teeny-boppers, they're just tender saplings. Marijuana merely increases the pitch, and frequency, of the tender-sapling giggle. When they're not stoned they worry about breaking a fingernail in typing class, or they pen letters to Donny Osmond which they never mail but later rip into shreds so tiny their mothers will never, in a thousand years of rummaging through their waste baskets, be able to piece them together and read them.

Inside the building, in the gym where the band plays under the basketball hoop, these girls dance together in little circles, rings of fluttering elbows, knees, and torsos slender as green tulips. A boy of their own age who starts making his move, who sidles right in there, trying to tune in his quivering adolescent synaptic knobs to the right frequency—what wave are you on, Susie and Debbie and Terri and Linda and little Janine, I'm here to move!—Well, Susie and her friends keep twitching and fluttering away until, possibly, his nerve receptors get a little numb from the frozen stratosphere instantly forming around him. (A meteorological phenomenon very familiar to adolescents who are Too Obvious.) The goof. Get back where you'll be comfortable, on top of the folded bleachers where your friends perch with their shoulders hunched up like vultures' wings.

Six years ago at this same high school, around the time everyone had found out from reading the weekend supplements that the folkways and mores of the young were changing radically, that there was a sexual revolution underway in perhaps the very high school your son or daughter attended, and the new teen rebels were not James Dean and Natalie Wood — no, not those reckless, tormented teen-agers from the past, with their Wildroot and their charm bracelets, pony tails and the blue jeans with tough cuffs on them, sweet in the memory now that they have disappeared forever — this new bunch were far worse, their very brain cells were being stewed and mutated by exotic weeds and chemicals — at that moment in history, as I say, one could be more precise about what was going on at places like Malvern Collegiate Institute. Then one could see the revolution in progress, battle lines being drawn, promises of a new era, etc.

There were the hippies, and there were the Old Guard, the straights — in this case, the "Clubbers", kids who hung out at the Balmy Beach Canoe Club, wore sweatshirts and Clark shoes, natty suede Clark shoes with squeaky crepe soles — young studs of the boathouse with hair like Glen Campbell who made a big thing out of drinking beer and rolling hippies on the boardwalk, at night. They also made a big thing, of course, about getting something off their dates. These were the girls who, in the daytime, tottered around the halls on five-inch heels and black stockings. These were girls who, at the dawn of puberty, had bypassed the tender-sapling stage to enter directly into the stage of fourteen-year-old dollhood, girls with nervous rabbit faces and dusky vampire eyes, lipstick the colour of ski wax, cheeks the shade of strawberries just beginning to ripen, Nile River green pencilled over the eyelids, hair treated with smouldering alloys of hydrogen peroxide. Tough customers, you understand.

So you have one of the Clubbers getting his books out of his locker, and his pal snickers, "Heard you went out with a real sleazebag last night." And the first Clubber starts grinning, a little nervously, but he curls his upper lip so it comes out nasty, like an evil grin.

"You mean Sally?"

"Yeah, Sally the Sleazebag."

And there follows some raunchy dialogue, and the carcass of the dear girl's "reputation" is chopped up into the size of croutons.

Six years later, the Clubbers might still go out with sleazebags, and talk about it, but at least they wear their hair long, and they drink beer at the same room in the Ben Lamond Inn with the—well, not the hippies exactly, since the hippie has gone the way of James Dean and Natalie Wood in the gallery of social archetypes, but the kids who might have been hippies, who are as utterly rootless, passive, and distrustful of the adult world as the hippies ever were but have not — not at this moment, anyway, with their chins flopping down to their breastbones from swilling suds at the Bennie—the comforting illusion that they are participating in a revolution. The intervening years have had their effect on all these young, but the cumulative effect has been to blur old distinctions, to blur and confuse the old ground rules, for example, with which age-old dramas such as adolescent courtship and sex are played.

The girls dancing together: in a year or two they will no longer be able to do this. They will be expected to move on to the next stage of the game, which, under the old ground rules, would have been dating. Under the new ground rules, however, that next stage is . . . whatever they can manage. They are left with precisely nothing to go by, no hope of some adorable little wretch on the phone, asking them out to the sock hop on Saturday night and hoping, for God's sake, that they won't tell him they're washing their hair that night. Dating, as a social institution among adolescents, has crumbled beyond repair, it has almost vanished.

The result is a certain amount of confusion, particularly for girls. Girls who've gone past the sapling stage and are in that transition period in which one says to oneself, well, okay, here I am, ready for some honest romance, even for some teen heartbreak, if necessary. So where are the guys? Where are the nongoofs? Where are the nice, thoughtful, ordinary-looking males? Guys who don't spend every minute of their spare time working on the '59 De Soto they picked up for $35. Guys who aren't 100 per cent Clubbers or members of the "good group" (as Clubber types are sometimes referred to in other high schools) standing around in a circle in the halls fighting to get in the last word about next weekend's ski trip. Guys who aren't A-craving browners, or conscientious kids who belong to the library committee or the audio-visual club. Guys who don't get ninety-eight in physics and look at you sort of sideways out of quarter-inch lenses when you talk to them. Guys who don't spend their evening in the basement with their chemistry sets trying to figure out how to manufacture slugs you can put in turnstiles on the subway. I mean, where are they?

Please, this is a serious matter. We've had several years now of encounter groups, feminism, planned parenthood, fornication on the movie screen — a lot of truly liberating things here — frankness, honesty, and openness, hippies, suggestive lyrics on AM radio, hemp-smoking, tantric yoga sexual conditioning, youthful rebellion, and other such related phenomena. But you take a teenage girl who is a bit too cool, now, for dancing with the other maidens in the gym (she is looking for a genuine boyfriend, and not a lap dog like Donny Osmond or David Cassidy to cuddle; she is even, let us assume, able to talk to boys on an individual basis, and not just as part of a gang of other boys and girls hanging around the do-nut shop). What is her likely fate in this post-Ann Landers era? Is she really going to find a teenaged boy who, besides being intelligent and lively and all that, is both relaxed about sex and willing to pay serious attention to her? Is such a boy to be found without serious effort? Is he to be found, even, without a grim and desperate search?

The guys drinking beer at the Bennie, for instance. One of them is on his way out, in a space where he's going to laugh his way home. "You want to hear about this girl?" he says laughing, as he walks out the door. This boy, Steve, is not, let me tell you, some creep who hangs around dirty bookstores for hours, like they were reference libraries. It's a serious story he's telling, a case history, as it were. It illustrates the mores and behaviour of girls, you see, these strange people we call females. "This girl was a virgin, right? And she went to this party with the Bikers, and she, uh, had this virginal sweater with her tits all hanging out. Only a virgin would do that. Anyway, eight guys went on her—and she could only remember the first and the eighth. She got the virginity banged out of her."

Ha, ha, very funny. Watch you don't fall off the sidewalk there. "Yeah, at this party, they caused $3,000 worth of damage. They were throwing chairs out of the window, and everything. There was this girl inside a bedroom" (starting to crack up with laughter, now) "and a line-up of about fifteen guys outside. And she kept yelling out" (here his voice becomes a falsetto) "'more!'"

Now part of all this discourse is what is known as a gross-out, a typical male adolescent defence against exposing, in one's conversation about girls, too much of what one really feels. Adolescent boys have perfected the gross-out to the point where some of them sound like quite nasty little fellows. "If they're old enough to bleed, they're old enough to butcher." This one isn't saying that, mind you — he's quoting a friend of his, who goes to rock-concerts and (reportedly) sweet-talks girls in the following manner: "I just want to know one thing. Do you ____?"

Still, this is pretty rough talk from boys who, all in all, look like the nice neighbourhood kids one's mom might ask to help her in with the groceries. But they're agitated in some way. In confined spaces, like in a hall after the last class, they bounce around like gerbils. They won't sit still until they've been pacified with marijuana, in which case they tend to loll on the carpet like exhausted Foreign Legionnaires stretched out on the desert rocks waiting listlessly for the Arabs to come screaming up and murder every last one of them.

Steve, for instance, does not go home after he leaves the Bennie but heads, with four of his friends, to this girl Beverley's house where he finds Beverley and a second girl sort of hanging loose with some other male strays. Anyway, one of Steve's friends, who is really full of it this night, gets up in the middle of Beverley's living room and starts to hold forth. "Let's take a survey, guys. Would you like ten nice cold draughts or a good screw?" Steve, lying back in standard opium-den posture with his head resting on the warm air vent by the floor, cannot be bothered. "Gerald, you impress me," he says, like that, and playful Gerald spins around and comes at him with a death-dealing kung fu slash with his foot, just a sock on, you understand, but it actually hits Steve in the nose, and suddenly Steve is staggering over to the bathroom with an honest-to-God nosebleed.

Meanwhile, the two girls are sitting there, completely out of it, as girls tend to be in any gathering where they are heavily outnumbered by males. Beverley is practically being driven neuropathic by the situation, trying to keep the guys from burning holes in the rug with their cigarettes, and from time to time nervously stuffing dollar bills and Belvedere Kings down the bosom of her off-the-shoulder blouse. Brave girl! Would that she were a Gypsy wench in the same off-the-shoulder blouse, stuffing a pouch of silver kopeks down her bosom while some pop-eyed Gypsy horse thief in a walrus moustache was staring at her with dilated nostrils. This bunch of goofs, with their tales of gang bangs and dozey females they have known, would start pounding each other's ears in before they'd break apart and start any nostril-dilating business on their own.

Of course, there are other lads for whom the sexual revolution, the whole honesty and openness thing, has not been in vain. They're quite easy with girls — honesty and openness has done wonders as a nice short-cut to a lot of unnecessary small talk. "Hey, do you wanna make it? I mean, everything's out front here, okay? I'm not laying anything on you, okay? I'd just like to make it with you." You can chalk that one up to the changing social climate. More guys are coming on with a "direct" approach, and more girls, not just the sleazies, are actually feeling uncomfortable about refusing them.

At the Sauble Beach camping grounds Morris the Mechanic (so-called because he's wearing one of those splotchy white surgical outfits some mechanics favour when they go down into the grease pit) is trying to get this one girl he's just met into the back of his Ford station wagon. It's about two a.m. now, and he's impatient to get going. "C'mon, let's go." He's even got his hand on her upper arm, like Stanley Kowalski about to drag Blanche DuBois into the boudoir. He figures this girl is pretty well looped, and, y'know, why do chicks hang around camp grounds like this unless they want to get laid?

But you can see the girl is not too enthusiastic — old Morris there is nothing to write your girlfriend about. "Well, he's about five-foot-five, Sylvia, and he's got this adorable beard that hangs off his chin like a thin clump of Spanish moss, and just a few little tiny zits here and there where he didn't use his Phisohex." Besides, a little *savoir faire*, please. You've got to say more than, "C'mon, let's go," even if it is two a.m. and starting to drizzle, and you figure you've already got it made with this chick. So the girl starts dragging him around to various tents, and she sticks her head in each one and asks the people brightly, "Hi, where are you folks from?" and some of them are rude and some are kind of amused at this slightly drunken young lady, and the guy with her who has "Jesus Christ, let's go, eh?" written all over his face, and they offer her and Morris tokes, or a little swig of some sparkling rosé. Poor Morris. Every time this girl takes her head out of one tent and he tries to steer her back to the station wagon, she drags him to another tent and the routine is repeated. A somewhat roundabout and time-consuming method of resisting someone's advances.

Ah yes. None of that "I'm not that kind of girl" business, such as your working girl selling notions over the counter at Woolworth's might have said to a heavy-breathing greaseball in the 1950s. By all means, let us be more cool than that. You're not going to go home branded forever with the scarlet "S" for Sleaze if you do it once in a while with some guy who just picked you up. Still, most girls in high school today are just not primed to do that. The girl who goes around saying, "When I wear white on my wedding day, it won't be just because I like white"—well, all right, she can go out and hold hands with her boyfriend in the shiny wing-tip shoes (the kind who will say to *his* friends, "I don't have to drink to have a good time"). But let's get serious. We've agreed that sex is no longer the issue. We're still just trying to find some reasonable heterosexual love and affection for this girl who's waiting for it, who believes she is ready for it, who has been led to assume that it's hers for the asking, and no worry about "reputation", or guilt, or the traditional wages of sin such as pregnancy or VD.

Perhaps she goes to a party where there is a reasonably even ratio of boys to girls and she takes a hard look at the available line-up of talent. That boy there is a direct-approach man, for instance, and if she wants to stick with somebody for more than a week she might as well forget him. That one is cute, but he's already dropped out of school and is now trying to play bass guitar with a band performing in some bar for the black-satin-pants-and-T-shirt crowd, and he never really says much to girls anyway unless they understand the intricacies of playing bar-band music. But perhaps, at this party, she sees a boy she has had her eye on for a long time and eventually there comes a moment when, sitting by him, she signals to him with a gesture as simple as rubbing her right eyebrow with the tips of her fingers that she is, as they say, "interested".

She might even go so far—bold hussy!—as to say, "Oh, let me

see your ring" and hold his hand up to the light to examine the onyx or the amber as if it were a truly interesting specimen of the jeweller's craft. Meanwhile, the touch of finger upon finger is the first move in the age-old courtship dance of the adolescent, a dance where the boy, after this transparent Oh-let-me-see-your-ring play, may at some point in the evening proceed to hold her hand and then, if she gives some slight squeeze to his hand, proceed to intertwine his fingers with hers and then. . . .

Yes, there is a whole sequence to be acted out, signals passed back and forth, unspoken and sometimes unconscious, like the courtship dance of the kittiwake bird where the male kittiwake knows he's got it made if the female opens her beak and exposes the orange-yellow of her mouth. From putting his arm around her shoulder, to her nestling her head on his shoulder, to his first audacious kiss, and so on. Of course, the tempo and duration of the dance vary greatly among couples, and, you understand, it is usually a great deal less formal and tentative than it used to be, in grandmother's time. Sometimes whole sequences are passed over, in one's hurry to get to it, or when both partners are in high gear due to alcohol or dope.

And then, of course, it is still largely up to the girl to decide how far along this sequence she wishes to proceed. If she really likes this guy—perhaps he is exactly what she has been looking for, and, God knows, the pickings aren't that fat she can afford to be extremely choosy — she may wish to, well, *entice* him, without of course going too far. It's really difficult to talk about this, actually, because one is forced to use all these old phrases, these figures of speech, from eight, ten years ago. Like "going too far". (As in, "We went further last night than we really should have.") Or "fast" and "slow". (As in, "That guy's a fast worker.") The courtship dance being less formal and intricate and central to teenage sex (with the advent of the direct approach), these expressions have lost much of their meaning. But not all of their meaning. Unless he actually uses the direct approach, a male teenager still has to go through some form of the dance to discover what the female has in mind. And when

Mating Dances Beneath the Basketball Hoop **189**

you have a courtship dance, with its infinite variety of pace and tempo (from twenty minutes to twenty months), adjectives like "fast" and "slow" are very pertinent, almost literal in their meaning. (All this is obvious to teenagers. Adults sometimes forget it, though, because they really don't have a courtship dance. You don't "make out" at adult parties. To get a lady in bed you have to be witty or something.)

The point is, she wants this guy all right, but she wants it to be "serious". She wants a "relationship". She certainly doesn't want a one-night stand, or a one-week stand, or even a one-month stand. She wants, though this word will never be spoken, to be *courted*. She wants somebody to go out with, regularly. She wants somebody to take her to places where she couldn't go alone without being hassled to death. She wants somebody to call her up, even on nights when they're not going out. She wants somebody she can discuss with her girlfriends. So, at this party they might end up necking, but that's it. The rest is for later. A long-term liaison, she hopes, is about to commence here.

Perhaps one does. She starts going out with this guy on a regular basis. They start "going steady", in fact — another expression with an historical aura about it. (PTA discussion groups in the 1950s, for example, held talks on the following topic: Should teenage boys and girls "go steady"? And always a concerned parent with a story of some young couple down the street who insisted on "going steady" and constantly spending time with each other, holding hands in the halls between classes, petting and so forth, and then It Happened, and the girl got pregnant and of course they had to get married and the guy, instead of going off to university to study to be a brain surgeon as he planned, had to quit school and get a job checking out groceries for $60 a week, and now they're living in some tiny apartment with the girl spending her evenings taking care of the baby and weeping in her pillow because hubby is out with the guys bowling or drinking beer to forget his misery. Teenage tragedy!)

Parents still warn kids about "going steady", but the scenario is fast fading away — you might as well warm up the old story about the girl who decided to take "just one puff" of a marijuana cigarette at a party and ended up being kidnapped by a white-slave ring. Secretly, parents are often quite happy to see their daughter "going steady". They would rather have the girl going up to Sauble Beach with her "steady" than with another girl—at least Morris the Mechanic won't try to drag her into the bushes.

One evening the girl takes this boy that she's been going out with for a few weeks home for dinner, and in some deeply primitive and unconscious fashion this act places a semi-official stamp on their relationship. The mother likes him. The old girl is all smiles, one might almost say that she's flirting with her daughter's young man. "Oh, you don't have to bother with the dishes, you and Linda just go in the living room and watch TV." Nudge. Wink. There is such sweetness in the air! Of course, the father doesn't say much, and one gets the impression he'd rather see this kid melt back into the woodwork and stop fooling around with his daughter. He's in the living room while they're watching TV, reading his paper for what seems like five hours. But — forget it. He'll come around eventually.

Shortly after this occasion, Linda and her boyfriend will be together, and he'll say something like "I love these jeans — I want to get married in them," and she will reply "Would your wife wonder where you got the inkstain?" referring to a spot where a bottle of ink spilled on them one night when they were fooling around in his room. And he turns to her and shrugs — casual, not heavy like he's about to get down on his knees and propose right there, but, still, he says it: "I don't know. Maybe you'll be my wife."

Well, she gives this embarrassed smile, she changes the subject, but he has said it. Casual, not moony-eyed, or anything: he just said it like that, like, "Yes, well, what else could the fates possibly have in store for us?" And now it's out in the open. Marriage. True Love. This girl is only sixteen, but don't laugh. She really digs this boy. She has a fantasy of being married to him. She loves pottery and she can set up a little studio in a little house up north maybe, with some frontage on a lake, and he can practise his guitar and write music, and they can look out at the lake in the evening and go skinnydipping when it's warm, with the moon and stars and all, pollution-free atmosphere, scent of evergreen in the still night air. She can really see all this.

And one night, just to get this out of the way, the old courtship dance comes to its fevered conclusion, and they sleep with each other, one night when his parents are out of town. No big deal. Aside from the fact itself of defloration, the primordial significance of no longer being a virgin, it hardly seemed worth all the fuss. It seemed, at the time, more like some kind of technical operation, not unlike — if you want to know the truth — some gynecologist probing around with his rubber glove. She could hardly feel it, in a way, when it was happening. She almost found it difficult to believe it was really happening to her when it was happening to her.

It was certainly nice, though, don't get her wrong. It was just very strange — that this was the holy mystery of life everybody talks about. She felt about it the way a lot of kids felt when they expected the entire universe to blossom into a polychromatic art-nouveau display after their first inhalations of marijuana, and instead they got almost nothing. Almost nothing except the right to say to themselves: well, you've done *that*, now.

So where else can they go now? They are two teenaged lovers. Gradually, they start breaking off contact with the old gang at the do-nut shop, and become a well-established couple. Even Linda's father starts getting used to having this boy around, like another piece of Danish Modern in the living room. Linda herself can say good-bye to any more worries about going out someplace on the weekend. She is so unworried, in fact, that she is even beginning to speculate what it would be like to be on her own again, going out with a bunch of girls to a party to try her luck. And then she starts getting the old "When are you and Bill gonna get married?" routine from some of her girlfriends which, at a certain point, starts to sound like a very serious question.

What a question, though, to ask of a girl who is only about to turn seventeen. She doesn't expect to be married until they're at least ... well, eighteen. No sooner. Both their parents would have a fit.

In the meantime, they talk to each other regularly on the phone when they're not seeing each other, a phone call at least three nights a week, about an hour and a half long. These are no longer breathless conversations, exactly. They just fill each other in on what's been happening, you know, if they haven't had much chance to talk with each other during the day. Old Bill there, nothing much exciting happened in *his* day. And sometimes Linda starts chattering away about her girlfriends, very trivial stuff about who put down whom lately in conversation, but she can't help it, Bill doesn't say much and those ninety-second dead silences on the line are really uncomfortable, and meanwhile Bill's mind starts wandering and he remembers a homework assignment he's got to get done tonight. Then suddenly Linda, who has been going on about some friend of hers named Angela, asks "You know Angela, don't you?" and Bill snaps to and says: "Yeah, Angela. She's the one with the terrific boobs, isn't she?"

Well. Linda is silent for a moment, but the way he answers the question — *the one with the terrific boobs* — she is somehow very irritated. How can she explain it? He sounds already like one of the boys coming off the afternoon shift and saying to his pals, "Hey, let's stop off at the hotel for a beer, they have a waitress there with terrific boobs." He sounds already like a guy who'd say to his buddies, "Well, gotta get home now, the ball and chain's probably waitin' up." It's in his voice, she can swear it. It's the way he just gives her a part of his attention, like he can take it for granted she'll stick around while he attends to more serious matters. It's the way he can refer to other girls as if they were fair game for his lust — the goaty disposition of a married man who wants a little variety in life.

And he's barely seventeen! This is her own teenaged lover! Mother, you warned me about sex, but this! That two teenage lovers in this age of practically guaranteed sexual Opportunities for Youth could wind up like an old married couple with nothing to say to each other and clumping along from day to day just like — like mom and dad, and aunt and uncle and all the old boring couples who lived in the past ages before they heard of sexual liberation.

GOODBYE WESTMOUNT —
SALUT JEAN-CLAUDE!

Montreal, you charmer. Writers of guidebooks for tourists cannot get over the fact that people in this modern North American metropolis still speak French: phrases like "cosmopolitan", "Gallic", "sophisticated", "unique in North America", can't begin to convey their delight at this touching survival, on this continent, of a language which should have withered and blown away a long time ago — like the Dutch spoken along the banks of the Hudson River in the days of Rip Van Winkle. *Montreal's two and a half million citizens live with a flair timelessly Gallic ... preserving in their bilingual and bicultural atmosphere the two basic cultures of the Western world ... the resulting interplay of Gallic and Anglo-Saxon culture, plus the traditions of numerous ethnic groups, contributes to Montreal's cosmopolitan flavour....*

Keep up the good work, Montreal francophones! Keep preserving those two basic cultures, Armand, as you answer questions from the passengers on your bus in both French and English. Keep up that cosmopolitan flavour, Réjean, as you serve the Crêpes à la Bretagne to the folks from Cincinnati in your red flannel embroidered Breton waistcoat and Errol Flynn pirate shirt. Keep up that timeless Gallic flair, Geneviève, as you give directions later to those same folks in an accent heavily influenced by good old St. Hubert Street joual, the patois of home and hearthside our guidebook writers call "the Québécois' version of Brooklynese and Cockney rolled into one".

Only don't give this bilingual, bicultural, cosmopolitan, sophisticated, good-time, Gallic shit to Karen there, as she stands patiently trying to get the attention of this salesclerk in Ogilvy's who is talking to one of his confrères in authentic Montreal French, the kind where those marvellous French diphthongs get stretched and kneaded and rolled into shape inside the mouth like some tasty dough, and are then emitted from a mouth which has become a bit slack because the muscles have atrophied over the years (unlike the mouth of the lady who taught you in your adult-education French class, say — her mouth muscles, when she uttered French, were as disciplined and responsive as Toscanini's arms conducting the "Light Cavalry Overture"). This salesclerk is sort of just standing there talking when Karen asks him, in perfectly *good* French, I mean French she learned in Swiss summer schools, with the accent and the pronunciation under perfect control and everything, *excusez-moi, est-ce que vous pouvez m'aider pour une seconde* ... and he turns around in mid-sentence and says, almost without breaking the flat rhythm of his conversation, "Look, lady, I'll be with you in a minute, okay?"

This is the real interplay of cultures in Montreal. It has nothing to do, basically, with French or English or bilingualism. Those are just the party labels, the code words, the shorthand which points to the more basic reality of life in Montreal. This basic reality is the amazing ability of its native citizens to size you up and instantly identify what group you belong to. Karen, for instance, is actually of the same race and nationality as the clerk at Ogilvy's ... her last name, Greenwood, was her father's translation of Boisvert ... and her first name was the most un-Latin, un-French one her French-Canadian father could produce to christen a female child ... but her genes are as Québécois as a clay pipe and a wool toque and thirteen kids running around in a farmhouse on a back concession lot. Her French, as well, is certainly good, understandable French. The point is, however, that she does not *belong* to the Montreal French, and the clerk realizes it. In his practised eye she's nothing more than a Westmount *anglaise*, and it doesn't matter how many summers she spends in Switzerland learning French.

Well, as a matter of fact, Karen did grow up in Westmount. That is a fact of her life she cannot deny. She will tell you she is not entirely divorced from her ethnic heritage, because she did go to convent school as a girl and learned from nuns who told her that boys did not want to marry "spoiled fruit", and that they'd be mighty proud of you if you never kissed anyone before *them*, your loving husbands . . . nuns who asked the girls to raise their hands if their mothers wore shorts (a sin against modesty). She spent years of her childhood and adolescence sitting in a room watching a succession of these women troop in, lugging books, test tubes, Bunsen burners, globes — lugging them in patiently along with their invisible load, which was that ancient Catholic wisdom handed down to them unaltered since the day Samuel Champlain built his first stockade in Quebec ("and for the whole of his married life, girls," they would say, "this saintly man respected the virginity of his wife Elaine"). So you can't tell Karen she doesn't have a little of that three-hundred-and-fifty-year-old Quebec *weltansicht* bred into her very bones, even if the nuns who had helped with the breeding and marrow transplants were, in point of fact, Irish sisters who couldn't pronounce the "t"s in "bottle", and said Richaloo in World History class to refer to a famous French cardinal.

But all that hardly weighs much alongside the fact that she did grow up in Westmount, and she never heard anyone speak French in her neighbourhood except the plumbers and electricians who came to her father's house, and — it's so absolutely stupid to mention it, it's like saying you had a portrait of the Queen in your living room — their, uh, French maid. Yes, old Suzette, who hauled the vacuum-cleaner up and down the stairs all the years of Karen's childhood, Suzette with the fleshy arms and the sour odour clinging to her on hot days when the sweat mingled with the dust of Karen's house, Suzette would say to her, *ça va, ma chouette*, that sort of thing . . . and that was about it for the French language around the Greenwood neighbourhood. And Karen remembers ladies talking to her mother in their living room about such and such a restaurant being located in the "French quarter". The wrought-iron-balcony-staircase casbah, as it were.

Well, the other day, a lawyer friend of hers, a Jew who grew up only a couple of streets away from Karen, told her he was twenty-six years old before he knew there was such a thing as "Vieux Montréal". Vieux Montréal! Old Europe in the heart of Montreal, so beloved again of our guidebook writers, who rhapsodize over Vieux Montréal, left-bank types drinking espresso in cafés, and youths with guitars and blue jeans and wool knit sweaters heavy and bulky enough to be worn by the Aran Islanders, performing colourful French folk songs and dances on the Vieux Montréal cobblestones, in front of the very gaping eyes of the couple from Cincinnati...this friend of hers had never been down there until one day he had to make his way to the old courthouse on Notre Dame Street. I mean, who in Westmount *needed* Vieux Montréal?

No, the only time she really mingled with French kids when she was a child was during the summer when her father rented a cottage in a small village north in the Laurentians . . . summertime in Montreal being an excellent time for any bourgeois Montreal family to be anywhere else but in Montreal. You just take the polio season, for one thing . . . a youngster could catch polio like *that* in the summertime . . . one dip in a municipal pool, and you might as well sit back and wait for the fever and chills . . . it was like hanging out in the swamps of west Africa and watching the anopheles mosquitos swarm over your naked torso. You got out if you could. Anyway, it was much easier in this summertime haven to relate to French kids—the little girls swam together, played together, were chased together by their older brothers threateningly waving chicken legs acquired from the butcher's truck, fresh, dripping legs that jerked when you pulled the nerve hanging out at the end. No separate territories, camps, communities, or factions among the summertime refugees from the polio-ridden city. . . .

But how unreal, how ... *negligible*, such experiences seemed once one was back in Montreal, back to the serious business of growing up, going to school, learning who you were supposed to be. The cottage, the lake, the Laurentians, were like an asteroid you lived on for three months of the year—an asteroid where the immutable laws of life in the big city, life on the home planet, Ile de Montréal, were suspended. Green, pleasant asteroid! How nice it would have been to take all your lessons in life inside that particular schoolhouse. Years afterward, in Karen's late adolescence, she sought other asteroids, other zones of life, where she could forget she was part of the Westmount lawn-and-shrubbery ghetto, could get rid of a certain identity ... she and her best friend the only two girls in their high school to read Hermann Hesse, hating to see themselves as two more nice Westmount girls wearing cotton turtleneck sweaters and corduroy jumpers, two more girls with a hint of Maybelline creme blush to cover two cheeks scoured with Phisohex ... so instead they took to wearing black stockings and black wool turtleneck sweaters, with maybe a silver pendant in some demi-arabesque design and a grey flannel skirt to go with the young-experimental-dance-student look they were achieving here ... hanging out at places like *le bistro* with the zinc-covered bar, or *le bleu toit*, which the English kids called the blue twat, doing the disco scene (mid-sixties), and being rather more ... *open* to French kids than to the Westmount and NDG boys with their English Leather after-shave and aluminum hydroxide anti-perspirants corroding the pores of their underarms so no funky natural human scent would permeate their Arrow shirts.

Even at that stage of the game it was painfully obvious that the French kids had more *esprit* than the boys Karen knew. Maybe their complexions were a bit more sallow, and they had more of a tendency to grow scraggly beards before the hormones were completely ready, and also their deltoid and pectoral muscles were not as finely toned because they didn't go in as much for invigorating tennis and squash games, but their eyes were undoubtedly more sensitive (like the eyes of underdogs everywhere) and they seemed more, well, hip to the randomness of life, if you can understand. I mean, the French kids were more likely to pile into a cab six or seven at a time, at three in the morning outside some Mountain Street discotheque, and one of the girls would ask the cab-driver if he'd like to join them at a party at Jean-Guy's place, and if it wasn't a Saturday or a Sunday morning, hell, he'd probably accept; the general axiom of their life seemed to be something along the lines of live fast, die young, and leave a beautiful corpse, which of course was not something to be stated outright with any degree of seriousness (because it conjured up the picture of all these cornball Arthur-Rimbaud teenagers) but at the same time that was the formula at the back of everybody's mind.

Esprit. Karen's current boyfriend is French, actually, and possessed of more *esprit* than he knows what to do with. The way they met, in fact, was a perfect example of *esprit* in action. Karen was sitting on the bus going by the University of Montreal and across the aisle was Jean-Claude in his blue jeans, yes, and his Aran Islander sweater and his sensitive eyes — sensitive, you may be sure, not only to the randomness of life but to the ironies, large and small, about us everywhere. Obviously not an anglophone, in other words. There he was sitting next to some guy in a goatee and caramel-coloured leather topcoat, some guy going on about his Ph.D. thesis on Blaise Cendrars, and not since Lane Coutell bragged about the "A" on his Flaubert paper to poor Franny Glass has there been such pomposity heard in the land. Karen looked at Jean-Claude and Jean-Claude looked at Karen, and he smiled, and the irony-sensitive eyes said to her, *qu'est-ce qu'on peut faire?* What do you do if you've been trained all your life to be polite and sociable and to suppress your yawns no matter what? I mean, what do you do?

As it happened they got off at the same stop, and because they had already exchanged these messages with their eyes and because they were walking in the same direction, they started up a conversation, and that was how the whole relationship began. *Esprit* was obviously at work, like some restless karma itching to be realized. Now Karen seemed to have discovered at last her ticket to living with that timeless Gallic flair. Now she seemed to have found her way through the walls and the dividing lines and the *cordons sanitaires* of her native city, a way out of that Westmount identity and into the *real* interplay of Gallic and Anglo-Saxon cultures. A French lover—but of course. Now she and Jean-Claude go off to some little chalet in the Laurentians and it's as if the asteroid is there once again, a little haven, a little refuge, something that was probably there all along, waiting for Karen to make that one little move, to plug right into somebody's live *esprit*. Now they can sit in the chalet and drink out of gallon-jugs of wine and go snowshoeing when the energy moves and spend the rest of their time in bed, making love and reading Paris *Match, Le Devoir*, the Sunday *New York Times*.

Except that the two of them never go to the chalet alone. There are always six or eight other people along with them, six or eight fun-loving Montrealers from Jean-Claude's part of town. That's just the way things are done, *ma chère*. You don't love me alone, you love my cluster, my gang, my happy convivial *cercle*. Well—that's okay. This is what Karen wants, after all, Gallic flair with a vengeance, getting into the culture, moving and grooving in that other solitude . . . and it's perfectly hopeless. Jean-Claude's friends are always nice to her, they smile and they ask her questions about her work and her life, they pass the gallon-jug to her whenever her glass gets empty, and she never *ever* feels that it makes the slightest difference. It's no use. She just can't get interested in staying up until three in the morning arguing over whether *Aut' Chose* is just another poor-boy imitation of the Rolling Stones or finding out which high-level *péquiste* party functionary is responsible for the latest sell-out, or reminiscing about outings to the chalet in years past with boys and girls long gone, boys and girls who once drank wine and smoked hash and made love in the very same room they are sitting in but who are now off working for the government in Ottawa or married to a civil engineer out in Longueuil.

No, she can't do it. It's not a question of language after all—

anybody finds themselves *listening* more when they're in a group speaking a language they have learned after the age of fifteen, of course, but with Karen it's more than that, it's — it's like she knows the official meaning of the words they speak, but she is also aware that there are unofficial meanings which she does not know, and never will know. Once, one of Jean-Claude's more obnoxious friends, a stringy, intense-looking young man with a moustache fine and sparse as the hair on a cat's ear, and this passion, which he continually mentioned, to convert the MCM into a real vanguard political force, came up drunk to Karen at a party and said something like, "You know Karen, you'll never really be a Québécoise until you can swear like one," and she smiled a tight little anxious smile, as if to show desperately that she really understood François to be joking, ha ha, and she said something like —— ——, François. Will that do? And François shook his head seriously, like a customer at a restaurant being shown a very inferior wine list, and said, no, Karen, you still sound like you've come out of that convent school for proper young English girls.

Well, how about this, François, go —— ——, you —— ——. Yeah. Only she doesn't say it. She has an idea what he means by this. She's supposed to say something like *maudit tabernacle tiré par un team de Christ*, or some other ridiculous backwoods oath. She supposes she could actually do it if she practised, but the words coming out of her mouth, even when she screwed her face into a real grimace, would somehow lack . . . conviction. Of course. To attain that conviction she would have to know what it's like to kneel down with the whole family in the living room and say the rosary as it was broadcast over the radio from Mary Queen of the World Basilica. She would have had to have grown up, not in *her* Catholic Church, but in *their* Catholic Church, and the little world which that Church permeated . . . to have had a mother who looked forward to playing bingo at the parish hall every Saturday night instead of a mother who looked forward to bridge with the neighbours every Wednesday night, to have had, instead of a father who watched the *Canadiens* on his colour console while drinking Heinekens and nibbling away at a mixed snack of Camembert cheese, pretzels, and Shreddies, a father who took his sons with him to the Forum on the metro, right down into that part of town where the Jews and the English thrived, and immediately after the game, took his sons straight home, back to the roily, festering "French quarter", the joual-ridden depths of the East End where every kitchen had a little statue of the B.V.M. (robes of cream white and sky blue) on a stand screwed into the Gyproc, along with plastic, two-dimensional Canada geese or some other wall décor they picked up to beautify their home.

So since she didn't grow up in that world she can't swear with conviction, and she can't really grasp the specifically down-home, Canadian flavour of the words she learned in continental cafés and youth hostels and in the pages of her trusty Larousse, and furthermore she has no real interest in Quebec rock groups and Quebec singers and Quebec politics and Quebec movies and theatre, and so what the hell is she doing with this group of people? She figures she might have had a chance if it were just Jean-Claude and her alone on their own asteroid, but — fat chance! — Jean-Claude, like a great many other young, vital French-Canadian Montrealers, can't go downtown for lunch, practically, without bringing those six or eight soul brothers and soul sisters along.

No, it was never as simple as learning another language. One could always do that in a year or two. It was never as simple as shedding one's conscious prejudices and stereotypes around French Canadians, of adopting strenuous pro-French attitudes. (Indeed, nothing was more ironic than the spectacle of anglophone intellectuals — who almost always came from somewhere outside of Quebec—becoming fervent *péquistes* as soon as they found themselves living in Montreal, watching French channels on TV to perfect their command of the language, teaching themselves Pauline Julien songs on the guitar, greeting even fellow anglophones with a hearty *salut!* Such tolerant smiles this francophilia generated among Jean-Claude and his friends. It was like those white radicals in the United States who started dressing funky and talking like brothers from the ghetto, unaware of the snickers in the corner from Jomo Lamumba there, the genuine black revolutionary with the pimp sunglasses . . . or those poor men who swear off sexism forever, help with the house-cleaning, fix dinners for the wives, and then watch those same liberated wives make eyes at the brute who walks into the party with that age-old macho strut. . . .)

It was instead a matter of a certain identity which would keep revealing itself, treacherously, through the smallest detail. It might be the subtle inflections of the voice, so that Jean-Claude, for instance, talking to a stranger on the phone in English, a stranger he assumes is an anglo because, well, the guy speaks English like Lloyd Robertson — Jean-Claude will pick up, almost unconsciously, a signal from some phrase or word this man utters, and all of a sudden they are asking each other with mild delight, *vous êtes français, vous?* and slipping into their true native tongue like a man changing his shower from cold to warm. The salesclerk at Ogilvy's, in the same way, takes a look at that sixty-year-old lady at the notions counter, and if she's wearing some tweedy outfit, where the herringbone twill in the jacket clashes in some vague way with the herringbone twill in the skirt, and she's got these fur mukluks on, or some godawful pair of clumpy vinyl boots that you slip over your feet, he knows for sure she's *anglaise*. A French woman of her age and social class would still look sexy, for God's sake. On the other hand, if it's a person from the lower classes, the clerk doesn't even have to check out the clothes—just the physical condition. If he is a man of thirty-five with recidivism of the gums, he would bet a year's salary that he is one of your honest-to-goodness, salt-of-the-earth French Canadians. Yes, recidivism of the gums, or sallowness of complexion, or concavity of the chest, or wheeziness of the breath — aside from the winos who are a sort of international brotherhood, no group of people in the city are as collectively unhealthy as the folks who live, say, in that East End patch south of Sherbrooke Street around Pie IX Boulevard

... a neighbourhood which is to the French Canadians as the Southeast Bronx is to the Puerto Ricans, a kind of dark homeland, a ruined stretch of their national turf.

Of course, sometimes one's radar is not working at full strength, and one becomes careless, as it were ... the same Ogilvy's clerk goes to Steinberg's, say, and says something to the cashier in French, out of a habitual assumption that, okay, she's just the cashier, she must be French, and the cashier gives him a dirty look as if to say, don't take it for granted that I'm one of your kind, buster (a dozen years ago, before the whole city became more educated, she might have said simply, "I don't speak French, and I don't care if I ever do"). The clerk is taken aback, for one second, and thinks to himself, well, I might have known from her healthy pink cheeks that this one here has been fed lots of milk, and gets a lot of fresh air and sunshine, and is probably Irish or German or some damn thing.

Small wonder, incidentally, that this clerk had no trouble placing Karen. Karen still has the creamy complexion of her schoolgirl days, and the bright-eyed, wholesome look of a model for *Miss Chatelaine*. Is it possible she is really French Canadian? Yes, indeed she is. Her father just made sure she got healthy doses of that Westmount hygiene every day of her life. Her father, the man she despised for his treachery to his own race, his selling out, his practically identifying himself with the English conquerors ("The English built this city," he would tell his daughter. "Do the French think they can take it over just like *that?*"), even his anti-French jokes. ("Did you hear about the two flamingos who moved into Laval and put a plastic French Canadian in their front lawn?")

Ah yes, the classic case of the *vendu*. How often has Karen felt a certain remorse that her father decided to become upwardly mobile, to move as far away spiritually as he could from his cousins in the East End, to become anglicized, to change his name, even, to pass for white. If he had never done this, she reasons, she could probably have fitted in with Jean-Claude and his friends all right, she would have had her purchase on *esprit*

. . . and who cares if that might have meant having the polio scourge every summer. At least she wouldn't have had to feel like a stranger, an interloper, in her own city, looking for that asteroid where no one cares if you're an anglo, and clerks would answer her back in French.

But these days, actually, Karen is beginning to understand a bit more why her father did flee his ethnic heritage, his identity as a French Canadian. It was, of course, not easy for her to understand, because he had never talked about it, never spoke of his family, his childhood — for all that she could tell from his conversation he might have been Albert Greenwood who served in the RAF during the war and grew up in Northumberland where his family raised sheep — but, thinking back on it, Karen can guess a bit.

One time Karen overheard a friend of her father's make some remark about "pea soup" and then her father, who had been working on his fourth glass of Chivas Regal, snorted and replied "You mean to tell me your mother never kept a big pot of pea soup out in the back porch?"

"What d'ya mean, a big pot of pea soup?"

"I mean a big pot of pea soup. My mother made about ten gallons of it each winter, in this big bloody pot. You put the pot out in the back porch and you got ten gallons of frozen pea soup."

"What the hell do you do with ten gallons of pea soup?"

"Well, every night at dinner time your mother goes out there with an ice pick and she cuts out a whole big chunk of it. Then she heats it up on the stove, you see, and she rings the dinner bell, and you all sit down to a nice pea soup dinner, all sixteen of you. Goddam delicious pea soup. That's what kept us alive a couple winters, Charlie."

He said it all without any trace of bitterness, but Karen could tell pea soup was no joke to her father, not really, and neither was a family of sixteen where a few brothers and sisters always departed this vale of tears before they managed to even hit puberty. It was her first clue as to why her father went in so much for that Westmount hygiene of swimming and tennis and lots of oranges and grapefruit in the wintertime and separate bedrooms for mom and dad, and ... well, Karen could understand, too, because one night she had this vision while she and some of Jean-Claude's friends were sitting around at the chalet, and one guy started playing the guitar and singing a song he had composed, which was a dirge-like lament for his lover who would never settle down and give him some full-time loving, and suddenly all of the people in the room came into focus for Karen ... Jean-Claude, and the singer, and all the rest of the girls and the boys drinking that cheap Bordeaux and passing joints around and looking like these super-intense, exquisitely sensitive youths, so laden with *esprit* that it was beginning to torture them in the very pit of their souls, and, in fact, they were consuming themselves with their compulsive *esprit*, burning their candles at both ends ... only Karen was seeing it all through the eyes of her father for the first time, and it seemed like they were no different from those generations of Quebecers who preceded them, ill-fed farm children, boys and girls intimately familiar with death from wasting diseases, pneumonia, tuberculosis, mysterious ailments of the kidneys and the liver, alcoholism, arthritis, gout, colitis, bleeding ulcers, rheumatic fever ... perhaps even in some of them now the insidious microbacterium tuberculosis was beginning to eat away at the fabric of their lungs, like moths gnawing away at an old scarf, spreading tiny lesions and cavitations as yet invisible to X-rays. Of course, it was ridiculous! Their life expectancy would be similar to hers, anybody's in this country, their lungs were just suffering from too many successive coats of tar and nicotine, that was all their coughing meant, and the Edam-coloured skin was just due to staying up every night until four or five in the morning, and the skinny, feeble-looking thoraces and rib-cages were caused by lack of exercise, yes, and too much red wine and marijuana instead of fresh green vegetables ... and deep inside, Karen has this terrible feeling that she has, like her father, already crossed the line in some mysterious fashion and is no longer even remotely a Boisvert, but a true Greenwood instead, and like everyone in this harshest of Canadian cities she has grown to accept and even embrace her given identity: Westmount anglo! Because this is how she *sees* them, and she knows she will never re-shape her identity and her outward appearance to be like theirs, she will never be one of them, she will never think like them, and the clerk at Ogilvy's is perfectly right to talk back to her in his insolent English.